The author, Neil Liebowitz, M.D. is the founder and director of the Connecticut Anxiety and Depression Treatment Center in Farmington, Connecticut. This second edition adds 9 new essays and annotates the first edition's collection of essays that tell clinical pearls about the evolution of modern psychiatric treatment. These are personal stories of the author and his patients that illustrate some of the dilemmas and possible strategies to approach common psychiatric problems. From growing up on suburban Long Island to residency training at Yale, to an academic career at the University of Connecticut, lessons were learned about how best to understand psychiatric problems and a strategy to treat them. Not a psychiatric treatment manual but more than a simple memoir, not a scientific treatise but more than just stories. Its stories and ideas are meant to help others to become better patients and clinicians. The author hopes that some of his ideas might be tested in the future with more rigorous investigative techniques to either provide support for or show them to be inaccurate observations.

Dr. Liebowitz graduated as an Echols scholar and Phi Beta Kappa from the University of Virginia in 1978. He worked as a research assistant at Stanford University during a year off from college in 1977. He graduated from Stony Brook University Medical School in 1982 including psychiatry clerkship at Long Island Jewish/ Hillside Hospital during the release of DSM III. A Psychiatry sub-internship was completed at Columbia University Psychiatric Institute in 1981. He completed his psychiatric residency at Yale University in 1986. After completion he joined the Psychiatry faculty at the University of Connecticut where he remains an assistant clinical professor. He opened the Connecticut Anxiety and Depression treatment center in 1994. Now celebrating its twenty fifth year. This volume represents his effort to document clinical knowledge he seeks to pass on to his patients and trainees.

PSYCHIATRY IN TECHNO COLORS

A PSYCHIATRIST'S MEMOIR OF LESSONS LEARNED ABOUT DIAGNOSIS AND TREATMENT OF ANXIETY AND DEPRESSION

Second edition

By Neil Liebowitz, M.D.

Director, Connecticut Anxiety and Depression Treatment Center

Assistant Clinical Professor, University of Connecticut, Farmington, CT

First edition Copyright © 2010 Neil Liebowitz, M.D.

Second edition Copyright © 2019 Neil Liebowitz, M.D.

All rights reserved.

ISBN: 978109748799

Cover photo: *The joy of dancing on a rainbow* quilt, courtesy of artquiltsbyjudyross.com

Psychiatry in techno colors

A psychiatrist's memoir of lessons learned

About diagnosis and treatment of anxiety and depression

CONTENTS

Acknowledgements 8

Preface to second edition 10

    Forward (By William Glazer, M.D.) 12

    Preface: Extending the boundaries by getting real about stigma and patient advocacy 16

    Introduction: The phoenix rises from the academic ashes 21

    Ode to Freud and latter day disciples 30

    The evolution of my psychiatric faith 39

    Battle of the titans and how I survived my psychiatry training in turbulent times 48

    Seeing is believing, and why I stopped listening to Prozac 58

    Psychiatry in techno colors 64

    Bad drugs, good medications 76

    Marketing of a slightly better medication 89

    What's my diagnosis, does it matter and who cares? 96

    Confessions of a reformed bipolar over-diagnoser and how to see residual ADHD 109

You can't teach old dogs or neurons new tricks- when undesirable medication combinations maybe best 119

The RAM Hypothesis and why remembering everything may make you depressed..124

Origins of panic 131

Life, liberty and the pursuit of happiness; assessing risks and benefits 138

"I must be the worst patient you've ever seen": My theory of relativity 144

Suicide and the need for hope.......................................154

A danger to others 161

Study conclusions, lies and statistics 171

Afterward-the future 185

Appendix: Depression Treatment Paradigms..................190

How to understand psychosis-we all can speak schizophrenageeze 203

The clinical relevance of differentiating obsessing and dwelling in patients with anxiety and depression..............................213

Dying in balance and my organ is more important than yours- managing treatments from different specialties...........218

Complex or Difficult cases: Assessment strategy 227

Treatment non-compliance or failure to gain acceptance of illness? 235

The first shall be last: An alternative approach to the psychiatric intake evaluation 241

The role of the not so simple 15 minute "medication check"........247

A Multiple Models Assessment and Treatment Strategy for Depression and Anxiety 250

How to do a medication trial 266

Choosing medication cocktails: Top shelf brands "neat" vs. mixed generic "well" drinks 271

Acknowledgements

I would like to express my appreciation to the thousands of patients that I have seen over the years who have helped me gain the experiential knowledge needed to write this book. I have learned from many brilliant educators through the years (including Dr Glazer who graciously wrote the Forward) but it has been my patients who tell me what the truth is. As I learn from you, I try to pass this information on to help others.

Thanks to my wife who has supported me through many years and many difficult challenges. She has always been the most insightful person and knew what the right things to do were. I appreciate the several therapists who have guided me in times of decision-making. I do believe in psychotherapy even though I focus on pharmacology.

In memory of my mother whose struggles inspired my interest in psychiatry? I know she is still bragging about her son, the doctor (and yes psychiatrists are and have always been real doctors.)

To my children, who have endured having a psychiatrist as father. I haven't counted the number of years of therapy you may need to undo the cruel limits and embarrassing comments I might have said to you. To Dan who helped edit this book and still decided to go to medical school (you know my son is going to be a doctor! - add another 3 months of therapy for that comment).

(Second edition addition: I give thanks to the residents who I have supervised whose quest for knowledge motivated me to be more articulate in translating clinical practice into words.)

⌘ ⌘ ⌘ ⌘ ⌘

Preface to Second Edition

It has been over ten years since I wrote most of the first edition. I am older and more solidly in the Erikson stage of generativity. Or so I have thought. I looked up this stage again and saw that it should have been from age 35 to 55. But now, isn't 60 the new 50? As I enter the last Erikson stage "ego integrity vs. despair" or as I have read, "wisdom," I see the urgency for me to update my book. I have since written new essays which I have given to supervisees over the years to try to explain my thought processes in clinical care. Time constraints and a new grandchild have preoccupied my time. I had feared that I would have to rewrite all that I have written in the first edition, thinking that half of what I said I wouldn't believe anymore. Much to my surprise, after finally sitting down to read through my first edition, I realized not much has changed in my thinking. In addition, I didn't want to change the flow of each essay as they held together in storybook format. So I decided to just annotate the original work with my current thoughts. I corrected some of the grammar and poorly worded sentences, but the gist is not much altered. I did not correct the misuse of "forward" instead of the more conventional "foreword" in the first edition as one of my patients pointed out it might have been either deliberate or a Freudian slip, implying I was moving forward. I liked that interpretation.

I created a new section for the additional essays, significantly lengthening and expanding the book. This second edition adds more practical strategies for diagnosing and treating anxiety and depression. It is difficult to put clinical acumen into words that others can understand and use, but I tried. I made efforts to create a better framework to conceptualize this complex topic. I made a partial effort to layout an algorithm for treatment decision making. I encourage anyone who would like to expand on this or create a program using my ideas to do so. I would be happy to collaborate. I think this edition will be more useful to clinicians as well as patients trying to find strategies for improving the outcomes of their psychiatric interventions.

No volume can truly replace good clinical judgment nor can treatment be reduced to a mechanical algorithm. Patients aren't always accurate in their presentations of symptoms or histories. Clinicians must listen and translate these symptoms into meaningful data points before treatment decisions can be made. The wisdom of aging clinicians must be reconciled with new research data. This means that good clinicians are very unlikely to be replaced by vending machines. I hope that my book helps future generations become better clinicians and speeds the recovery of those who suffer.

⌘ ⌘ ⌘ ⌘ ⌘

Forward (By William Glazer, M.D.)

As prescribing psychiatrists, whether we like it or not, we incorporate three very specific kinds of information into our decision making process. The most desirable category of information is *"evidence-based"*. It is desirable because it is grounded in varying grades of scientific evidence that inform us what to do next about our patient. The evidence base is available in forms ranging from the *gold standard* randomized controlled trial to the *lowly* observational study. What a world it would be if there were data available to apply to every clinical encounter that occurred in our practices, from the 16 year old adolescent female who cuts herself to the 38 year old suicidal mixed-manic veteran with PTSD and nowhere to live, to the suspicious and combative 83 year old former school teacher who cannot recognize her own daughter. If only we could punch in a key word and be presented with a treatment protocol that would effectively end or relieve the misery and suffering of these patients and their loved ones.

But we can't, so we must rely on a second category of information that we incorporate into our decision making process: *our own clinical experience*. Academics, payers and policymakers complain about this type of information because as each practitioner has his/her unique experiences the potential for variability in decision-making is enormous. For example, payers for care often emphasize studies that demonstrate that when left to their own devices (rather than "the evidence base"), admission rates to psychiatric hospitals vary 10-15-fold. In continuing educational programs, our clinical experience is given a back row seat – "show me the data"…."give me a reference" are the knee jerk retorts of lecturers in continuing medical education programs that are supposed to be designed to "update" clinicians in the strategies and tactics of treating clinical challenges. I doubt that anyone can seriously challenge my assumption that the vast majority of clinical challenges that we encounter on a daily basis are not informed by at least a single study (of any quality).

We read textbooks and attend continuing education programs and hear the evidence base, but we always leave these experiences feeling a little hollow and intellectually hungry – still disconnected from the realities that we immediately face in our offices/clinics/wards/units.

The third category of information that we rely on for clinical decision-making is the *uniqueness of the individual*. As Dr Liebowitz demonstrates in this book, depression has as many faces as it has sufferers. He approaches each patient as a "pharmaceutical artist" drawing from "a palette of medications that are tried and tested" that he combines in combinations that are tailored to the unique clinical needs of the patient. Liebowitz sees *blue* (serotonin) as a cool color that calms anxiety while *red* (norepinephrine) is needed to add fire to those whose depression renders them unmotivated. And dopamine serves to alter the hue. He creates the right shade of purple that reflects the proper pharmacologic balance matching the individual need of the patient.

Dr Neil Liebowitz has written a courageous book – a main course for the unsatisfactory meal that constitutes our evidence base. Dr Liebowitz has taken upon himself to tell it like it is. There is not one reference in this book because as Liebowitz explains, it is an amalgamation for his readings of the evidence base, his interactions with his educators and colleagues at meetings and over 25 years of clinical experience.

I have never seen a book like this one. As a seasoned clinician myself, I felt a little voyeuristic as I peered into Dr Liebowitz's inner thoughts about how to treat depressed patients. If you are like me (I recommend this book for the experienced practitioner as well as the knowledge-seeking patient) you will identify with much of what he has to say, and you will also take issue with some of it – all of us have our unique experiences. But at the end of the book, you will feel less alone in your office when a non-responding depressed patient looks you in the eyes and presses you to find a remedy for his or her incredible suffering. You will also feel more effective in the ability to carry out your work.

If only more clinicians of Dr Liebowitz's caliber would "confess" to the way they actually treat depressed patients. In very little time, these confessions would contribute to the evidence base and inform that "best practices" process that is so desperately needed in our field. Thank you, Dr Liebowitz, for sharing your professional life with us.

William Glazer MD

Menemsha, Massachusetts, October 2010

(Second edition note: Sadly Dr. Glazer passed away 2013. I have replaced his brief bio with his obituary that appeared in the New York Times:

GLAZER--Dr. William M., of Menemsha, MA and Key West, FL, died at home in Menemsha on Sunday, June 23 surrounded by his family. The cause of death was appendiceal cancer. Dr. Glazer was born March 31, 1947 to his parents Irma and Harry Glazer of Newington, CT. He graduated from Clark University in 1969, and the University Of Connecticut School Of Medicine in 1973. He completed his residency in psychiatry at Yale University in 1978. After completing his residency, he went into private practice and was the President of Glazer Medical Solutions. He was a clinician, researcher, lecturer, consultant and had been involved with continuing medical education since he began on the faculty of the Departments of Psychiatry first at Yale University (1978-1994) then at Harvard University (1994-2006). His research and teaching has generated the publication of hundreds of papers, chapters and multimedia educational materials. He lectured nationally for over 25 years on themes related to the diagnosis, treatment and management of severe and persistent psychiatric illnesses. He was a recognized expert in the areas of schizophrenia, tardive dyskinesia, managed care and psychopharmacology. He leaves behind his wife Roseline, children Aaron, Hilary and Jacob along with daughters-in-law Dalia, and Illana, grandchildren Solomon, Dvorah Leah, Samuel, Isaac, and Ziva. He also leaves behind his father Harry, brother Dan and sister-in-law Paula. Dr. Glazer was Commodore of the Menemsha Pond Sailboat fleet for 20 years. He was loved and admired by many friends and colleagues on the Vineyard, Connecticut and Key West along with his patients for whom he cared very deeply. He looked forward to Vineyard summers as two-star general of his "Menemsha Army" of five grandchildren. Donations may be made in his name to Daybreak Clubhouse, Vineyard Haven, P.O. Box 1993, Vineyard Haven, MA 02568.
Published in The New York Times on July 2, 2013)

⌘⌘⌘⌘⌘

Preface: Extending the Boundaries by Getting Real about Stigma and Patient Advocacy

All through my psychiatric training emphasis was given to maintaining good boundaries between the patient and the psychiatrist. This was necessary to maintain therapeutic neutrality and objectivity. The psychiatrist was not to become a patient's friend or worse romantically involved. Truly there needs to be a boundary to be objective in therapeutic decision making as well as preventing exploitation of the patient in the trusting doctor-patient relationship, but this boundary can seem cold and unnatural. Sometimes it seems like psychiatric apartheid. The psychiatrist must not reveal anything about his or her personal life so as not to contaminate the therapeutic relationship. During my residency, when my wife was pregnant, I had to tell my patients that I would be taking a week off in the next month but didn't know exactly when that would be. I couldn't explain my ambiguity, as it would be revealing too much of my personal life including that I was married and about to have a child. My withholding of these simple and commonplace facts led to all sorts of fears, anger and confusion in my patients. The withholding of information seemed to be a much greater contamination of my patients' treatment than when I chose to reveal these facts prior to the birth of my second child two years later after residency.

Psychiatrists have fostered a magical and almost mystical aura about their art. The aloof and distant psychiatrist is all-knowing, can read minds and holds the key to one's recovery. Yet this critical knowledge is withheld until just the right moment when the patient is ready to receive it. Rather than admit that the psychiatrist didn't know an answer, he would ask why the question was asked. I was never very good at this charade and soon began to make cracks in this therapeutic neutrality. My first breech was the offering of suggestions early in my treatments. Next I tried being more real in my interactions with patients. One elderly patient, who had seen many psychiatrists before me, told me that I wasn't like the others. When I asked her what she meant by this she said, "you talk to me, answer my questions and tell it like it is." She liked that.

As a junior faculty member I began seeing a few private outpatients. One of my early patients was Dr. Karen Kangas who has since become a well-known pioneer in the community, advocating for people with mental illness. She has been widely recognized for her advocacy work in Connecticut and nationally. She expressly asked me, in fact insisted, that I use her full name in this piece stating, "Full disclosure is a goal to overcome stigma."

When I first met her she was in her 40's, divorced and recently discharged from a Montana psychiatric hospital after a manic episode. She was working as a school principal when her mania struck. Her symptoms were severe enough to lead to hospitalization. Instead of expressing sympathy for her illness, the school superintendent went to the hospital and proceeded to yell at Karen. During this visit he informed her that she would be fired upon hospital discharge. There were no Americans with Disabilities Act (ADA) protections at the time. Her illness caused her to lose her high paying job. In addition, her manic behavior had alienated her from her husband and family. She was devastated and angry with all of the losses in her life. Her children didn't want to talk with her and the few remaining old friends seemed awkward around her. She felt like a leper who couldn't talk about her illness to anyone lest they might catch it. When she came to Connecticut she began doing research on who would fit the bill to help her rebuild her life and more importantly offer hope for her future.

As I worked with Karen I helped her overcome some of her despair. But this led to anger. She wondered if others felt the same as she did. She was angry that mental illness was viewed so differently than physical illness. There were support groups for people with heart disease and cancer but not for mental illness. She looked throughout the state for a support group but only found a small group over an hour away that met secretly. I decided to start my own group for some of my patients with bipolar disorder. She found this group interesting but it was small and its private nature did nothing to destigmatize mental illness. Upon applying for a job as an advocate for people with mental illness at a state hospital, Karen used my name as a reference and I was more than happy to oblige. I felt no hesitation in breaking boundaries again when I provided her with a heartfelt high recommendation for this important new position.

My father-in-law was a noted psychologist and in his study I found and read an old copy of Clifford Beers's book, *A Mind that Found Itself*. This was a personal account of Beer's treatment in Connecticut Valley Hospital and later founding of the Mental Health Association. I learned about some researchers who were looking into self-help groups for mental illness as there were for addictions. I had a sense from efforts to move patients from state run facilities to the community that greater involvement of patients might be appreciated. I suggested to Karen that she translate her anger into action and recommended a few contacts.

I didn't realize that my few simple recommendations would lead to what she did. Combining her intelligence, education and leadership background with some hypomanic energy she single handedly began bipolar support groups throughout the state. One position led to another. As she advanced in her new career, she helped build an increasing infrastructure for patient or "consumer" involvement in programmatic changes of state run programs. Karen has won many awards including the National Clifford Beers Award and a new award was created and named after her! The Dr. Karen Kangas award is now given to people who exemplify advocacy and compassion for those with mental illness. Perhaps the most significant achievement was regaining the trust and respect of her children.

Her leadership brought empowerment to patients and gave me great insight into a patient's perspective of different aspects of mental illness not taught in residency, namely coping with the stigma. Psychiatrists perpetuated this stigma by making their offices different from other doctors' offices. Many had double doors with an entry and exist so that one patient never saw another. As a teacher of the psychiatric residents at the University of Connecticut, I thought these insights should be taught. I breached a boundary with Karen, and invited her to give a grand rounds presentation with me on overcoming stigma. I reciprocated by giving a joint presentation to the Connecticut Self Advocates group. Unlike Dr. Szasz who felt that to overcome stigma one had to not label the mental illness, we felt we needed to embrace the illness and work to cure it. You can't cure an illness if you seek to deny its existence. More importantly, getting better means getting over one's own stigma of the illness, and treating it like any other physical illness. This includes not being embarrassed by the need to take medications to feel well.

Over the years I have encouraged my patients to become their own self-advocates whether that be: at home, work, with family or in the community. Quite a number have followed Karen Kangas' lead and become active in the consumer movement.

This ever-growing consumer movement has led to greater awareness of the needs of patients and the inequities of treatment. The ADA now helps protect some patients' jobs during recovery but inequities are still evident in the differential insurance coverage and reimbursement for mental illness. To this day an internist will receive a higher reimbursement for a visit from Medicare if he labels a patient as having fatigue instead of depression. With the help of strong consumer advocates, Connecticut was one of the first states in the union to legislate parity mental health benefits, meaning there needs to be the same co-pays, deductibles and limits for psychiatric visits as any other illness. Parity coverage is part of the new national healthcare bill and will be phased into Medicare over the next several years. Unfortunately, carve-outs for mental health undermine the spirit of parity. By carving out the responsibility for mental health benefits to a third party at a fixed fee, the insurance company is limiting payment for one specialty while allowing the rest of medical care to consume whatever it needs. This shortsighted approach almost guarantees higher medical costs due to delays in psychiatric evaluations that might obviate unnecessary medical testing.

I am breeching another boundary in writing this book. As Dr. Glazer has noted, I let you into my inner thoughts about how I conceptualize certain mental illnesses and how I decide on treatment. I have pulled away the wizards curtain to let you see what I do. In addition, I describe my own personal experiences that led me to theorize certain concepts and strategies. Psychiatry has so much to offer yet psychiatrists carry the same stigma as their patients. This is most evident in medical schools where so few students choose to go into psychiatry. Current estimates predict severe shortages of psychiatrists nationally and worldwide. While I criticize some of the approaches taken by psychiatry in the past, I hope to encourage psychiatrists to be proud of the work that they do. The practice of medicine is still very much an art integrating a broad range of scientific knowledge with clinical experience in order to help the individual patient. Lab tests and diagnostic studies in other specialties give a false sense of certainty that masks the underlying ambiguities about when and how to treat. The effects of psychiatric treatment on the other hand are clearly evident in the functional well-being of our patients. No other field does so much to improve the quality of life of people. While a surgeon or internist may save a person's life, it is the psychiatrist who helps that person want to live and be productive. Both outcomes are equally important.

(Updates for second edition: Full parity has been achieved with Medicare and most insurance companies since the first edition came out. Many carve-out companies have been eliminated as well as some of the unnecessary time consuming treatment plans since parity makes them not cost effective. For the first time in many years, more medical students in the United States have chosen to go into psychiatry residencies.)

⌘⌘⌘⌘⌘

INTRODUCTION: THE PHOENIX RISES FROM THE ACADEMIC ASHES

In my last rotation of my psychiatry residency I was chief resident on a unique Neuropsychiatric Evaluation Unit. It received referrals from around the state including patients with acute and vexing psychiatric conditions. The unit promised, for those who could afford the two-week stay, comprehensive evaluations, medical, psychiatric and psychological. The expectations on the staff were grueling. At a time when average lengths of stay were a leisurely several months to several years, we had to complete ten plus page evaluation summaries of our findings including complete psychiatric histories with accounts of every hospitalization and treatment trial, six plus hours of neuropsychiatric testing, and any lab and x-ray study we could think of.

The prior year, the unit had a chief resident and an advanced fellow (fifth post graduate year after medical school or PGY5). Only four years were required for a psychiatrist to become eligible to take the exams necessary to be awarded certification from the prestigious American Board of Psychiatry and Neurology. So a fifth year was an unnecessary elective one took to gain more experience. This fellow, feeling overworked in this elective position, quit mid-rotation. The following semester, in order to prevent another bolting resident, this advanced fellow position was converted into a mandatory rotation for a junior resident (PGY2) who couldn't quit without jeopardizing his graduation. The head nurse interpreted this as a snub by reducing the importance of their mission but felt the same quality and quantify of work should be done by the less experienced resident. This PGY2 resident felt so abused that he complained to the residency-training director. The staff on the unit were admonished about their treatment of the resident; and informed that if they abused the next PGY2 then they would lose the position altogether. Unfortunately for me, the staff was never admonished about abusing me, the new chief resident (PGY4). The attending on the unit was very bright and meticulous, but her compulsiveness led to piles of data that never got published. Her day of reckoning had come. She was being asked to leave the Yale ivory tower. She had not published enough and so perished. Since she was such a diligent worker, she had accumulated so much vacation that needed to be used or lost before the end of the semester. She took off over two months before the end of my six-month rotation, leaving me in charge. (Second edition note: She obtained a better position at another institution who clearly appreciated her expertise.)

The staff avoided the PGY2 out of fear of retribution, but placed all their demands on me. While under this burden of responsibility, I had frequent consultations with professors and interviews to decide what I would do after graduating from residency at the end of this rotation. Yale is the type of ivory tower institution that brings awe to every trainee. The professors are brilliant and you want to somehow have that brilliance rub off on you. They lure you into remaining on as a PGY5 at a stipend 30% lower than a PGY4 by feeding into your sense of relative incompetence. It is like the captivating *Hotel California* in the song by the Eagles

> "We are all just prisoners here, of our own device
> And in the masters chambers,
> They gathered for the feast
> They stab it with their steely knives,
> But they just can't kill the beast...
> ...You can check out any time you like,
> But you can never leave!"

And play upon my sense of incompetence they did. One professor interviewing me for a low paid Yale fellowship accused me of proceeding "ass backwards" in my search for a position because I dared to look at a variety of opportunities including private practices and academic positions outside of Yale. The head nurse on the unit accused me of being "the worst resident that they had ever had" for failing to order a gastro-intestinal consultation for a constipated patient. She accused me of altering charts and threatened to report me to the hospital chief of staff so that I would never get a job, "anywhere!"

I feverishly looked through all of my notes to see if she or I had altered anything. The only thing I could find was a single slash through the letters "ob" as I changed my mind from writing "obstipated" to "constipated." These are two terms that address varying degrees of difficulty having a bowel movement.

I was overtaken by a sense of panic. I became paranoid that she would do something awful to ruin my career. I could not believe that my career would be ruined because of a patient's difficulty in having a bowel movement! I called the secretary to the chief of staff to see if the nurse had made an appointment to talk with the chief as she had threatened. She had not. Fortunately, that year I happened to be the president of the residents' association and I met regularly with the chief of staff. I got reassurance from his secretary that she would call me first if this nurse tried to make an appointment with him. After setting this early warning system, I called the chief of psychiatry who was my supervisor in the unit chief's absence. He immediately realized what was happening, and proceeded to make more regular visits to the unit to calm the head nurse. He subsequently provided me with some of the best advice on leadership as well as career guidance.

The chief of psychiatry, Malcolm Bowers was one of the nicest supervisors I had. He had supervised me for several years in my psychotherapy training and now was my direct supervisor in the absence of the Unit chief. I sought and trusted his advice for many issues and now asked for his guidance in my career choice post residency. He told me that if I had any inkling towards academics, that I should do that first, His reasoning was not what most would think, such as the difficulty in getting a position. He realized that academic physicians made less money than private practitioners (this was especially true at Yale) and that it was hard to readjust your lifestyle. I was married with a young daughter, and my wife worked full-time and wanted to reduce her hours and have another child, making less than I was as a resident was not going to sustain those goals. The expectations placed upon junior faculty were enormous and would put a strain on any relationship. I looked at all the professors at Yale that I respected and none was still married to their first wives. I had to leave the Hotel California. This would mean getting back into psychotherapy and interviewing more broadly for jobs.

I was offered an assistant professor position at the University of Connecticut as a consultation-liaison psychiatrist at a small Veterans Administration Hospital. A consultation psychiatrist was responsible for evaluating patients with psychiatric problems when on medical and surgical units. The salary was better than Yale and we could manage with my wife working only part-time. It was a position with very light duties that would provide ample opportunities to do research and write. Within my first two months there, three of the five full-time psychiatrists left. I had to take over an additional position as director of the mental hygiene outpatient clinic. I was seeing more patients in a month than I did in my whole residency. I loved it. Within six months in my role as an administrator, I worked out bugs in the scheduling system such that the clinic went from losing Federal reimbursement money to becoming one of only two sites in the hospital in the black. This achievement was rewarded, in classic government style, by having one of my staff positions eliminated. The budget was based upon data that was two years old and the fact that I had turned this around was irrelevant. The chain smoking financial officer still entered financial data with pencil in a large ledger book. He freely used the eraser to change any numbers that stood out too obviously from the prior year so as to not attract attention of a government audit. He implied that my success was smoothed out just as the other numbers, no aberrations to stand out and call attention to any potential problems, past, present or future. He had only a few more years until retirement so he wasn't going to risk his neck. From his ashen complexion, hacking smoker's cough and cachectic appearance he looked like he might not live to retirement. Such was my introduction to government accounting.

After two years of my directing the VA mental hygiene clinic, the only other full-time psychiatrist decided to leave. He ran the inpatient unit upstairs from the clinic; he was the upstairs maid, and I was the downstairs one. I was asked to take his position since it was more critical to resident teaching while a new psychiatrist was hired for downstairs. The unit ran full and efficiently, but once again irrationality struck causing the unit to close after a year of my being chief. This time the cause was a battle between the leadership of the VA and the University.

The VA director wanted the university faculty to devote more hours to the hospital, feeling the pinch of government cuts during the Reagan administration. (Ironically, plans were being made to build a new multimillion-dollar replacement hospital while the director was threatening to close the facility. I guess this was just another example of planning based upon creative government accounting.) The university department heads complained to Washington to try to have the director removed for his interference with academic pursuits. I couldn't imagine working harder than I was and still teaching. The director survived and, in retribution against those who tried to remove him, he chose to selectively close several programs key to the University. One program cut was the VA's drug and alcohol program since it was a piece of the University's world-renowned alcohol research center. Can you imagine cutting a drug and alcohol program where 80-90% of the patients had problems related to substance abuse? The chief of psychiatry fired back by pulling me out along with the psychiatry residents. The VA director retaliated by closing the psychiatry inpatient unit. I ran a full census until the final closing when patients were transported to a different VA hospital. I was transferred to run the outpatient clinic at the University Hospital. Construction on the new VA hospital began in the fall without an inpatient psychiatric unit and no substance abuse program.

At the University, I ended up caught in between yet another battle, this time between the hospital and the psychiatry department. Allocation of overhead expenses was blowing the budget of the department. The hospital was charging psychiatry the same overhead as it did surgery even though our needs consisted of a few desks and chairs. The chairman could not get an itemized budget so decided to move the clinic off campus where expenses would be more transparent and controlled. He had a large government research grant that could use the vacated space. Overhead costs would not be a problem because the government negotiated overhead directly with the University as part of each grant. It was a savvy plan except it required approval at multiple levels of committees up to the governor's office. One such committee refused to sign off on the move until consideration was given to a building 5 miles away presumably owned by a political crony. A threat by the chairman to expose this to the local newspaper moved the process along and I helped to design the interior space of our new clinic across the street from campus.

Things seemed to be going well for me. I was teaching, seeing a good number of patients and being an administrator. I did a little writing and some research projects. It was coming time for me to apply for promotion. That year the chairman, facing increased pressure from managed care companies to improve the efficiency and competitiveness of the psychiatry department, decided to reorganize all the clinical program leadership. Reorganization was the latest buzzword and imperative in the corporate world and now was being applied to our department's clinical operations. As with other reorganizations I saw, logic was not a major factor in reorganization decisions. Reorganization decisions were driven by the latest buzzwords. In this case the word was "seamless." In order to make our department more competitive with the growing managed care organizations, the chairman was to eliminate all the directors, including my position of clinic chief. This meant that there were no separate inpatient or outpatient directors. A new position of "super director" was created, which meant that there was no onsite leader. The super director was to be available to all the different programs located in three different buildings and two separate floors. It might have worked better if he were superman and had a phone booth installed on each unit to change in. Cell phones did not exist at the time and the new super director spent much of his time in a director's chair in the clinic parking lot tethered to a landline with a 30-foot extension cord.

I was a team player and wouldn't have complained except that a leadership role was one of the criteria used for a promotion that I planned on applying for later that year. I was worried, so I spoke to the chairman who had always been supportive of me. He suggested I come up with a title. I thought of "Prince" or "Duke" but didn't think that would be recognized by the promotions committee. He anointed me head of mood disorders, whatever that meant. The committee didn't understand it either and rejected my application for promotion to associate clinical professor.

I was angry, upset and felt that I was set-up to fail. I knew that I did not publish enough to be promoted on that criterion alone, so I consulted with the chairman for solace. He gave me what he thought was fatherly advice, but I saw it as an attempt at a psychoanalytic cover-up. He advised me that when others didn't get promoted it was due to deep-seated emotional conflict blocking their pursuits, and then he advised me to seek counseling. I had run every service he asked me to, sat on every committee, taught every lecture, but I didn't have my own grant. I was upset and did what any good psychiatrist would: I agreed that a return to therapy was in order. For a week, I tried to recall the name of my last treating therapist who I went to for six months during my last months at Yale. I remembered his address and even the pass code to his locked outside door, but couldn't recall his name. Searching through old bills, it finally came to me. His name was the same as my chairman, was Freud right or what? It didn't take long in therapy to appreciate that my Freudian block was telling me it was time to leave the University. I had perished and it was a fair and square battle. I could have stayed to have a repeat match, but I was not going to end up like my unit chief at Yale who was pushed out. I wasn't meant to remain in any ivory tower.

I have no regrets for spending the time in academics. I view it as a higher paid six-year fellowship. It afforded me so many opportunities and unique experiences. I was clinical director of three different programs. As director, I attended leadership meetings from the Federal government's VA programs and State sponsored committees. My research activities brought me to many conferences in interesting places such as the World Health Organization in Geneva, Switzerland where I participated in the evaluation of a new international diagnostic system in psychiatry (ICD 10). I attended invitation only meetings with psychiatric leaders at the NCDEU (New Clinical Drug Evaluation Unit), where researchers interacted with the pharmaceutical industry in presenting new data and theories in the development of future treatments. As a faculty member, I would have private luncheons with visiting speakers from master therapists to controversial authors like Thomas Szasz. I took classes in statistical analysis and research methodology in the School of Public Health. It was truly a great learning experience that made me better at everything I do now and provided the knowledge of leadership skills to open my own private practice clinic three miles from the university. My clinic, the Connecticut Anxiety and Depression Treatment Center is the fulfillment of my chairman's last assignment for me. We see more patients in a year than either the VA Mental Hygiene Clinic or the University outpatient clinic did when I was director of each.

This collection of essays represents my return to writing after my transition from full-time professor to full-time private practice. It represents an accumulation of what I have learned from my many varied experiences. When I was an assistant professor of psychiatry at the University of Connecticut I struggled to find research topics that I was not only interested in researching but was capable of doing and able to pass scrutiny of peer review. Once I sent a case report of a patient whose heart stopped after an ECT (electroconvulsive therapy) treatment. I thought the case revealed an important clue to making the procedure safer; instead I received a scathing rejection that included the remarks of one anonymous reviewer, "publishing this piece would obfuscate the literature." I was crushed by the harshness of the rejection and shelved the paper until a hyper-graphic chief resident of mine helped re-edit it and got it accepted in a lesser journal. I struggled to write papers after that, fearful of the critiques that would follow.

Now over twenty years since finishing my residency and seeing thousands of patients, I have a lot to say. My training has spanned many years of transition in psychiatry. I have many clinical pearls that I learned from my patients and tales of the evolution of psychiatric ideas. I had attempted to write some of my ideas to submit to peer review journals, but the rigors of academic publication have gotten so intense since the old days when Freud and his followers could write chapters about just one patient. Without extensive references and structured rating scales, publication opportunities are limited. I might be able to find an obscure journal that no one reads, but why make the effort. Then it struck me, everyone is writing a memoir. I am not that old, but if Brooke Shields, Lance Bass and Marie Osmond could write memoirs, why not me. Anyway, this is not a true memoir. It is a vehicle to tell a variety of insights that I have obtained over the years and how I came by them.

Each essay was designed to stand on its own yet is interconnected to the others by virtue of being part of my life's journey to explore human behavior, its flaws and remedies. I have not mentioned the names of living individuals to protect them from my possible misrepresentations, false memories of events, or unflattering portrayals. I hold no resentments or ill feelings towards any of them. Names mentioned are of individuals who are either deceased or portrayed in such a flattering manner that anyone would delight in such reverie. My descriptions of patients are composites with details altered to obscure their identities. Any patient thinking I was talking about them should realize that I've probably seen several patients with similar details. At any rate, I hope they can appreciate that the purpose of telling their stories is to help others learn from the experience.

A note of caution to any students of psychiatry; don't trust anything I say without fact checking first. I don't have to worry about being promoted, so I have liberated myself from the rigors of true peer review authorship. I have bypassed the onerous tasks of hunting down references and rely on my memory and occasional Google-ing of a name. I give the same caution to any patients hoping to treat themselves, work collaboratively with your provider. I am reminded of a statement made by the Dean of the Stony Brook nursing school at my wife's graduation. I paraphrase what she said, "unfortunately half of what you have been taught is untrue or incomplete. Worse yet, I can't tell you what half." If my collection of essays gives any insight into a possible avenue of treatment, discuss it and ask if it applies to you. I hope these pieces bring resonance if not enlightenment to a broad audience.

⌘⌘⌘⌘⌘

ODE TO FREUD AND LATTER DAY DISCIPLES

In my teenage years I read a lot of psychiatry and psychology books. The field of psychology was fairly diverse with differing theories of behavior ranging from psychoanalytic to behavioral. The behavioral theories were generally based upon experiments with animals and then applied to humans. There was an intuitive logic to the behavioral theories with notions of rewards and punishments shaping behavior. Analytic theory was more imaginative and had notions of unconscious motivations, which inevitably were connected to some, repressed sexual notions. In my readings, I became increasingly interested in new biologic theories that were evolving as new medications were discovered to treat mental illness. Since only physicians could prescribe medications, I decided becoming a psychiatrist rather than a psychologist would best fulfill my interests in psychology.

My interest in going to medical school certainly pleased my Jewish parents. The psychiatry nonsense was hopefully a phase I would outgrow and they never took seriously until I actually got into my psychiatry residency. "Why do you want to waste your medical degree?" They said, not appreciating that you needed to go to medical school to become a psychiatrist. My aunt bragged about her son, the psychologist. "You know it is harder to get into a psychology program than medical school." She would taunt my mother.

There were new programs that allowed you to get a medical degree in 6 years from high school. My father, the accountant, saw great cost savings in this strategy. I saw it as avoiding the competitive process of having to apply both to undergraduate and medical schools. I detested the rivalry among my fellow high school students who also had aspirations to get into medical school. I applied to all the six-year medical school programs we found, which was about six. One fellow classmate, quietly applied to a program that just opened and was the only one to get in to a six year program my year, much to the dismay of the others who thought that they were more qualified. I was selected for interviews at two programs. I went to a program in upstate New York for a series of interviews. When I got there, I found out that one of these interviews was with a psychiatrist. I was excited about this since I had never met a real psychiatrist. I had read a lot about psychology, psychiatry and mental illness, but this was my first encounter with a bona fide psychiatrist.

I was uncomfortable in my suit and tie. I had to try to act mature, which was not very easy for me. The psychiatrist was a very somber and soft-spoken man. He sat down in a chair across from me, not across the desk like the other physicians who interviewed me. "So tell me about your interest in going to medical school," he asked. I went on freely, telling him about my long-time interest in psychology and psychiatry. I told him about all my readings, especially how I read every *Psychology Today* magazine for several years. He waited for a pause in my eager presentation and asked me to tell him about two articles that I had read recently. I stumbled a bit, paused until some titles came to mind. I was a little nervous with this seeming pop quiz type question. I was pleased when my anxiety lifted enough for me to recall two titles. I think he stroked his chin prior to asking me, "Both of these articles have sex in the title…"

My mind went into overdrive. I don't remember if he said anything else. He was a Freudian, I thought. There are actually doctors who believed this stuff? What am I supposed to say to him? What is the most appropriate response to this remark? I can tell you, I did not give him the right response and I knew that for sure. I just burst out laughing. I couldn't believe that he would ask me about sex in my medical school interview. As a Freudian, didn't he already know what every healthy 18-year boy thinks about anyway? Did he want me to confess all of my sexual fantasies? I wasn't going to do that. The rest of the interview was a blank. It was my first traumatic experience invoked by an analyst. He spared me from entry into a program that I was not ready for. I ended up getting into all the undergraduate universities but none of the six-year programs. The schools I went to turned out to be better than the ones with the six year programs and I was able to graduate in 7 years anyway not including taking a year off.

When I began my training in psychiatry I was bombarded with statements about "listening" to my patients. Psychoanalytic oriented psychiatrists were enamored with Freudian theory whose basic premise was to have the patients come to understand their repressed early childhood conflicts by recalling them in psychotherapy sessions. The patient was supposed to tell the therapist the first thing that came to their mind and continue with whatever thoughts flowed from there in an uncensored fashion. This was called free association. Psychoanalysts were supposed to say very little, so as not to influence the patient in this free association, aside from encouraging the patient to "go on" in their free association. Any feelings towards the therapist, including anger at the paucity of feedback from the therapist would reflect the patient's prior experiences and prior relationships. This was referred to as the development of a transference reaction since the patient was transferring his feelings from a prior relationship onto the therapist who by being a blank slate could not possibly have influenced these feelings. As the transference develops the patient forms a regressive dependence on the therapist in what is called a "transference neurosis." Regression is a turning back to an earlier or more primitive way of dealing with conflicts. The therapist tries to encourage this regression in order to learn what early patterns of social interactions the patient had. At this point the therapist can analyze the primitive transference interactions and hopefully re-parent the patient to have more mature interactions. Most analysts say this therapy will take years to accomplish. First there is the need to develop this transference that breaks down patients' defenses or resistance. Then therapy tries to recreate more adaptive defenses through the transference relationship to the therapist. The couch comes into the therapy so that the patient doesn't see the therapist's facial expressions that could contaminate the transference.

Taken from the perspective of a skeptic, this process seems ideal for sustaining a therapist's practice. Creating dependence was part of the process and it would take years to recover from this. If the patient should glance back and awake the therapist from a snoring slumber, the patient would be blamed for not producing interesting enough dialogue. If the patient did not improve, it was the patient's fault for hiding important details. If the patient asked a question of the therapist, the response was to ask why it was asked. One of my first therapy patients was a young art student. She was to have her first art show and wanted to invite me to attend. My supervisor encouraged me to ask the meaning of the invitation and I obliged. It was painful and unnatural for me to be so withholding of my response to such an innocent invitation. After several fruitless sessions, she angrily assumed I would not attend. Counter to my psychoanalytic advisors, I "contaminated the transference" by going to see her artwork, since I was truly interested in seeing it. Our sessions became more productive afterward and I was more inclined to disobey what I was being taught.

    I was becoming more impressed by the power of medications to treat patients than by this vague psychoanalytic therapy. My analytic supervisors denounced medications as quick fixes that resulted in relapses. In fact, patients did relapse more often than not when medications were discontinued. The analysts claimed to have the cures for psychiatric disorders. It would take years to become an analyst and their treatments also took years. I retained this lingering fear that I was short-changing my patients by not being a good enough therapist and having to rely on medications. All the chairmen of departments of psychiatry were analysts, so I thought that there must be some truth to their theories. After finishing residency, my faculty appointment at the University of Connecticut afforded me the opportunity to attend monthly seminars with nationally renowned "master therapists." While honing my pharmacotherapy skills in my clinic appointments, I retained the thought that if I could only give the patients the right therapy, medications would not be necessary. Insurance companies were just beginning to question the merits of long term therapy that analysts said was essential for cures, at which point the therapists began blaming the insurers for failures of treatment instead of the patient.

    I was working at a Veterans Administration Hospital clinic when I encountered, Joe Panic. Joe had just been released from the Institute of Living (IOL), a world-renowned psychiatric hospital in Hartford, CT, after a 9-month inpatient hospitalization. He said that they wanted to keep him for over a year, but his insurance ran out at 8 months. They kept him the extra month for free, reinforcing the message that the insurer was the cause of any treatment failure. I asked Joe what brought him to the hospital initially. He was 38 years old and a successful employee at a financial institution. He served 4 years in the Army in a non-combat role and had an honorable discharge. He reported that he had been the victim of sexual abuse at an early age but never dwelled on it. He had problems in relationships and focused on his work instead. One day, at work he began experiencing panic attacks. This frightened him so much that he went to the emergency room where he was referred to admission at the IOL. The psychoanalytic hospital staff latched on to his sexual abuse that he never dealt with. After spending nine months in the hospital, he felt incapable of working anymore and struggled with day-to-day intense feelings of anxiety and insecurity. I asked him what he had learned at the Institute of Living. He told me, "Prior to the hospital I did not feel. After the hospital all I can do is feel." This was the therapist's goal to help the patient "get in touch with his feelings." But this was supposed to help you, not make you more dysfunctional. It didn't seem to matter that in doing so he became a broken man. Although it seemed that the IOL had ruined him, the IOL had begun a treatment strategy that would take years, but his insurer stopped paying, interrupting the treatment. Could the IOL be to blame if the insurer stopped a surgeon in the middle of surgery and the patient was left to hemorrhage? They did try to patch him up in the pro bono one month of hospitalization after all.

  The treatment was a classical psychoanalytic approach that focused on breaking down defenses to get at the core troubling feelings. This process was expected to make you worse before you got better. Joe was well defended prior to the hospital and covered up his feelings from the early childhood abuse, but this allowed him to function. Removal of these defenses brought him in touch with his feelings, but now he couldn't function. The patient and I both shared in the mistaken belief that if only he had been allowed to stay another year in the hospital, he could have rebuilt his stronger defenses that would have "cured" him. I was upset that they attempted a treatment that they must have known could not be finished. Now, without insurance, he had to rely on the symptomatic relief from the new medications I prescribed for him and whatever limited therapy the VA could provide. My belief in the potential for a cure from long-term intensive psychotherapy lingered like a young child's belief in the Easter bunny or Santa Claus. Just like that child, I kept looking for evidence to prove or disprove this belief. Any time I had an opportunity to speak with an analyst, they would tell me that the Easter bunny was real. It would take several more years to obtain the evidence to convince me that the bunny was just a fantasy that, after years of psychoanalytic training and thousands of dollars invested, was too painful and humiliating to give up.

One critical intervention made by an analyst was giving an interpretation. This was like the defining play of a quarterback in the Super Bowl or the aria of a diva in a very long opera. After months of remaining quiet and encouraging free association by the patient, the therapist would make a connecting statement. This was to be a brilliant connection between past experiences and their associated emotions with the present difficulties and their associated emotions. This interpretation would be given only when the patient was "ready" to hear it. Ready, implied a time when the interpretation would not be rejected and the brilliance of the analyst would be confirmed. The interpretation was to be truly meaningful for the patient in his quest for insight into his problems. In residency I took a whole seminar just on interpretation. The professor's research was on developing the perfect interpretation and the change it provoked. I was quite good at coming up with interpretations. If I threw in a few sexual references, the professors would revel at my brilliance. I saw it as an absurd game in which the obvious was made into the ridiculous by invoking speculative theories.

I attended many master therapists seminars learning a variety of therapy approaches. Most were focused on making short-term interventions that helped the patient as much if not more than long-term therapies. Most were very sincere in their approaches and shared a common thread of empathic appreciation of the patient's problems and offered practical solutions. The one exception was Thomas Szasz.

Thomas Szasz was trained as an analyst and got his notoriety from his book, *The Myth of Mental Illness*. His premise was that mental illness was a fabrication of the psychiatric profession used to subjugate individuals by labeling them as mentally ill. He stated the society had to change so as to accept individuals who were different. He reported that patients could be cured by psychoanalytic therapy. In his seminar, the audience was able to observe him interview a patient while on stage. The patient was diagnosed with schizophrenia and was in our partial hospital program. Dr. Szasz questioned the patient's taking of medication for his condition. The patient lacked insight into his illness and complied solely because his parents threatened to kick him out of the house if he didn't. The patient did acknowledge that he had become violent in the home. Dr. Szasz seemed to demean the patient for listening to his parents and not being his own person. One week after this interview the patient stopped his medication and made a suicide attempt.

Just before the lunch break we had a question and answer session. I asked Dr. Szasz if he really believed that conditions such as bipolar disorder and schizophrenia didn't exist in view of increasing evidence for a biologic basis and the benefits of medicinal treatments such as lithium and antipsychotic medication. He stated in front of the audience that there was not convincing evidence for this and that he stood by his belief of the myth of mental illness. After I asked my question several individuals thanked me for my question and comments since they were parents of mentally ill children and felt Dr. Szasz was blaming them for their children's illness. Traditional psychoanalysts spoke of the schizophrenogenic parent who caused their child to become mentally ill through erratic parenting.

As a faculty member, I had the opportunity to have lunch with the speakers. As I walked with Dr. Szasz to lunch, I again asked him incredulously about his statement that there was no biological basis for mental illness. This time he admitted to me that he indeed thought that certain conditions such as schizophrenia and bipolar disorder had evidence for a biological basis. Upset by his contradiction, I asked him why he didn't say this publicly. He told me, "I don't have to say anything publicly." I began to wonder how many other famous people hid their true beliefs in order to maintain their public persona for personal gain.

In the mid 1980's some of Freud's letters to his friend, Fliess were published revealing his doubts about his own theories of fantasized sexuality in his patients. In his therapy of his wealthy Viennese patients he couldn't believe that so many had been sexually abused. First he proposed a seduction theory that his neurotic patients suffered because they were seduced at an early age. He then wrote that these seductions were actually fantasies indicative of repressed early sexual feelings. Repressed sexuality causing psychiatric symptoms was one of the tenets of psychoanalytic theory. His private letters revealed what he wouldn't say publicly, that he suspected that many of these women had indeed been molested as children. (Second edition comment: Things might be finally changing. Think Me-too.)

I once attended a lecture given by a psychiatrist who was "analyzed" by Freud. He told us that Freud was actually somewhat shy and sat behind the patient because he was uncomfortable face to face. He was also very active in the session, talking a great deal, so much for the therapist being a blank slate. He was impatient with patients. If they didn't get better by six months of treatment, he saw them as hopeless and ended their treatment, so much for therapy lasting for years. His impatience was evident in his early technique of getting patients to talk about their repressed feelings. He would press on both temples hoping the images would pop out. He later settled on a less invasive method of free association in which the patient was encouraged to say the first things that came to mind.

Freud was also looking for biologic treatments as well. This led to a period of cocaine addiction. The speaker speculated that if Freud were still alive, he would be doing biological research into the causes and medicinal treatments of mental illnesses. While Freud is best known for his psychoanalytic theories, he deserves more credit for sparking new interest and hope for treatments for mental disorders at a time when patients were just locked away in institutions. My experiences tell me to be wary of charlatans promising natural cures or expensive lengthy unproven therapies. Also, be cautious of anyone who is overly confident that they have all the answers. Much is yet to be learned and much of what we think we know is wrong.

⌘⌘⌘⌘⌘

THE EVOLUTION OF MY PSYCHIATRIC FAITH

I can't pinpoint the precise day I got interested in psychiatry, but I do know it goes back to somewhere between the ages of 13 or 14. I began reading books on psychology in the library. One interesting book stood next to another, a phenomenon missed by the internet generation who consider bookstores and libraries so last century. By the time of my high school graduation, I had read all of the books in the psychology stack of my local town library as well as every edition of *Psychology Today* over the previous five years. I wrote my first term paper in the field in 9th grade. It was on suicide, although, I never experienced suicidal ideation nor knew anyone who expressed those thoughts to me at the time. I recall reading the 19th century French sociologist, Emile Durkheim's book on suicide. He tried to discredit seemingly unscientific explanations of changes in length of daylight as causes of winter depression and increases in suicide rates during the spring. Instead, he postulated changes in social expectations around major holidays as leading to increased depression, and later loss of social support in the spring for the increase in suicides.

Durkheim didn't predict later discoveries of the suprachiasmatic nucleus that connects the retina in the eye to a master rhythm generator, the pineal gland, in the brain. The effect of decreasing length of daylight causes dysregulation of the pineal gland's release of the hormone, melatonin. This in turn leads to desynchronization of sleep-wake cycles with other stress hormone cycles and is believed to be a contributing cause of season affective disorder (SAD). The seasonal pattern for depression is very common with worsening in the fall and winter months. Depressions improve as the length of daylight grows in the spring. The paradoxical increase in suicide rates correlate with transitions in depressed individuals becoming energized enough to act on prior suicidal thoughts just before their mood is set to improve. This phenomenon is also noted in the initial phases of response to antidepressants, such that the FDA has included warnings of increased suicidal ideation after beginning antidepressant medication. These warnings are less of a reflection of any side effects of the medications but a renewed awareness of the observation that energy symptoms may improve before mood and rational thinking in many depressed individuals. Increased suicidal ideation has been reported even with light therapy for SAD.

The more I read, the more fascinated I became by human behavior and interaction. I must confess trying to understand my mother's behavior was a significant motivator of this activity. She had erratic outbursts usually followed by profuse apologies. One of my earliest memories was of my sheets being ripped off my bed, with me in them at 9am on a Saturday because they needed to be washed, and my mother was not going to wait one more minute. She was very concerned with discipline and order. She would stop the car in the middle of the road to yell at stranger's children for their dangerously playing in the street. "If their parents won't discipline them, I will." She said, while I tried to hide under the dashboard in embarrassment and fear of retribution. There were seemingly spontaneous episodes of rage that would end as quickly as they began. Over time, I observed some patterns. The outbursts seemed to have triggers. The triggers generally had to do with some fear of harm to someone, particularly a family member. I gradually learned how to pre-empt these fears to avoid triggering an episode. If I weren't able to prevent one, carefully chosen words of reassurance given after a period of cooling off would be quite effective at thwarting her irrational fears.

When I was 15, I planned to go into Manhattan for the first time with two friends. One was interested in buying an 8mm camera for making movies for a school project. Both of these friends' parents approved, as they were regular commuters to NYC, which was less than an hour away by train. But NYC might as well have been Beirut during one of its uprisings. The three of us were sitting calmly at the kitchen table when I presented our sensible plan. We would travel with one of my friend's father during his morning commute. My friend was familiar with the subway stops to take us to near the camera district. We would take a commuter train home. My friends had done this before and their parents were comfortable with their competencies to know where to go and where to avoid. As I spoke, all could see my mother escalating into a frenzy of fear and loss of control, screaming an emphatic "no way and I don't care what other parents say." Recognizing her embarrassing loss of control she escaped upstairs to her bedroom.

"I guess you can't go." One of my friends said with a hint of sarcasm and disbelief at the recent display of primitive irrationality.

"No, I don't think it is over yet." I replied. My intuition knew my mother better. She had left clearly embarrassed by her display and had to redeem herself as a rational person with legitimate concerns. "In 15 minutes she will come down the stairs, apologize for her behavior, and tell me I can go if I am very careful," I continued like the Amazing Kreskin. At precisely 9:15, my mother came down and followed my predictions as if they were scripted in a play. My mother had to be given additional reassurances that we didn't have sinister intentions because my friends were struggling to contain their smirks and giggling that reflected their marvel at the accuracy of my predictions. I think it was then that they knew that I would have to work in the field of mental health. Who else could not only remain calm in the face of such madness, but also make subtle interventions that could convert an irrational beast into a sensible parent? We never told our parents that we were almost mugged on this trip if an astute postman, who spotted the teenage punks grabbing my friend's jacket, didn't save us.

My friend, the film buff, trusted in my psychiatric skills enough to suggest that I try hypnotizing him. Inspired by the movie, *The Manchurian Candidate*, in which hypnosis was used to implant a complex plot to kill a politician, he was hoping to use the technique for his own less sinister gain. He wanted me to use post-hypnotic suggestions to implant all the knowledge he needed for a test, obviating the need for him to study. It was a simple yet naïve plan; put him in a hypnotic trance, and then read all the notes to him. With a simple code word all would magically come back to him with 100% accuracy. I read all the hypnosis books in the library. I tried dangling watches, floating arms and even attempts to awaken him from a sleep to put him in a trance. My test was pricking him in the arm or leg to test his depth of hypnosis. All these efforts failed, and he may still have small pinpricks scars to this day. The time would have been better spent studying. I was humbled; I couldn't learn all I needed from just reading books in the library. It would be almost 20 years later that I actually hypnotized a patient. By then I learned that only certain individuals could reach the depth of hypnosis observed in stage acts. Also that hypnosis was really just a heightened state of suggestibility, so he wouldn't have had any easier time memorizing for the test than he would from studying.

I continued to read psychology books. Freudian concepts seemed strange and difficult for me to understand. Everything seemed to be about repressed sexuality and didn't seem relevant to the uninhibited 60's. What I found intriguing was behaviorism as written about by Watson and B.F. Skinner. In tenth grade I wrote a paper on Skinner and his experiments. Huxley's *Brave New World* and Kubrick's *A Clockwork Orange* helped point out some of the pitfalls of behaviorism, but I learned some techniques that I used to control my mother's behavior. Also observing the misadventures of my two older brothers helped demonstrate ineffective dealings. My oldest brother used a direct, confrontational technique with her. He tried to challenge her craziness head on, ridiculing and disregarding her admonitions. This resulted in loud and violent confrontations ending in my brother storming out of the house and mother putting a "Jewish curse" on him. "You should get hit by a car and die, then I will go and stomp on you to make sure you're dead," she said regretfully. I knew she didn't mean it but she had little control over herself when she got in one of these states. Like a caged animal threatened, she would lash out with all she could muster without regard to the consequences.

My second brother used the opposite tact. He told her nothing. Everything was secret. This caused my mother to redouble her efforts to spy on him. My mother worried about every bad thing a kid could do, but he would not give any reassurances to her. Mum's the word. He knew she was spying on him and rummaging through his chest of draws for incriminating evidence. One day he decided to call her on this cat and mouse game and put some capsules of blue pig dye from his biology class in his top draw. When he returned from school, she frantically asked him what was in those capsules. He took brief delight in thinking he had taught her a lesson as blue dye was visibly coating her tongue and running out of her mouth. The victory was brief however as it didn't address the underlying problem. He got little relief from her irrationality or respect for his craftiness.

Psychiatry didn't have a name for my mother's condition until a decade later when DSMIII (Diagnostic and Statistical Manual 3rd edition) came out in 1980. One of my therapists in calling it Panic disorder gave me the unifying piece of a puzzle, which I had been working on for most of my life. But I had already learned how to "treat" her. I took a different approach than either of my brothers. I tried to present her with only positive news. I withheld anything negative. I pre-empted any potential negative reaction by repackaging anything potentially perceived as negative with a positive spin and in a relative context. I might preface a less than optimal outcome with a tale of how awful it could have been. This helped prevent blow-ups triggered by less than positive news that I might tell her. It didn't rid her of spontaneous episodes, such as might be triggered by leaving something out of place. For that I had a contingency plan - holding my breath. Most of these episodes occurred when guests were present, upsetting the natural order of things. I rarely brought friends over. My parents, aware of this pattern and thinking it was due to a lack of friends and their desire to keep a closer watch on our behavior, bought a swimming pool. If I caught a glimpse of my mother running out of the house, I knew something was up and I headed underwater. I remained there long enough until her spell would pass, coming up only for quick gasps of air. She inevitably would leave and tell my friends to have me come into the house. When I would innocently ask what she wanted, she had forgotten what was so urgent. The time frame for this was between 15 and 60 minutes, about the length of a typical panic attack.

Panic attacks, like obsessive-compulsive disorder (OCD) were conditions that psychiatry thought were deeply rooted in psychological conflict and prime candidates for psychoanalytical psychotherapy. Therapy was focused on identifying early childhood traumas that produced fears and insecurities later in life. Freud's essay on his treatment of the "Rat man" formed the rationale for long-term psychoanalysis for OCD. As recently as 1983 my biologically oriented supervisor taught me that OCD needed treatment by an analyst. The following year, research with the serotonergic medication Anafranil changed all that. OCD was soon discovered to be one of the most biologically based conditions most likely related to an interaction with early childhood infection affecting genetically vulnerable individuals. Likewise panic disorder was found to be responsive to medications and a different type of therapy. This therapy named Cognitive Behavioral Therapy (CBT), focused on reframing irrational negative thoughts and telling individuals to simply resist doing useless rituals. It sounds very similar to how I dealt with my mother. I was doing CBT with my mother by reframing any potentially negative event or thought with a positive one. I also recognized that the attacks were time limited and by waiting long enough rationality would return.

One CBT technique I teach patients with panic attacks is called A.W.A.R.E. It recognizes that during a panic attack, the individual can't do anything to stop the attack and needs to let it pass. During a panic attack, the individual is at a reduced capacity to think clearly and needs a simple tool to help with reassurance of a positive outcome. Recalling the simple A.W.A.R.E. acronym provides a reminder that a panic attack is not serious and will pass quickly if not reinforced. The major liability comes from avoiding situations where a panic attack occurred which leads to agoraphobia. The acronym stands for: A: accept that you are experiencing anxiety and not anything more serious; W: watch for the pattern of escalating then falling anxiety adding a sense of predictability to what is a terrifying event; A: act through the attack to prevent the development of avoidant behavior; R: repeat the preceding; E: expect the best.

Interestingly the psychiatrist, Aaron Beck, who developed CBT, was analytically trained. His background helped him to identify problem areas in patients. In psychoanalytic, therapy, anxiety and depression are viewed as symptoms of past traumas and unresolved conflicts. The patient is encouraged to free-associate his thoughts until he gains insight into the origins of his problems. The goal is insight into the causes of the problem and symptom reduction is a byproduct of this insight. The patient, with his new found insight would come up with his own solutions to his past maladaptive patterns. CBT on the other hand focuses on the here and now. The cognitive therapist actively offers psychiatric solutions, techniques and assignments for the patient to do to help with symptom reduction. CBT appreciates that just getting insight into the origins of your problems not only doesn't help most people but also may not even be necessary. Whereas psychoanalysis can take years to progress, CBT is designed to be brief.

      My mother's agoraphobia was mostly limited to driving. She also thwarted my dad's efforts to relocate. Her fear of driving got so bad that my father tried to help her by accompanying her for a ride. He sat in the passenger seat while she backed out of the driveway and proceeded down the street. They hadn't gone more than 100 yards before my mother slammed on the brakes in panic. My father, not wearing his seat belt jolted forward, cracking the windshield. That was the last straw. He overcame his prejudice and acknowledged that she actually needed to get some psychiatric help.   After a few therapy sessions and a little Valium, she was back driving, except on the highway. Their HMO only had limited coverage.

      My mother suffered fears for most of her life. Valium was her little helper that kept her from severe agoraphobia. But the real therapy came in the form of death therapy as demonstrated in the movie, "What about Bob?" I was backpacking across Europe and had no contact with my family for 5 weeks. This was before the Internet and long distance telephone calls were prohibitively expensive. When I returned, I learned that my mother had a modified radical mastectomy for breast cancer. There were no nodes positive for cancer and it was a small tumor so no additional treatment was advised at the time. Her mother had died of breast cancer about 8 years after a diagnosis at a similar age, but there was hope that this was caught early. After the diagnosis, her behavior changed somewhat. Real fears replaced irrational ones. Life became too precious to "sweat the small stuff." All fear was not lost, but perspective was gained. I've noticed this phenomenon in a lot of my patients. We fear more the unknown than the known. We imagine outcomes worse than reality. It is better to prepare patients for the negative possibilities than give falsely rosy expectations.

Most panic disorder patients treated with antidepressants will experience an initial worsening before they improve. This often occurs in the first two weeks of medication initiation. Patients referred to me by primary care physicians often will claim they are hopeless since they failed every medication. When I review their history, they usually stopped each medication prior to 2 weeks, never getting past this period of brain adaptation. If I were told that a medication will help me and I get worse, I would stop it as well. However, if told that getting worse initially was common and a sign of the medication working, I would be likely to stick it out. The same patient puts up with chemotherapy side effects because they are told what to expect. I find that my patients are more likely to stick with treatment if I give them an honest prediction of what side effects that they should be prepared to tolerate.

My mother's cancer returned 5 years later. It was mistakenly assumed to be arthritis until I suggested she have her physicians order a bone scan. Bone metastases then became liver metastases. Chemotherapy and radiation options were exhausted. Liver failure led to gastrointestinal bleeding. She was hospitalized for transfusions only to be re-hospitalized several weeks later. I spoke to her after the second major bleed and asked her if she wanted me to take off to visit. She seemed remarkably calm. It was a calm I had never heard before. I immediately called my siblings to say that she was going to die. She refused all further intervention even intravenous fluids. My family had to sit vigil to prevent eager house staff from their persistent efforts to put an I.V. in her non-existent veins. One would have expected this anxious woman, with prior panic and now not able to take any medication to be as anxious as she ever was. She knew she was going to die in a few days but was at peace. Seeing this convinced me that fear of dying was infinitely worse than dying. Perhaps if every anxious person knew this, they would be much better off. Anxiety is a normal part of life. It serves as a motivator and an alarm when danger is present. To eliminate all anxiety is to die. To accept ones fears and use them to motivate healthy change is to live.

So I must confess after my own psychoanalytic oriented therapy, I realized that my need to understand my mother might have sparked my interest in psychiatry. The ability to understand problems and help individuals is the greatest reward in psychiatry. The unknown and the unusual become comprehensible and treatable. After my mother's death I learned from my aunt that their mother had been hospitalized for a year or more leaving my mother alone as a teenager with her hard working father, while my aunt moved to another state with a relative. Maybe this explained my mother's efforts to provide the kids in the street the parental discipline that she never got. I have come to believe that Psychiatry, more than any other field, is able to improve the quality of life of those suffering. I never give up trying to find a remedy and have been rewarded in many seemingly hopeless situations.

⌘⌘⌘⌘⌘

BATTLE OF THE TITANS AND HOW I SURVIVED MY PSYCHIATRY TRAINING IN TURBULENT TIMES

I did my third year medical school psychiatry rotation at Long Island Jewish and Hillside Psychiatric Hospital in 1980, the year the Diagnostic and Statistical Manual third edition (DSMIII) was published. The DSM was the American Psychiatric Association's bible of diagnoses. It was to be used by most mental health professionals even though billing was still done using an old diagnostic coding system used internationally by all other specialties, the ICD 9 (International Classification of Diseases). DSMIII marked a revolution in psychiatry and Hillside Hospital was one of the places in the forefront. Regular seminars and grand rounds were being held during my rotation on the topic of the new diagnostic criteria. My supervisors were learning the new diagnoses at the same time that I was. Most of my 6 week rotation was spent in one of the smoke-filled "cottages" that served as freestanding, open (unlocked) psychiatric units. Medical students did all the admission physical exams and followed two patients through their hospital stay. My supervisor was a British born psychiatrist with a wonderful upstairs accent and a wry sense of humor. One of my two patients was a depressed heroin addict.

I was excited about my first rotation in psychiatry. I had just come off a very difficult surgical rotation at a county hospital where the medical student did all the "scut work." That meant transporting patients to X-ray, waking up in the middle of the night to draw blood and even putting IV lines in patients. I got very good at this and even got an IV in a heroin junkie after the resident failed several times, using the "Intern's vein" in the thumb. I also wrote most of the post surgical notes while the residents were in surgery. It was a hospital that patients came to be because they had to, not because they chose it for its reputation. My first day on surgery, I got paged at 6pm, as I had been assigned call the first day. The overhead page was "medical student to the OR." It took several calls for me to realize that they were calling me. There was an emergency cardiac bypass surgery to be done and the attending liked to have the medical student be first assistant.

I was told to scrub in for surgery and was assisted in the technique by an OR nurse. After putting on my gown and gloves I was directed to the patient's chest across from the surgical attending. The residents were positioned at the legs of the patient to harvest veins for grafting. I followed orders to scrub the patient's chest with providine, a brownish antiseptic. Then I was handed a scalpel and directed where to cut. Nothing happened, I didn't press hard enough. "This couldn't be for real," I thought. "This is my first day on surgery. Did he know this?"

"Press harder," the attending commanded me as he guided my hand holding the scalpel. I was getting nervous and beginning to sweat through my gown. After the skin was open, the bone saw was introduced to the scene. I looked down at the residents working on the leg. They gave me a look of distain and jealousy; first assist was a position of prominence that they should be in. The attending took control of the bone saw and instructed me to use the suction device to keep the area clear of blood. I was also told to put special bone wax on to stop the bleeding from fresh cut bone. Fortunately, I had used bone wax before in a research project in college. It was the only familiar thing so far.

The sternum was cut through. Now a clamp was put in place with a turn crank. I was to turn the crank separating the pieces of the freshly sawed boney sternum. This is a lot harder than it would seem. It made a creaking sound that convinced me I was breaking something with each successive turn. I was. Beads of sweat were forming on my forehead. My eyeglasses seemed as if they were slipping down my nose. The attending noted this and before my glasses could slip into the patient's recently opened chest cavity, he instructed one of the nurses to tape my glasses to my forehead. She put two long pieces of surgical tape from the bridge of my glasses to my forehead and over the surgical head covering, partially obstructing my vision. We cut open the pericardium, the thick membrane that surrounds the heart. I was busy sucking the blood from any crevice from which it might come.

"Did you ever feel a beating heart?" he asked. "Go ahead, touch it." I did with tentative and gentle hands. It was now almost an hour into the surgery. The tape was starting to come loose from my forehead. The leg vein graft was almost ready. Was I going to have to assist the attending throughout this procedure that I knew nothing about? My back was starting to hurt from leaning forward. I had a desperate urge to scratch the itchy tape on my forehead. The answer came with a tap on my shoulder as the second attending appeared from behind me. This was going to be a grueling rotation. I don't recall if the patient survived, but I learned that the hospital wasn't licensed to do bypass surgeries except in emergencies. So I guess the attending didn't expect the patient to live anyway, but I didn't know that.

That was probably the highlight of my surgical rotation. It was filled with long hours of hard work and stress. One day while on rounds with the residents and attending, I dared ask a question. The attending thought it was a good question and deferred the answer to the chief resident. He got it wrong. The residents, except "samurai surgeon" from Japan who liked doing amputations, mostly came from "off shore" medical schools because they didn't get into American medical schools. After the attending left, the chief resident jabbed me in the side and sternly told me that attending rounds were for the residents and "if I should ever ask another question on rounds...." I actually blocked out what he threatened me with.

The medical students did have their own lectures. One of our lectures on cancer was given by a general surgeon who chain-smoked throughout the lecture. People were still allowed to smoke in many areas of hospitals back then. He lit his third cigarette of the hour with his book of matches refuting the claim on the pack that cigarettes caused cancer. "It's the benzene in the lighter fluid that caused cancer." He choked, gave a phlegm filled cough and finished, "that's why I only use matches."

The last week of the rotation we had practice oral exams. It was Monday and mine went poorly. I was told that if I did this poorly on the final, I would fail and have to repeat the rotation. I panicked. I couldn't imagine a worse fate than repeating the rotation. I got out a 600-page surgery text from the hospital library and read it cover to cover before the final on Friday. I got the highest grade of anyone on the exam. I started my psychiatry rotation the next Monday and immediately began looking for psychiatry residencies.

Let me get back to my heroin addict. He was a very personable fellow, somewhat like the McMurphy character in Ken Kesey's *One Flew Over the Cuckoo's Nest.* He needed a methadone detox from the heroin, and he really wanted to straighten himself out and get on the right path. I met with him daily and we chatted about his goals in life and his relationship problems and how his family didn't understand him. When I met with his family, his mother talked about how she could never predict what condition he was in. He would pass out at the dinner table with his face falling into a plate of spaghetti. She had to call an ambulance regularly because of his overdoses. He convinced me he was better when he completed his four-week detox. I was enthusiastic in presenting him to my attending.

"I really think this time will be different," I said.

"Don't get your hopes up." The attending said cynically in his British accent. He was clearly trying to break through my naiveté, but I wasn't buying it. I felt that I really connected with this guy, and he had promised me. We discharged him. Just as the attending had predicted, the patient was back in the ER two days later with another overdose. My disappointment didn't shake my interest in psychiatry, nor did my attending dissuade me with his admonition not to go into psychiatry. He, like many psychiatrists of his generation, saw the end of psychiatry, as he knew it. They weren't optimistic about the advent of new diagnoses leading to new treatments. They didn't foresee that the next decade would be labeled "the decade of the brain" as advances were coming at a rapid rate. I saw the hope of new medications and had read in articles in high school and college about the advances in basic neurosciences that were going to lead to new treatments. Psychiatry was becoming a new field with new hopes for cures. Patients rarely died or were seriously maimed. Staff was understanding and compassionate. The only problem was the plume of cigarette smoke that hovered seemingly everywhere psychiatry was practiced. When I later learned that I could tell patients that they couldn't smoke in my office, my only obstacle to going into psychiatry was removed.

I met with faculty in psychiatry to plan electives for my fourth year. I was able to obtain a psychopharmacology elective at Columbia University with one of the leaders in this new field, Donald Klein, and his associate Fredrick Quitkin. Don Klein was analytically trained as most of his generation, but was looking for biologic treatments. They had recently published one of the first textbooks on clinical psychopharmacology. They were working on a project to test the validity of a new diagnosis, atypical depression, which manifests with symptoms different from typical depression. In atypical depression patients overslept, over ate, were worse in the evening and had mood reactivity. These individuals would not want to do anything, but if dragged out, they would seem to have a good time. This was evidence that their mood was reactive to the situation. Another feature was their extreme rejection sensitivity. These symptoms were the opposite of classic depression where patients had insomnia, decreased appetite, were more depressed in the morning and didn't react to the prodding of others. They would still be depressed if they won the lottery. As an analyst, Dr. Klein would have considered these patients with atypical depression as having borderline personality and needing intensive psychotherapy, but he saw otherwise choosing to try only medication. There were many of these patients among the actors and actresses in NYC.

His research group studied whether patients with atypical depression responded better to tricyclic antidepressants (TCAs) or to MAOIs (monoamine oxidase inhibitors).

This was the first time a clear difference was seen between the effectiveness of two types of antidepressant medications for a subtype of depression. This research group several years later was able to show that selective serotonin reuptake inhibitors (SSRIs) worked almost as well as MAOIs.

During my rotation I got to observe their interviews with patients to see if they met the atypical criteria. Since these were new criteria, they included some patients who were missing one (QB1 acronym for queer bird) or two (QB2) of the criteria. Short of the humorous word play, they were very serious about making sure these patients met their criteria. I learned a lot about research and medications. One important lesson was that these patients (for whom most psychiatrists would have advised long term psychotherapy and would not have considered medication) got dramatically better with just medication. This was true for most of the QB patients as well.

While at Columbia, I also did a 5-week sub-internship at the Neurological Institute. I got to study with a prior employer and mentor from Stanford who had taken a prominent faculty position there. Five years earlier, I had decided to take a year off from undergraduate school at the University of Virginia (UVA) and went out to live in Palo Alto with some friends. I had no support for this "frivolous" activity from my parents and needed a job. Since I had done a research project in my second year at UVA, I figured that might be the only skill I had to get a decent job. I called various professors in the Stanford University Department of Neurology. After the first cold call rejection, I learned to ask for names of other professors who might need help. When I called these people, I would say the previous professor had referred me to them. I was pleased with the results of this minor deception and got a job in a few days. What I didn't realize was that I had actually had a real skill. I had successfully kindled seizures in rats; something that the researchers at Stanford had tried and failed. My supervisor at Stanford was a neurologist, the second one I had exposure to. The first was working in the same Neurosurgery research lab where I did my independent research project at UVA. Both encouraged me to pursue Neurology instead of Psychiatry. After my sub-internship, though, I still preferred Psychiatry because psychiatric patients were more likely than neurological patients to show improvement with existing treatments. My neurology experiences contributed to my neuroscience knowledge and contributed to my conviction in the biologic basis for most psychiatric illnesses.

Despite multiple professors and my parents discouraging me from going into psychiatry, I applied. And in spite of my car being stolen the day of my interview and the Rent-a-Wreck rental car breaking down several times on my way to the interview, I ended up at Yale for my psychiatry residency the following year. Yale had a large psychiatry department. The chairman, Morton Reiser, was struggling to hold together masters of their field with very divergent concepts of psychiatry. There were leaders in psychoanalytic theory like Stephen Fleck and pioneers of psychopharmacology, like George Heninger.

The attendings who taught us at Yale were young, brilliant and have since become leaders in their field. Another resident and I had joint supervision with Dr. Heninger. Dr. Heninger told us about growing up on the grounds of a state mental hospital where his father was superintendent. Rather than being isolated and frightened, he wandered and spoke with the patients who where unmedicated and psychotic. His thought processes were so quick and complex that we had trouble following him. As he spoke, his eyes would roll back into his head so that only the whites were showing. It was as if he were reading from his own brain. As my fellow resident and I tried to understand what he was saying, we appreciated how the other attending had helped translate his insights into language that mere mortals could understand.

One attending was competitive by nature and not shy about his prowess both intellectual and physical. In my first supervisory session, after learning about my exercise regimen he asked me how much weight I could bench-press. He boasted he could press 300lbs. I reassured him of his superiority and left it at that. Later when faced with a treatment refractory patient who seemed to have symptoms of atypical depression, I suggested treatment with Nardil, a MAOI used by my mentors at Columbia. He remarked, "I wouldn't trust anything that Fred Quitkin said." Instead he recommended a very similar MAOI, Parnate. To this they added lithium.

The addition of lithium represented a carefully thought out strategy based upon the serotonin permissive theory. Antidepressants were thought to work by increasing the amount of norepinephrine (adrenaline) in the brain. This made sense since depressed patients seemed slowed down and adrenaline charges people up. The problem with this hypothesis was that although increased levels of norepinephrine could be measured in animal models as soon as the drugs got into the brain (it would peak in about 5 days), it took up to 4 weeks to see any antidepressant effects. My attending co-authored a seminal paper pointing this out and hypothesized that the antidepressant effect came from a subsequent reduction in the number of norepinephrine brain receptors (down regulation) that resulted from this flood of extra neurohormone. The timing of this effect better correlated with antidepressant response. In other words the benefits from the antidepressant weren't due to a direct action of the medication on norepinephrine levels in the brain (which would have been almost immediate), but due to an opposing delayed reaction to the prolonged presence of the medication. In addition, animal studies showed that an intact serotonin system was necessary for this norepinephrine receptor down regulation to occur. This was called the serotonin permissive theory because the serotonin permitted the norepinephrine to be down regulated. In the year 1980 (5 years BP, Before Prozac) the only medication known to have a stimulatory effect on serotonin was lithium

Thus emerged the lithium augmentation strategy for treatment of refractory depression. On our research unit, when a patient failed to respond to an experimental medication protocol, which was often, they inevitably received a combination of Parnate and lithium. Results were often dramatic. Lithium augmentation of major depression was one of the first theory driven psychopharmacology protocols and surprisingly took several years to be widely received. This may have been partly due to the relative toxicity of both drugs involved. Both medications had multiple drug interactions and narrow therapeutic indexes (meaning the dose needed to treat was not much lower than a lethal dose.) But it worked in some of the most severely depressed patients. Resistance to acceptance also came from academic rivalries leading to regional differences in treatment.

When I finished my psychiatry residency I decided to take a four daylong review course for my Psychiatry Certification Board test. After seeing the differences between treatment theories and practices between Columbia and Yale, I wasn't sure whose ideas might dominate the test. So I decided to take a Harvard review at McLean Hospital, near Boston. A major thought leader who wrote a well-respected psychopharmacology text taught one lecture, on treatment of refractory depression. He outlined a comprehensive list of strategies from high dose anti-depressants to the addition of thyroid hormone. When he seemed done, I raised my hand and asked, "What about the addition of lithium as an augmentation strategy?" He frowned and said that this was not an effective treatment. Not accepting his answer yet not wanting to disrupt the class, I waited to confront him after class. I told him how we had been adding lithium for several years at Yale with excellent results. He responded with a condescending tone, "Those patients are just Bipolar and you just misdiagnosed them." The implication was that those at Harvard didn't trust what was done at Yale.

So much for my attempt to find consensus in treatment, I couldn't even find two to agree at my own institution. For years afterward, when I saw a patient who had been treated by another psychiatrist, I could surmise where their previous psychiatrist had trained by what medications they were given. If they were on Nardil then they came from New York. If they were on lithium and not Bipolar then they had a Yale trained psychiatrist. If they were on high doses of medications with thyroid supplements, chances were that they were treated in the Boston area.

As time has passed, new treatments have emerged and new research completed. None of the theories taught to me was completely accurate. Bipolar disorder is more widely diagnosed, supporting the Boston notions, but controversy grows about how we make diagnoses. The combination of a serotonin medication and a norepinephrine medication has become the most common pharmacologic augmentation strategy, but the addition of psychotherapy rivals that. Neither Nardil nor Parnate is commonly used, yet lithium survives.

In medicine, an old adage says that if there are multiple theories about a condition then the likelihood is that none is correct. Theories of serotonin and norepinephrine imbalances in depression are only part truths as other brain hormones such as BDNF (brain derived neurotrophic factor) have been discovered. Theories based upon response to medications may be flawed as well when we learn that medications thought to be selective to serotonin, such as Prozac, may not be so selective after all. It might be that two seemingly contradicting theories are both true to some degree and complementary. We must avoid being trapped by our theories, as some of the analysts were, and miss the bigger picture. For instance, it might be that the cigarette and the benzene in the lighter fluid both contribute to causing cancer, but understanding why people smoke in the first place and preventing it may be more important.

⌘⌘⌘⌘⌘

Seeing is believing, and why I stopped listening to Prozac

It was the first day of my outpatient year of my psychiatry residency, which was to be all orientation sessions. I had just finished a traumatic last week of my inpatient psychiatry assignment at the Veterans Administration Hospital. On my last day on call I had discharged a petite woman, who was not a veteran, but had been admitted because of a special arrangement with a local HMO. This arrangement provided a better gender mix for resident training and presumably a low cost hospital care for the HMO. She was reportedly threatening to kill herself and a coworker called the police who barged into her apartment at 2 am and took her barefoot and half drunk to the ER. When I had the opportunity to evaluate her the following day, she denied any suicidal intention and was appropriately scared by the large psychotic and manic men on the inpatient unit. She was sober, pleasant and reassured me that she would be safe back at her parent's house where she was living. I compassionately consented to let her go after consulting with my attending via telephone. Two days later, I was informed that she jumped out of her fourth floor apartment to her death. The friend, who had been with her the night in the ER, was asleep and her husband refused to wake her up to answer another distress call. I was shaken and distressed by my first patient who actually committed suicide. I spent hours discussing the case with supervisors and colleagues, getting support and trying to learn whatever lessons to be gleaned from the grim details that could prevent another catastrophe. I looked forward to the less acutely ill patients of my outpatient rotation.

I was in the first session of the day and was getting my first page. I ignored the first one. The outpatient secretary tracked me down after the third page to tell me that one of my assigned patients, John, was threatening to kill himself. She suggested that I come down to the clinic to meet with him immediately. I didn't want my second suicide to occur within a week of the first, so I discreetly left my orientation meeting to find the clinic. The secretary introduced me to John. She knew him well as he had been a schizophrenic patient there for many years. She pulled me aside and quietly told me that she didn't think he would harm himself and I could calm him down if I gave him an appointment. He was a heavyset man of about 30, with an acne scarred face and moderately disheveled, not unlike a number of individuals seen pushing shopping carts of empty bottles around the nearby streets. He didn't appear to be in any distress, certainly nothing like the inpatients with paranoid schizophrenia I had just worked with at the VA.

I introduced myself to John and asked him what was the matter. He said he wanted to meet the new doctor. I asked him if he had intention of hurting himself, which he denied. He seemed satisfied that I offered him an appointment for the next day, after my orientation, but he said he would wait until the end of the week. I realized this was his way of getting my attention so he could greet me. It was going to be a rough year. In fact, rougher than I realized when I got to meet my other assigned patients. I also learned that the secretaries often had the most helpful advice.

During my classes we were taught how to "listen" to our patients. This was repeated often. We were assigned two supervisors for therapy. One of mine was an analyst. His office was in a building next to the clinic. I went up the stairs to his floor. The stairwell smelled of urine. His office was dark, separated from a small waiting area by two back-to-back doors with only 5 inches separating them. He kept the shades drawn and only dim lights on. There were books on Freud and the Holocaust everywhere. "Tell me about your cases," he asked. I hoped I could learn how to treat John, so I presented him first. After only a few sentences he stopped me. "No, not him." I went on through my whole caseload of distressed patients and he negated the learning value of each one. Finally, I presented a young woman with a mild depression who was dating an older married man. "Yes, her. You can learn from her." Hiding my disappointment, not to mention abject fear that I wouldn't have adequate supervision for my difficult patients, I consented to present Julie. This would consist of reconstructing our session as close to verbatim as possible by writing process notes when the session was done or whenever I had enough time.

The following week I got to present my first session after the intake appointment with Julie. I read the first line from my process notes of the session. He stopped me. "You've ruined the whole session!" Amazing, she asked me what she should say and I told her that the time was hers to present what she wanted to. This ruined everything? It didn't seem to stop her from telling me her story. I went on with my process notes. When I was done he seemed pleased. He explained how she was a classic example of an oedipal conflict and that her involvement with the older boyfriend was just a substitute for her father. I naively asked him what I should do or say next. He responded appalled that I even asked such a question.

"What do you mean, say? Say nothing. Let her tell you her thoughts and feelings and after several years she will come to appreciate that she is just longing after her father."

"But," I began, "My rotation is only a year long."

"That is the problem with your rotation; it shouldn't affect what you do in your therapy."

My therapy with Julie lasted only three months. In January, she told me she was feeling much better and didn't see the need to continue. I was terrified. What would I tell my supervisor? Her treatment was to take years and I had failed. It was only a "transference cure," my supervisor told me. She was better, but I had failed because she didn't know why she was better and I had no other appropriate patients to present to my supervisor. In my last session with Julie, I presented what my supervisor told me, how she had only gotten better and therefore would risk recurrence of her depression. I think I might have sounded a little desperate. I was losing my only patient acceptable to my supervisor and God knows what other patient I would get to replace her. It was rare to get someone who really didn't need help that I could present to this supervisor. Julie was inconsiderate in insisting on terminating with me, while profusely thanking me for helping her. It was an "it's me, not you" kind of breakup, except she was leaving because she got better and didn't need me anymore. But I needed her and what was I going to do? I did what any self-respecting resident would do, I requested a new supervisor.

This time I was more assertive with the chief resident assigning supervisors and made certain that I would not get an analyst. This was heresy in the early 1980's, since everyone knew that analysts made the best therapy supervisors. The chief resident annotated the list of supervisors pointing out the best and most revered by residents past. All were senior analysts. Nevertheless, I insisted, "no analysts." My next supervisor was a young, practical psychiatrist. She happily listened to the problems with all of my difficult patients, especially John.

John spoke in neologisms. These were made-up words or phases that didn't seem to make sense, liberally peppered with swear words in between. I dutifully listened to them, half confused and half frightened. One day he called me and gave me a particularly frightening diatribe of meaningless phrases. I was frightened and didn't know what to say. He talked so fast and incoherently that I couldn't trust myself to repeat it to my supervisor. So I quietly grabbed my pocket tape recorder and gently pressed the record button and then placed it near the telephone earpiece. The next session, John accused me of recording him. I sat terrified that I violated his trust by recording without his permission. But how could he have known. My recorder didn't make a noise. I took every precaution to avoid a sound from the recorder. I listened passively, trying not to reveal any of the truth about what I had done. It worked; he calmed down and seemed to let his paranoid, yet true accusation pass. I eventually realized he was just presuming this and that like many psychotic patients they had a sixth sense about others.

I presented the recording to my supervisor. I said, I didn't know if John was severely decompensated and needed hospitalization or was just playing games with me. My supervisor then gave me one of the most profound words of advice of all my training. "Why don't you ask him?" I did just that in my next session with John. I asked him whether he was playing games with me or was really getting worse. To my amazement, all the gibberish went away. He told me how hard it was having a different resident each year and that he didn't know if he could trust me. He then brought in pictures of himself when he was a handsome young boy untainted by the side effects of the antipsychotic medication. He told me of the abuse he endured when in psychiatric hospital and the abandonment by his girlfriend and family due to his illness.

These experiences were the beginning of my realization that just listening to my patients was not enough. Patients told lies. They minimized symptoms to avoid being placed on more medications with terrible side effects or for fear of being hospitalized. They exaggerated symptoms to impress upon me how much they suffered when family members thought they had it too good. It was easy to be deceived by words, but it was much harder for them to hide their appearances. The lack of make-up, disheveled appearance and sad eyes gave away the depths of depression. The meticulously groomed complainer gave away the hidden obsessive-compulsive behaviors. The way John could recompose himself after his rambling sessions was his showing me that I didn't need to commit him to the hospital.

I needed to see my patients. What they say may be less important than the way they appear. Also, listening to patients without responding critically to what they say is a foolish and often hostile act that is rationalized by so called 'therapeutic neutrality." If I challenged the woman on the incongruity between her appearance and the assurances that she gave me, that day in the VA Hospital, I might have not let her go so easily. When, Julie told me she was better, I would have trusted her improved affect and sincere smile to mean that she really had improved with my brief treatment. If I only saw John's pain sooner and told him I didn't understand his meaningless babble, he would have opened up sooner.

It is now over twenty years since the completion of my psychiatry residency. I don't let people ramble on nonsensically anymore. If they ask me a direct question, I answer it first then ask why they asked it. I look at them to see how they appear. If they tell me that they are fine but clearly look in distress, I challenge their statements. If they present with exaggerated symptoms, I have them explain why they don't seem as bad as they look. I help them find and define the words for their feelings rather than let them fumble and use inaccurate descriptions. If my patient is a medical or mental health professional, I don't let them use only clinical words to describe their symptoms. They must explain what they mean by those words in plain language that is a personal reflection of how they are feeling. The affect must match the description. I avoid phone sessions, because I've come to distrust them and realize I miss more than half of the data I need for an appropriate assessment. If I give them Prozac, and they look better but they don't acknowledge it, I point out why I see them as better. That allows me to be more precise in finding out what is not better and what additional treatment might be called for. Many patients would stop their medications thinking they were not working, when in fact almost all but a few symptoms had significantly improved. Depressed patients routinely focus on the negative, neglecting the positive. These residual symptoms might be best addressed by adding another medication rather than abandoning what progress has been made from the current treatment regime.

 I've stopped "listening to Prozac" because it has very little to say. I've been seeing the colors of the rainbow that a variety of different medications can paint on the faces of my patients. I work hard to find the right colors that can turn up the frowns, calm the wriggling, and reanimate the lifeless. This is when I know I have done some good. Psychiatry drifted away from the rest of medicine when it was pursuing the talking cure. Freud sat behind the couch to avoid the patient being influenced by his facial gestures, but in doing so, he missed seeing the patients' ones. In my pediatric rotation in medical school, I was told the most important thing was how the child looked. Appearances told you how urgent the problem was. It also gives a wealth of other information, and psychiatry is no different.

⌘⌘⌘⌘⌘

PSYCHIATRY IN TECHNO COLORS

After September 11, 2001 when the new Homeland Security Department's director presented his color-coded terrorist alert system, my initial thought was how amazing it was that he could simplify an incredibly complex notion of national threat to a handful of colors. Each color represented a synthesis of threats and presumed actions that needed to be taken. One afternoon, while eating my tuna fish sandwich brought by one of the many pharmaceutical representatives vying for my attention and loyalty to their medications, I was asked how I chose to use one antidepressant over another. I began reminding him about the fact that while a majority of patients benefit from traditional choice of medications based upon traditional diagnosis and selection of FDA medication, less than half have complete remission of symptoms. To obtain a more complete remission of symptoms most patients go through seemingly random multiple medication trials. I was in a colorful mood that afternoon. As I was describing my understanding of the effects of different medications it came to me, in techno color. I could simplify what I was doing by using colors as well. I've been interested in art and dabbled in painting so I understood color mixing. I have always been a more visual learner and color added a new depth to this learning process. Artists see things differently than the average person. They try to express what they see in their art. I have tended to see things differently than most psychiatrists whom I've spoken with and have used my vision to create different strategies for treating mental illness. I use a palette of medications that are tried and tested but combine them in creative combinations that others have suggested may help clusters of symptoms. In this process I have to carefully tease out what my patients truly mean by their labeling of specific symptoms and then find the right medication or combination of medications that might ameliorate these symptoms. Patients can be capricious in their use of labels; even patients with medical backgrounds can be particularly confused in their labeling.

People with mental illness are often referred to as colorful people, except when they suffer from the blackness of depression.[1] Wouldn't it be nice if we could add color to these depressed individuals as some artists paint on black velvet? For the less creative psychiatrists, I could help them if I were able to develop a color by number system. The relevant colors were evident to me. Blue was the cool color that was needed to calm my anxious patients. Red was the warm to hot color that was needed to add fire to my depressed and unmotivated patients. The result was to create a shade of purple that put the reds and blues into perfect balance. I have begun to think of myself as a pharmaceutical artist when I work to select the right color medication to paint on my patient canvas.

At one recent American Psychiatric Association annual meeting, I attended a presentation where several thought leaders were debating about adding a dimensional aspect to our categorical diagnostic system. Our current diagnostic system puts mental illness into categories. The categories are determined by the presence of a certain number of symptoms from a list of possible symptoms. This may mean, for example, that a diagnosis is made by the presence of 6 of 12 symptom items. The problem with this system is that two individuals may meet criterion for the same illness with a different set of 6 items. For example, two people may meet criteria for major depression with one having poor sleep, weight loss, and low energy, while the other having too much sleep, weight gain, and anxious energy. Both patients may share only the symptoms of depressed mood, suicidal thoughts and loss of interest.

These patients while sharing the same diagnosis may respond better to different types of medications. The difference between patients may have a genetic basis that in the future genetic testing can

---

[1] It is interesting that the color black can be viewed as the absence of color or the combination of all colors. The latter, by analogy, represents the end result of a being overwhelmed by too much emotion or color. The former represents the shutting down of all emotion.

facilitate the best medication selection. In other cases the difference may reflect a progression of disease state. For example, a medication that may be effective early in the course of illness or after only a single episode may not be effective after many episodes when the illness has progressed. The observation that antidepressants seem to be less effective in children than adults may be reflective of this progression of illness hypothesis. Giving a label to clusters of symptoms instead of just making a categorical diagnosis adds a dimensional aspect to our diagnostic system. The dimensional symptoms can reflect a subtype of an illness, a prodrome (i.e. a precursor to an illness) or a sub syndrome (i.e. a milder form that doesn't quite meet full criteria but is troublesome nevertheless.)

    Several psychiatrists have been speculating how these clusters of symptoms, or various dimensions of depression and anxiety disorders, are associated with different neurotransmitter pathways. Serotonin deficits are associated with a variety of anxiety symptoms including, panic, obsessions, compulsions, and generalized anxiety as well as a sense of well-being, interest, and concentration. This concentration problem comes as a result of myopic attention to detail while missing the larger picture, rather than the concentration problems noted below. When patients feel overwhelmed and can't stop crying, a serotonin medication dries the tears. Further evidence comes from the fact that selective serotonin reuptake inhibitors (SSRI) have gotten FDA approval from studies demonstrating efficacy in treatment of anxiety disorders including: panic, obsessive compulsive disorder (OCD), post traumatic stress disorder (PTSD), social anxiety, and generalized anxiety. To the serotonin medications I assign a shade of blue.

    Norepinephrine (NE) or adrenaline dysfunction is associated with loss of drive, impaired concentration and aches and pains. Medications such as Cymbalta and Elavil that affect norepinephrine (it's unclear how much if any pain relief comes from these medications' serotonin effects) help patients that suffer from unexplained aches and pains. NE also helps with concentration. The lack of concentration here comes from being too easily distracted by external stimuli.[2] One of the first treatments for attention deficit hyperactivity disorder or ADHD (when it was called minimal brain dysfunction) was the tricyclic antidepressant, desipramine. The newer medication, Strattera (atomoxetine) that is approved for ADHD, is primarily a norepinephrine medication. The tricyclic antidepressants primarily affect norepinephrine, while the newer selective serotonin reuptake inhibitors (SSRI), do as their name implies, work on serotonin selectively. In my psychiatric color metaphor, the norepinephrine medications paint the patient with red tones.

A number of medications also affect the neurotransmitter dopamine. Dopamine is the neurotransmitter of movement (mental and physical) and intensity. Dopamine is most affected by stimulant medications like amphetamine and cocaine. On first take, they seem to have a similar effect to the red colored norepinephrine medications but this is not entirely true. Early studies using cocaine and amphetamine for treating depression caused surprising results. Depressed individuals noted that their depression became more intense. What these dopamine drugs seem to be doing is intensifying the current mood state. Stimulant medications have a warning against their use in depression because of this risk. Recall that the street name for amphetamine is speed. In the psychiatric color wheel, dopamine seems to affect the hue or intensity of the color.

Medications that increase dopamine acutely increase energy but may cause agitation or restlessness (too much uncontrolled energy). Dopamine is the major neurotransmitter affecting movement. Patients with Parkinson's disease have deterioration in their dopamine systems in the basal ganglia deep in the brain. They appear slowed down (bradykinesia), stiff, and have trouble walking. When a patient with Parkinson's disease takes too much of his l-dopa (a dopamine stimulating medication), he gets more pronounced jerking movements.

---

[2] Interestingly, there is a third type of concentration problem that is associated with too much dopamine as seen in psychotic disorders. Here the distraction comes from excessive internal stimuli and impaired thought organization.

Some may recall Rush Limbaugh ignorantly suggesting that Michael J. Fox was faking his Parkinson's movements because they were not classic tremors. What he was most likely observing was Mr. Fox's excessive use of l-dopa in an effort to overcome the Parkinsonian stiffness paradoxically causing abnormal movements. Children with hyperactivity have a paradoxical calming response to dopamine stimulating medications presumably due to dopamine deficits in the inhibitory front of the brain and by helping focus. Patients with psychosis appear agitated (hyperactive) and have rapid or racing thoughts. They have too much dopamine in the limbic areas of their brains and are benefited by dopamine blocking medications. Patients with tic disorder with uncontrolled movements are also benefited by medications that block dopamine.

Dopamine may be the "joy juice" neurotransmitter. Various studies implicate dopamine as a common pathway for many additive behaviors and addictive drugs. Lack of dopamine may be associated with a lack of enthusiasm or intensity for life. Patients often describe feeling flat instead of depressed when they have partially recovered. One of my patients who had a chronic depression responded to a combination of Effexor and Remeron (as labeled by Stephen Stahl, California Rocket fuel because it impacts so many neurotransmitters). He was able to remain well for several years with just the Effexor but later complained of lacking the "joy juice." He didn't want to go back on Remeron because of its prior weight gain problem so I added Abilify (aripiprazole) that modulates dopamine. This produced a rapid and dramatic benefit.

One very astute and recurrently depressed patient of mine has remarked that when she is depressed it is as if she doesn't see colors or the luster of objects. It is as if her eyes don't function well enough to see the details. She has always required antidepressant medication that affects all three major neurotransmitters, serotonin, norepinephrine and dopamine in addition to mood stabilizers such as lithium. The problem has been that dopamine receptors seem to burn out periodically. This seems to occur in most patients that I've seen who use stimulants such as Ritalin or Adderall to augment antidepressants.

The new medication, Abilify has been unique in that it can stimulate the dopamine receptor without overdoing it. I have been using it as an augmenting agent for depression since it came out and it recently got approval for this purpose.

Abilify (aripipizole) is classified as an atypical antipsychotic medication. All other approved antipsychotic medications block the effect of dopamine, which is too high in some brain areas in psychosis. However, when you block dopamine in other areas of the brain you can make people feel flat and depressed. Abilify is a partial agonist, which means that it can stimulate dopamine receptors only partially. If there is too much dopamine around, as in some psychotic states such as agitation, the presence of Abilify actually competes with the available dopamine resulting in a blocking effect. This gives it the unique ability to simultaneously act as a stimulant of dopamine in areas of the brain where dopamine is deficient and block its effect in areas where there is excess.

When Abilify first became available, I was faced with two patients with complex psychiatric problems. They both had cocaine addiction problems and attention deficit disorder and depression. Stimulants would be indicated for the ADHD but they had abused these medications in the past and antidepressants had only a partial benefit. I decided to try Abilify warning them that it was only approved for schizophrenia, but because of its ability to adjust dopamine affects, it might have some benefit. Both of the patients took the lowest dose that was available at the time, which was 10mg. Both ended up relapsing with cocaine abuse within one week. But because they were intelligent and observant individuals I had them describe their experience to me.

Both told the same story. When they first took the Abilify their depression began to lift in a few hours. By the end of the day they started to feel almost high as on cocaine. The next day they tried again to get that good feeling back, but taking subsequent doses of the medication made them agitated. That brief good feeling made them crave the initial effects of cocaine. What was clear to me was that the dosage of the Abilify was too high for them. It didn't come in a lower dose at the time. Subsequently, I was able to give a dose that was one quarter the amount every other day with good effects. Abilify now comes in dosages as low as 2mg, which is an appropriate starting dose for use of this medication for augmenting antidepressants. I use it as one on my tools for tweaking the dopamine system in depressed patients who describe their mood as flat, lacking color and get agitated on dopamine enhancing medications such as stimulants or Wellbutrin (bupropion).

(Second edition addition: There are now two additional dopamine partial agonists like Abilify: Rexulti (brexpiprazole) and Vraylor (cariprazine). There are slight differences among these medications in their receptor binding profiles and relative effects on the dopamine receptor that might make one medication more beneficial than the other to some patients. They all have very long half lives which make dosing difficult to do. This is because at low doses they stimulate the dopamine receptors but block them at higher doses causing almost the opposite effect. In other words, they work like antidepressants at low doses and antipsychotic medications at higher doses. If the medication seems to work well initially but then seem to poop out, consideration should be given to reduce the dose before a decision to raise the dose is made. It is nice to have these other choices that gently stimulate dopamine without the blasting associated with stimulant medications.)

So with my color-coded system, I can try to see whether the patient needs some blue colored serotonin, red colored norepinephrine or to have their color intensity increased by dopamine enhancing medications or reduced by dopamine blocking medications. The final result is a happy, motivated, calm perfect shade of purple. What we need to know next is what each medication does in the brain. We need a color chart for each medication to know what it looks like on the patient canvas.

To determine what color a medication paints I have used information from both scientific studies of receptor binding and clinical observations. The problem is that most medications that were thought to be selective are not that selective. Pharmacologists are able to assess what neurotransmitters medications attach or bind to by determining a pKa value. This measure alone doesn't tell you all the information that is needed since some bindings stimulate and some block the receptor in question. In addition, some medications don't get into the brain so easily because of a separation called the blood-brain barrier. A medication that doesn't get into the brain easily may have more side effects relative to its clinical effects than ones that get into the brain more easily. Paxil and Effexor have similar bindings to both serotonin and norepinephrine, but Paxil doesn't get into the brain as easily and doesn't demonstrate as much "red" effect clinically. They do share norepinephrine side effects such as dry mouth, blurred vision and constipation, which don't require getting into the brain. Also most medications bind to other receptors that produce other side effects. Paxil has significant antihistamine binding which causes sedation and weight gain. It also has anticholinergic effects that produce dry mouth, blurred vision and constipation. These effects are less in Paxil than in the older tricyclic antidepressants like Elavil (amitriptyline) or imipramine.

      Not all side effects are necessarily bad. The first antipsychotic medication, chlorpromazine or Thorazine was derived from efforts to find antihistamines to augment anesthetic medications. The tricyclic antidepressants were derived from similar molecules and retained some of these effects. Other medications were designed to have just the side effect of some of these older medications. Detrol is an anticholinergic medication that is used to treat over active bladder. You can get the same effect from an old tricyclic antidepressant like Elavil. I give desipramine, another tricyclic antidepressant, to patients with irritable bowel disease with comorbid depression and anxiety because the anticholinergic "side effect" treats diarrhea and cramping. This side effect of desipramine is similar to the primary desired effect of the widely used gastrointestinal antispasmodic medication Bentyl (dicyclomine). One of the most potent antihistamines is the old tricyclic antidepressant medication, doxepin. This makes it very sedating, but it is more effective and longer acting than Benadryl for allergic symptoms.

In selecting a medication we can look at both the color it paints and also any secondary effects (side effects) that we may want or want to avoid. Over the years medicinal chemists have carefully designed new medications that were more specific and selective in their effects. This reduced side effects, such as creating antidepressants that didn't have anticholinergic or antihistamine side effects. However, in this process of creating "cleaner" or more selective medications, the medications may have lost some of their punch. This has resulted in psychiatrists doing more combinations of medications. This polypharmacy used to be frowned upon because it used to lead to side effects and dangerous drug interactions. With the enhanced safety of these newer medications and our better knowledge of drug interactions, it often turns out that combinations of several medications may be better tolerated than a high dose of one of the older medications.

Below is a simplified chart of relative effects that I have observed and compiled from various publications. It doesn't precisely correlate with publications because I have modified it based upon my clinical experience. Using this table one can come up with combinations that may have similar benefits but different side effects. I like to compare this to the *Jelly Belly* jellybean recipes where various flavor jellybeans can be eaten together and create new flavors. For example, combining Effexor XR 75mg with Wellbutrin 150mg produces a similar clinical response to Cymbalta 60 but a given patient may prefer one medication or combination to the other. The combination of desipramine 100mg with Effexor 75 might look like it too would be similar, but this should not be done because of a serious drug interaction that causes the desipramine level to rise dramatically with toxic side effects.

While most patients will improve with a relatively straight forward random selection of an FDA approved antidepressant, we need to do better and work towards symptom remission. The colorblind psychiatrist doesn't interpret the various symptoms as indicative of missing colors. He chooses medications based upon habit and not color or chemical effect. He may go through many medication trials that differ little in their mechanism of action or "color" making the patient feel hopeless and incurable. When, in fact, the patient has really tried on only one color of medication. This patient might feel much better in blue than in bright red. The colorblind psychiatrist is often afraid of side effects and may never try an older medication that may be more effective and whose side effects may help another condition the patient has. Finally, the colorblind psychiatrist may miss the need to adjust hue. Agitation, requiring a dopamine blocker, may be misinterpreted as anxiety and mistreated with high doses of addicting tranquilizers instead of a low dose of a major tranquilizer or mood stabilizer.

How does a patient encourage their prescriber to make more rational medication selections? Ask questions about why a medication or combination was chosen. Does it make sense or is it just random. Try to be honest and descriptive of one's symptoms to help provide a basis of medication selection. Keep track of what medications you have tried over the years and what benefits and side effects occurred. Keep your own file of these trials. Also find out what other biologic relatives have tried and their outcomes. There are many other ways of selecting medications that may be just as useful as my color-coded one. What is most important is that these trials are done in a logical and methodical fashion with attention to symptoms, and how each medication works including its effects, side effects and drug interactions. Fortunately, most of the psychiatrists I encounter now have seen the light and every color of the rainbow.

(Second edition note: Glutamate is a neurotransmitter that has become more important recently in depression treatment. The glutamate antagonist medication, Lamictal (lamotrigine,) has been approved for bipolar disorders but has utility in other conditions. There are several medications with glutamate antagonistic properties including: Namenda (memantine), Nuedexta and most recently ketamine. I haven't included this in the color coded system but it may be

like dopamine, a hue controller. It seems to help reduce irritably, anger and impulsivity associated with mood disorders.)

Color chart for common medications

(on next page)

Notes for chart:

[3] Ach implies both true anticholinergic effects and pseudo anticholinergic effects due to peripheral NE effects.

[4] Paxil and Prozac are strong inhibitors of P450 2D6 resulting in a significant number of drug interactions

[5] Strattera because of short half-life may work better as 40 mg twice a day for depression than 80 mg once a day as used in ADHD.

Medication (mg)	Red (NE)	Blue (5-HT)	Hue (DA)	Ach[3]	Histamine	note
Lexapro (10)	-	+++	-	-	-	
Celexa (20)	-	++	-	-	+	
Zoloft (100)	-	++	+	-	-	
Paxil (20)	+/-	++	-	+	++	4
Prozac (20)	+/-	++	-	-	-	4
Effexor (75)	+	++	-	+	-	3
Effexor (225)	++	+++	+	++	-	3
Cymbalta (60)	+/++	++	-	+	-	
Wellbutrin (150)	++	-	+	-	-	
Strattera (80)	+++	+/-	-	-	-	5
Desipramine (100-150)	++	-	+/-	++	+/-	
Imipramine (100)	++	+/-	+/-	+++	+	
Protriptyline (25)	++	-	+	+++	?	

BAD DRUGS, GOOD MEDICATIONS

    I grew up in the 60's when liberal meant open or broad minded, as in liberal education. People around me were experimenting with a variety of drugs, while I was reading articles and books about them. I watched friends hallucinate on "natural" psilocybin or magic mushrooms, which, I learned, tasted like the manure it was grown on. In my high school there were always at least one or two students who had passed out in the hallways by the end of the day after imbibing too much of a variety of substances. I was open to learning about others experiences but a healthy fear kept me from trying these drugs. On a camping trip with several friends, one boy was trying to "expand" his mind with nature's bounty. He picked random plants in the woods, dried them in tin foil over the campfire and rolled them into a "joint." As he smoked it, he offered his "natural joint" in a neighborly fashion to other campers. I felt compelled to follow him so as to warn the unsuspecting guests of the origins of this "joint." A year later this poor fellow was hospitalized with a psychotic break as a freshman in college. I later learned that he was diagnosed with schizophrenia from which he never recovered. I always wondered which caused what, the schizophrenia leading to his attempts at finding a natural cure or his herbal remedies (which included marijuana, psilocybin and peyote among others) causing his psychosis. I tend to think it was a combination of both.

    A few years later, I took a year off from college and moved to California with some high school friends. My parents were terrified that I would succumb to the evils that lurked in that hippie-infested State. I might end up like a cousin who was rumored to have opened a head shop in San Francisco. (Interestingly, he later returned to the east coast, went to medical school and became a psychiatrist.). I can reassure my parents the worst drug experience that occurred there was my passing out from one margarita a friend's parent gave me on my twenty-first birthday. I now realize that they were alcoholics and underestimated my low tolerance. My experiments were mostly with inexpensive

California Zinfandels and an occasional Cabernet. My housemates included a vegetarian and an avowed carnivore who couldn't tolerate vegetables because of his irritable bowel syndrome. The latter got a job typesetting for a local newspaper and would come home with banner headlines to post in the kitchen: "**Ground Beef is Beautiful**" and "**Down with Mung**." Mung was our term of non-endearment for the overcooked vegetables our vegetarian prepared for himself.

One transient boarder who moved into our house taught us how to make bread. Bread making, along with moving to California were his efforts to change from the toxic New York lifestyle, which he felt caused his dad's untimely heart attack. In making his own bread he could be certain of its contents and relieve some stress. He had recently moved from New York City and was determined to live healthier. He described the bread making process in his thick New York accent, which had an angry edge, as he pounded the thick dough, kneading it "like a breast." I pitied any woman whom he might find to go out with him. It is possible that his move to California was preceded by a recent break-up. The contradictions in California abounded. The soft-spoken anti-nuclear protesting longhaired student of particle physics contrasted with the loud domineering woman who shouted to me to "mellow out, please!" whenever I dared to speak as loud as she. All of these experiences helped me to develop a healthy skepticism for quick fixes, fad dietary recommendations and "natural" remedies as espoused by seemingly intelligent people who clearly had little basis to support their advise. It is not uncommon for me to encounter the victims of these schemes, whose only flaw is the overwhelming desire to try to help themselves.

Barbara was a 39-year-old woman who never married and dedicated her life to her job and care of her aging parents. She had gained fifty pounds over the years due to long hours divided between her full-time job and full-time care of her parents while neglecting her health. This put strain on her back, resulting in multiple herniated discs. With increasing pain and stress from the increasing needs of her parents, she had to quit work and move in with her parents. She lived on her savings, which were rapidly being depleted. Too proud to apply for disability, yet unable to afford medical insurance, she became increasing anxious about her situation and sunk deeper into depression. Without health insurance, she sought the advice of her health food store staff and began taking multiple supplements and herbal remedies. Eventually, after several severe panic-attacks she presented to my office for evaluation. She was taking at least ten different preparations costing over $200 per month with limited improvement in her symptoms. As she could no longer afford these supplements, she tried to stop them but felt worse. I prescribed a low dose of Paxil 10 to 20mg per day, which at the time was only available as a branded medication and cost about $70 per month. Within a month she had dramatic improvement that exceeded the benefits she experienced from hundreds of dollars of herbal treatments. I prescribed a higher dose so that she could break the tablets bringing the monthly cost to less than $40 and she stopped all her supplements except for a multivitamin. The same medication is now available in generic form for as little as $4 per month.

I often have patients tell me that they don't want to take medications since they don't want to be dependent on drugs. These same people smoke 2 to 3 packs a day of cigarettes, drink several cups of coffee, often smoke marijuana and have experimented with other drugs such as cocaine, ecstasy or opiate pain pills. They may ask for natural remedies such as St. Johns Wort and others that have had limited efficacies, yet are terrified of using lithium which is actually a natural mineral comprised of the third element on the periodic table. Prejudices and misinformation abound about the field of psychiatry. "Are these medications safe?" I'm often asked in comparison to the multitude of "natural" remedies sold as "all natural and safe." I think these questions are valid but the answers are complex. I will attempt to present my rational oversimplification about how I interpret the risks and benefit of various substance options. I choose the term substance to contrast with psychotherapy options which I value highly, but require another discussion.

For the purpose of this essay I am dividing substances that individuals use to treat mental conditions into 4 general categories: 1) FDA approved pharmaceuticals generally prescribed by a licensed medical provider, 2) Natural supplements obtained with or without guidance from a naturopath 3) Homeopathic remedies used with or without guidance and, 4) Street drugs including both legal and illegal obtained with or without guidance from a local drug dealer or "friend." I will review each category to discuss relative merits and risks.

Drugs of Abuse

I want to start with the most dangerous first, street drugs. In this category I include the legal substances of nicotine and alcohol. Other common classes include; stimulants like cocaine, methamphetamine and illegally diverted pharmaceutical like dextroamphetamine (e.g. Dexedrine and Adderall) and methylphenidate (Ritalin); opiates like heroin and diverted Oxycontin (and many others), hallucinogens including PCP, LSD and marijuana (yes marijuana is a hallucinogen; consider the changes in time perception, touch and paranoia). What all of these substances share in common is that they are powerful, meaning their effects are stronger than what is generally prescribed often reversing benefits of prescribed medications. (Recall the Jefferson Airplane song, *White Rabbit*, "one pill makes you taller, one pill makes you small, and the ones that mother gives you don't do anything at all...") These substances have rapid effects that are often felt in minutes or less. They also fade quickly, in minutes or hours, leaving the person wanting or craving more to sustain the feeling. I like to call these substances "drugs" to differential them from other "medicines" which are designed to treat or heal a condition.

William Styron, the famous author of *Sophie's Choice*, wrote a short book, *A Darkness Visible*, documenting his struggle with depression. It was a brilliant portrayal of the illness but he failed to see one of the main reasons why he didn't improve in outpatient treatment. He readily noted that he drank heavily, while his psychiatrist tried various antidepressants to no avail. He justified his alcohol use by stating that it was the only thing that gave him a reprieve, no matter how brief, from his depression. He didn't improve until he got hospitalized, which presumably ended his drinking long enough for the medications to work. Alcohol has been shown to deplete serotonin in the brain. Antidepressants improve the functioning of the serotonin neurons in the brain. Even a single episode of drinking can undermine the benefits of an antidepressant for up to a week. My experience suggests that episodic binge drinking of as little as four standard drinks for a man or two for a woman can undermine the benefits of antidepressants.

      Mary had been depressed for many years prior to seeing me. I began her on Lexapro (escitalopram), a selective serotonin reuptake inhibitor (SSRI) and she improved dramatically in a month. Over the next several months in addition to her brightened mood, her confidence and motivation improved. After years of not wanting to socialize, she reconnected with friends and planned a trip to Cancun with some old college friends. I saw her for re-evaluation a week after returning from her vacation. She said her depression was worse than it ever was and attributed this to having to return to work after a great vacation. I asked her about her vacation. She was at an all-inclusive resort with unlimited drinking. She drank more than she usually did but never passed out. As she enjoyed the drinking, she continued to drink more than usual at home saying this was the only thing that lifted her depression a little since she returned. After reminding her of the negative effects of drinking, she stopped all alcohol use. Within a week of stopping alcohol and no change in the Lexapro dose, she began feeling better again.

      The body generally seeks a state of homeostasis or balance. This is analogous to one of Newton's laws of physics that states that for every action there is an equal and opposite reaction. Drugs of abuse cause a rapid response which most people find intensely pleasurable but as this effect fades there is a terrible let down. As the brain is continually assaulted by the repeated presence of the drug, its chemistry is altered in such a way that the individual no longer experiences the intensity of the high, having become tolerant to its effects. In addition to a diminished high with continued use, the individual feels worse without the drug. The body has achieved a new homeostasis with the drug such that it no longer feels normal without it. Individuals, who didn't feel well before abusing the drug, often return to their miserable state while using the drug and feel even worse without it. This withdrawal effect leads to continued use even though the individual no longer seems to be benefiting from the drug. Tolerance, which leads to use of increasing doses of drugs in efforts to attain a diminishing high and continued use to avoid withdrawal symptoms, are two characteristic features of addiction. Addiction is also characterized by a decrease in functioning as increasing amounts of time are spent procuring the drug, getting high or in withdrawal.

The most tragic scenario I've seen occurs with opiates. I've seen this many times. John was a 25-year-old man with a history of severe depression for several years. Multiple antidepressant trials seemed to be ineffective. Although, he never manifested symptoms of mania, I started some medications used to treat bipolar disorder with some relief. These medications often take longer to work. Out of frustration with his slow progress and on encouragement of a "friend," he tried snorting some heroin. I saw him only two days after trying the heroin. He stated that after using the heroin he felt normal for the first time in years. I warned him about the rapid tolerance and its negative effects. After only one week of use, he felt compelled to continue to use the heroin even though it was no longer making him feel better. In fact, he began to feel worse than ever if he missed a day of use. After multiple unsuccessful attempts to stop the heroin he decided to go on a suboxone maintenance program for heroin addicts. I have come to appreciate that individuals with bipolar disorder might be the most vulnerable to becoming rapidly addicted to opiates. They often say that their first time using is the only time they felt normal, but this first time effect is rarely duplicated despite multiple attempts followed by almost certain painful addiction. This is a class of medications that should never be tried even once by someone with a significant mood disorder.

(Second edition notes: There is a recent effort to gain approval of an opiate partial agonist for treatment of refractory major depression. The FDA has been appropriately cautious about approving

this agent due to potential long term risks. Similar efforts have been reported with the use of tramadol, a synthetic opiate-like medication. I tried this in only one patient who had received tramadol for migraine and reported benefit in their depression. Over the course of six months the patient demonstrated classic addiction behavior with the drug, using ever larger quantities with fading benefits.)

Natural supplements

Natural supplements can be divided into essential vitamins and nutrients that have a known need by the body and herbal remedies that are not essential but act like medications. Most herbal remedies have traditional histories of benefit but little controlled scientific studies to support their use. In the United States laws have been written that have allowed natural remedies to go unregulated by the FDA as long as they claim only to be "supplements not designed to treat any illness." This is based on the argument that they are plant derivatives so presumably are safe. It's truly amazing that the Federal government strictly regulates what claims pharmaceutical companies can make about their medications that have been studied extensively in carefully designed clinical trials, yet "supplements" get a free ride. There have been some calamities with some supplements such as tryptophan that was banned for over a decade due to permanent neurological damage that occurred in several users of this supplement. St. John's Wort, a popular herbal remedy for depression was recently found to reduce the effectiveness of antiviral agents used to treat HIV/ AIDS.

There is no regulatory oversight as to the purity or content of natural remedies unlike in some European countries. The actual content of various preparations has varied in independent studies from having none of the claimed substance to many times the amount. Some herbal blends sold for weight loss and "male sexual enhancement" have been shown to actually contain unlisted prescription medications that could be dangerous in the unsuspecting individual. While the minimal necessary and recommended doses (RDA) of vitamins have been studied scientifically, the study of herbal supplements has been hampered by variability of each preparation and paucity of good controlled clinical trials. Most of the studies lack placebo controls and are subject to bias and placebo effect. A good naturopath may guide the appropriate use of these supplements but I feel those who sell their own products are subject to a greater conflict of interest than physicians who have been criticized for accepting pens and lunches from pharmaceutical representatives. Until there is greater oversight by the FDA and more controlled trials of these supplements, I advise caution in their use. I believe that some have good merit, such as probiotics, glucosamine and fish oil supplements, but I don't have confidence as to the relative safety, potency or accuracy of current labeling of various products. They may have benefit for people with mild symptoms, but I doubt most are as effective as pharmaceuticals or even psychotherapy alone for individuals with significant symptoms. The major benefit may be the sense that the individual is trying to help him or herself but this shouldn't be a substitute for proven traditional therapies.

Finally herbal remedies have been around for centuries and did not demonstrate the effectiveness of our modern pharmaceuticals. When I made a visit to our local state psychiatric hospital, the treatment logs resembled an herbal catalogue, yet few of the patients recovered enough for discharge. State hospital populations grew steadily until the late 1950's when new medications were discovered. Some of the best herbal medications have already been exploited to make pharmaceuticals including: lithium (a mined element), aspirin (from willow bark), digoxin (from foxglove), belladonna, Taxol (from yew), galantamine (from daffodil bulbs), chloroquine (cinchona) and many others. Just because a substance is natural doesn't make it safe. Many natural substances are very dangerous; think of cocaine, opium, strychnine and marijuana. I have had many patients, like Mary noted above, who came to see me while taking hundreds of dollars worth of supplements and herbs with only modest benefits. These individuals often improve dramatically with even low doses of pharmaceutical medications.

(Second edition note: Marijuana has been legalized for "medicinal" use in many states and recreational use is a few states since

the first edition. This has caused many people to think of it now as safe and an alternative to pharmaceuticals. While legalization has reduced the risk of adulterated product and introduced a measure of several presumed active compounds in the marijuana (e.g. THC and CBD), there is still a lot of research needed to understand the risks and benefits of marijuana. Marijuana is clearly implicated in reducing cognition and slowing function. My current recommendation is to assess the risks and benefits of its use. If there is a safe and effective medication with little side effect, why risk switching to marijuana? The long term risks are not any safer and may be much worse. However, for individuals with severe chronic illness, such as chronic pain requiring large doses of opiates, marijuana might be a safer alternative. Now that marijuana has gained a semi-legal status we can expect more research to be done on the risks and benefits of the various components in marijuana that should help guide us in the future. Just because alcohol prohibition ended in the US doesn't mean we should be recommending the use of alcohol. The same caution should be applied to the end of marijuana prohibition. Legalization was a way to reduce the ineffective and expensive criminalization associated with its sale and use, while hoping government will profit instead of drug dealers. Legalization of medical marijuana has allowed research to proceed on identifying risks and benefits.)

Homeopathic remedies

Homeopathic medications, while regulated by the FDA, are not required to prove their safety or efficacy like other medications due to long standing legislation exempting them. Homeopathic medications are dilutions of compounds to minute levels that don't have a detectable effect. This seems to me the definition of placebos. The FDA doesn't require that they be compared to placebos. In trials of pharmaceutical medications, placebos are often shown to have benefit in over thirty percent of patients regardless of diagnosis. In some trials, placebo rates exceed fifty percent. If a placebo works, I'm all in favor of its use. In my practice, I aim for much higher than fifty percent response rates and therefore choose medications with greater proven efficacy. While most would consider a placebo safe, continued use of an ineffective treatment for a severely ill patient with suicidal ideation can be lethal. When you look at the actual ingredients of homeopathic medications, they often contain some well-known toxic compounds. Since they have been diluted to presumably non-toxic levels, they have been assumed safe. The logic of this strategy is unconvincing and the absence of good placebo controlled trials of these medications makes me skeptical about their use. Although, I confess, being open minded to alternative strategies, I have tried a variety of homeopathic remedies for canker sores, colds and allergies without any observed benefit. At least they are generally very inexpensive. Their main benefit, I believe, is the sense that the individuals are doing something to help themselves while the body may heal itself. There are better things a patient can do to help him or herself than take homeopathic remedies.

Pharmaceutical medications

The US Federal Drug Administration (FDA) regulates pharmaceutical medications. Drug approval is a long process. A complete explanation of the process can be found on the www.fda.gov website. I will give an over simplification of the process. Compounds are discovered and patented. Most of these compounds will never be studied. Compounds are tested in the lab to have certain properties e.g. they bind to known target receptors and don't bind to others that are known to cause side effects. Safety studies are done, initially in bacteria models then animals. Only after these safety studies are done, and the compound looks to be promising the manufacturer can apply for permission to study paid human volunteers. Independent scientists approve of this next stage after careful review of the preliminary studies. This is just to understand its safety, tolerability and metabolism. Very few compounds make it past this stage.

The first trials in humans are referred to as phase I trials, which are mainly to determine safety and tolerability. In phase II and III trials, the compounds are given to volunteers who have the target illness. These studies have at least two comparison groups, one taking the new medication and the other a placebo. The compound not only needs to be demonstrated safe, but it must provide benefit for the patients' illness and be better than a placebo (an inactive compound). Requirements for approval of new medications have become more stringent over the years. Companies can't hide failed studies anymore. Approved drugs also undergo continuous surveillance by the FDA that includes reports from physicians and patients directly to the FDA. The FDA will issue new warnings regularly when additional data emerges as to risks of any approved medication and may pull any medication thought to pose greater risk compared to its benefits. This type of oversight and monitoring is not done for any of the above categories of compounds. FDA regulation is not perfect, but provides a fair degree of confidence in the relative safety of compounds. There is also ongoing monitoring of the manufacturing standards of the medications. Although, some of this monitoring is currently lacking in medications manufactured overseas for importation to the US.

The advantage of FDA approved medications is not only in the above safety considerations. Their study has created a large database of how the medication works including its metabolism and appropriate dosing for a given condition. Since its purity and dose is standardized, unlike most herbal supplements, certain reliability is expected. It's interesting how some individuals become alarmed at the 20% variability allowed for generic medications yet tolerate unknown variably in an herbal product.

While FDA regulation gives a fair degree of confidence in a medication's safety there are still flaws in the process. Most of the problems lie in conflicts of interest in the funding of research. Almost all money for research comes from the manufacturers so that only new medications that have the potential for generating a profit from a new indication get studied. Companies are not likely to design studies comparing their medications to others that might risk an unfavorable outcome, although this has happened at times. In clinical practice, physicians routinely combine different medications, yet relatively few studies look at the effects of combining medications. Competing companies may fear that emergent side effects might be wrongly attributed to their medication and the FDA has only recently allowed indications for add-on medications. The National Institutes of Health has recently funded several large studies comparing a variety of medications to see which ones might be the best for a specific condition. These independent studies have failed to demonstrate superiority of one medication over another even when older generic medications are included.

When my patients come to me for help they want the "best medication." They often have friends or family members that have told them what the "best." was This is based upon what their personal experiences have been or what they heard through advertising or Internet blogs. More often they have strong opinions about what medications they don't want, such as Prozac because of the negative media attention. For an individual, the best medication is one that treats their condition and has no side effects. The reality is that each patient experiences a medication's effects and side effects differently. This is due to having different conditions, metabolisms and different co-existing problems. For example, giving a person with irritable bowel syndrome (IBS) and depression an antidepressant that is known to cause constipation may, in this individual, treat both the depression and the IBS. For someone who is not sexually active, a side effect of sexual dysfunction may not be evident or relevant. Mild sedation for one person may be felt as a calming effect for another. Some people have alterations in their metabolism of certain medications such that they become toxic on a low dose of one antidepressant, yet tolerate high doses of a similarly classed antidepressant that gets metabolized differently. Finding the right medication for an individual combines the art and science of medicine. This is good for me, since I don't feel threatened by the prospect of being replaced by a vending machine as some less informed critics of psychiatry have suggested.

Not all people who present with similar symptoms suffer from the same illness. A depressed individual may have had a mild manic state (hypomania) that was forgotten but will make a dramatic difference in their response to medication. One study done in Europe where patients' treatment records are available in national health system databases revealed that a significant number of patients presenting with depression failed to report previous hospitalizations for manic symptoms. Another study found that 25% of young patients presenting with depression went on to develop mania within ten years. So even under the best circumstances diagnostic considerations in selecting a medication may require revisions at later dates. Every time I give someone a new medication I not only consider this a treatment trial, but also a test of the individual's biochemistry. Even a failed trial can provide valuable insights into the biology of the patient's illness and metabolism, which in term guides the next selection of medication.

  Whatever the remedy you might be seeking, the general rule is that drugs that work fast often lead to longer-term problems. While many natural treatments may have fewer side effects and a placebo effect, these benefits are rarely sustained. The best medication for one person may be the worst for someone else. There are many healthy things a person can do for themselves, experimenting with different drugs is not one of them. Persevere with your psychiatrist to find the best medication and treatment plan for you. The best treatment plans don't rely upon medications alone. They combine medications with exercise, a healthy diet and counseling.

⌘⌘⌘⌘⌘

MARKETING OF A SLIGHTLY BETTER MEDICATION

When Prozac first appeared on the market in the mid 1980's, its effectiveness was not what was so remarkable. Most psychiatrists didn't believe Prozac to be as effective as the older antidepressants including tricyclics (TCAs) and MAOIs (monoamine oxidase inhibitors). The latter are more effective, in fact, for severe depressions than the newer SSRIs like Prozac if only patients completing a trial are counted. The problem was a patient's ability to tolerate the side effects. Side effects of the old medications were so troublesome that they had to be started gradually, often taking weeks to get up to a therapeutic dose. This delayed improvement if the patient tolerated staying on the medication long enough for them to work. MAOI medications had potentially fatal interactions with certain foods and over-the-counter medications. Common side effects included severe dry mouth, constipation, orthostatic hypotension (which caused patients to get dizzy and faint on standing), blurred vision, sedation and weight gain.

If a patient took an overdose of the older medications, often out of despair with the long wait for a response, the lethal dose was not much greater than the therapeutic one. This led non-psychiatrists to avoid treating depression or to use sub-therapeutic doses that reinforced a misconception about the treatability of depression with medications. The American Psychiatric Association, in its Diagnostic and Statistical Manual 3rd edition (DSM III), tried to formulate a subcategory of depression, labeled melancholic, that would identify patients who were uniquely responsive to medication to help limit who would need to be tried on these dangerous medications. In its revised edition, DSMIIIR, it went so far as to create a circular logic in the definition of melancholic depression that included the criteria of a prior history of response to medication.

Then along came Prozac, a medication that was so tolerable that it could be started at an effective dose, supporting the claim of a faster onset of antidepressant effect. Prozac was also very safe. So safe that it wasn't clear what a lethal dose was. Its ease of use and tolerability was so good that internists and other non-psychiatrists started prescribing it freely to their depressed patients. Mild to moderate depressions were responding as well. The melancholic label's circular logic lost its validity and was removed from subsequent DSM editions, since so many types of depression responded to the newer medications. A change in the way efficacy was measured also helped favor some of the newer medications.

A medication's effectiveness is measured by comparing its effect on a group of patients receiving the new medication to a group receiving a placebo or sugar pill. Alternatively, the new medication is compared to an older classic medication. Now it may sound simple when it is reported that the medication does better than a placebo or better than the old medication, but these conclusions can be biased. Not all patients entering a study complete it. Many drop out for a variety of reasons, most due to side effects. Some patients on placebos drop out due to "side effects" as well. What if someone drops out midway in the study? Do you report the results of only those patients who complete that study or only those who stayed in a certain period of time or anyone who even took just one dose? If you only count the results from those patients who have completed the length of trial this is called a completed cases analysis (CC). When you include all patients who took the medication at least to the first assessment this is called an observed cases analysis (OC) and the researcher takes the last observation and carries it forward (LOCF), analyzing this point as if the patient completed the trial.

Most studies used to report on only completers, which tended to show a greater difference between placebo and active medication. With the newer medications, which had fewer side effects, looking at all patients who took the medication often made the medication look better than older medications with more side effects. This was true because with more tolerable side effects, dropouts tended to occur later when the medication had a longer period to work. So manufacturers were able to show that the newer medications were just as effective as the older medications. Even though this might have been a bias due to lower side effects resulting in fewer dropouts early in the study.

Fewer side effects, greater safety and evidence of equal efficacy of the newer antidepressants to older ones led to an explosion in their use. As more physicians prescribed, the more they were convinced of the power of psychiatry but also of their own limits. Referrals started to pour in to psychiatrists. These referrals were more often partial responders, transient responders and treatment failures than patients who were never tried on medication.

With so many new patients being started on antidepressants, psychiatrists were confronted by patients who they may not have considered trying medications themselves but were clearly demonstrating a partial response. The patients were coming with the expectation that a medication would cure their depression if only the right one were found. Newer SSRIs came out, Paxil and Zoloft, which gave the opportunity to try different medications, but these switches rarely produced the desired effect. Psychiatrists are creative and adaptive people. They devised augmentation strategies by combining different antidepressants or other medications to see if a more complete response could be obtained. Old medications were combined with new ones, and new ones with newer ones. Blood pressure medications, hormones and the element, lithium, were added.

In all this chaos of combinations, psychiatrists became the first to really appreciate the minefield of drug interactions. While all of the SSRIs seemed to act similarly to boost the serotonin system, they had very different drug interactions. Researchers had identified an enzyme system in the liver called the P450 system, which metabolized a good proportion of our medications. Some of the medications and even some foods like grapefruit could interfere with P450 enzymes causing dangerously high blood levels even when low doses were used. Other medications and herbs like St. John's Wort could speed up P450 enzymes rendering some drugs ineffective, such as certain antivirals used to treat HIV/AIDS. Prozac and Paxil were two of the biggest offenders with strong blockade of the P450 system. The addition of either to a tricyclic antidepressant could raise blood levels 10 fold with risk of cardiac arrhythmias and other side effects. A combination with the over-the-counter cough suppressant, dextromelorphan could cause hallucinations. Only recently did researchers realize that use of Prozac or Paxil rendered the anti-breast cancer medication, Tamoxifen, ineffective.

Just in time for this awareness, Forest Labs introduced Celexa to the American market. It was a drug approved in Europe for many years and seemed like a "me-too" type of SSRI. In fact, Pfizer, the pharmaceutical manufacturer of the number three SSRI, Zoloft, held the marketing rights until Forest bought them. Pfizer didn't see any advantage to Celexa and chose to stick with its product Zoloft. Celexa had one unique property; it had minimal effect on the P450 system, similar to Zoloft at low dosages. Forest aggressively marketed it at a cost lower than its competitors and took a huge market share of the antidepressant marketplace within a couple of years with the help of both HMO formularies (who liked its lower price) and psychiatrists (who liked its drug interaction profile). Competing pharmaceutical companies where dumb struck by Forest's success. A small company, previously known for generic drugs, beat them. They cried foul by their marketing strategies, which to my experience were providing a lower cost medication with a slight edge in drug interactions.

While the competitors were still licking their wounds from Celexa and worrying about their patent expirations on Prozac, Paxil and Zoloft, they were again broadsided by Forest. This time Forest purified its blockbuster drug Celexa to produce Lexapro. Most critics saw this as a ploy to get a new patent as SmithKline did by reformulating its patent expiring Paxil into Paxil CR. However, Forest took bold steps that larger pharmaceutical companies seem afraid to do; they did head to head clinical trials comparing Celexa to Lexapro. They showed a slight but significant edge for the newer purified drug, Lexapro. They released the drug two years prior to the end of their Celexa patent, priced the drug 10% lower than their own Celexa and encouraged switches with free and plentiful samples. It worked. Patients were able to see the superiority of the newer drug that had fewer side effects. This wasn't as apparent in the clinical trials, but patients felt it. Sexual side effects were less; fatigue and appetite were less. By the time Celexa went generic, two years later, most patients wanted to stay on Lexapro, even when their insurance companies asked them to pay more for it.

In the interest of full disclosure, I received money from Forest for speaking about Lexapro to other physicians. However, I also have spoken for other companies' drugs and realize that I was selected for speaking after expressing my enthusiasm for the medication and not due to some brainwashing. Prior to speaking for Lexapro, I spoke for Effexor and prior to that, Paxil. The changes came as newer medications emerged that had some superior traits. Because of treating a large volume of patients, I have a large number of people who are dissatisfied with their current medication and want to try something new. My treatment philosophy is to tell patients that I will work with them until they are all better or the best they have ever been or they "cry uncle." (By which, I mean they tell me to stop messing around with their medication and they are content with "as good as it gets"). When I attend meetings with other high prescribing physicians where the manufacturers present their FDA approved promotional materials, it's difficult for them to deceive us. Sitting at a lunch table with two or three other "high prescribers," we have more patient experience than the clinical trials and we are able to see whether or not the findings are consistent with our clinical experience. This is why I have often told pharmaceutical sales representatives that their pitches are more likely to get me to use less of their drugs than more. This was most evident for my use of Effexor.

Several years ago, I was giving fairly frequent talks for both Effexor and Lexapro. These were my two most frequently prescribed medications. I liked Lexapro mostly for treating anxiety symptoms and Effexor for more slowed down depressed patients, so I didn't see any conflicts speaking for both medications. Clinically, Effexor seemed more like an SSRI with a calming effect at a low dose and like a dual acting tricyclic with more energizing effect at higher doses. This dual effect has been attributed to Effexor having a dual action on both serotonin (calming) and norepinephrine or adrenaline (energizing). As I was presenting this observation to my "target" physician in a lunch meeting, an accompanying enthusiastic and intelligent pharmaceutical representative pointed out that Effexor was dual action at all doses. After some brief argument, she backed off the discussion so as not to embarrass me in front of another physician. However she persisted several days later when she came to my office producing a research paper supporting her claim. It's important to appreciate that Wyeth, the manufacturer of Effexor, was claiming that dual action meant more effective and was claiming that this explained why their drug was capable of 33% higher remission rates. So the rep was doing her diligence in convincing me that Effexor was dual action at all doses.

I carefully reviewed the research paper. In order to demonstrate norepinephrine effects, researchers measured Effexors's effect on the constriction of the eye pupil at all dosages. This was called a pseudo-anticholinergic effect. Effexor did demonstrate other anticholinergic side effects that I never understood, since the manufacturer claimed that it didn't have anticholinergic binding effects. The "pseudo" antecedent is used because it has an effect like an anticholinergic drug but it really is due to another effect, in this case norepinephrine. This pseudo-anticholinergic effect explained why it caused more dry mouth, constipation, blurred vision and maybe even more withdrawal symptoms than more selective SSRI medications. Since at the low doses Effexor didn't clinically demonstrate any better stimulatory effects than the better tolerated, Lexapro, its use didn't seem warranted when only a low dose was needed. My use of Effexor plummeted and I was no longer invited to speak for the company. The diligent pharmaceutical representative moved on to another company. And the remaining Effexor representative wisely presented me chocolate instead of any new information.

I still believed that Effexor might be better for certain types of depression and so did many of my colleagues. The FDA reprimanded Wyeth for making its superiority claims that were not supported by a more thorough review of the literature. In a surprisingly daring move that challenged years of Wyeth marketing, the now somewhat bigger, Forest did two studies comparing Lexapro to Effexor demonstrating that they were equally effective for treating depression. As a speaker for both drugs who believed that dual action was more powerful, I was surprised Forest took this risk. They did the trials in such a way that played upon Effexor's weakness, its increased side effect risk and minimal difference at lower doses. In the first study they limited the dose of Effexor to 150mg, below which not much of its norepinephrine power was evident. In the second study they raised the dose quickly over 2 weeks to 225mg and had a high side effect dropout rate which made it not look as effective. (Remember as noted above, the new studies had to count these drop outs as if they completed the trial- last observation carried forward or LCOF.) Wyeth cried foul, but in the real world patients wanted a drug with few side effects that didn't need to be titrated slowly.

The conclusion of my exposition isn't that everyone should be put on Lexapro or that Effexor is a bad product, because it isn't. My purpose is to point out that each product has advantages and disadvantages. Studies can be designed to accentuate these good and bad traits and be deceptive to an untrained person. No medication helps everyone and there may be only small differences between some medications that may make a big difference for a specific individual. Pharmaceutical companies would love for their drug to be first line for everyone, even those who don't need it. I have a few patients who have done a lot better on old generic medications and have fewer side effects than they had on a new one, even Lexapro. It is still a fine art, matching the right medication to a particular patient. The clinician must work with the patient to figure out which medications might be best for them and hope that success is reached before needing to cry uncle.

⌘ ⌘ ⌘ ⌘ ⌘

WHAT'S MY DIAGNOSIS, DOES IT MATTER AND WHO CARES?

Prior to 1980, when the Diagnostic and Statistical Manual third edition (DSMIII) came out, there was chaos. If you got three psychiatrists in a room trying to diagnose a patient, you'd have at least 6 different diagnoses. The forerunner to DSMIII (The III is the Roman numeral for 3) was DSMII and it was largely based upon psychoanalytic concepts. The American Psychiatric community, flush with psychoanalysts who fled Europe around World War II, veered in its own direction towards psychoanalytic orientation in the 1950's. The rest of the world, including all of American medicine save psychiatry, used diagnoses from the International Classification of Disease or ICD system. Insurance companies required these diagnosis codes for billing, even for psychiatry (although there are lists of code correlations between the ICD and DSM systems).

It really didn't matter much what diagnosis you had then because there were very few treatments available. DSMII divided the world of diagnoses into two general categories: neurotic and psychotic. Neurotics, like Woody Allen, were less severe and could handle psychoanalysis. Psychotics got much worse and might try to harm themselves or you if you tried to get them on the couch. The distinctions weren't always so easy to make. Psychiatrists would argue for hours about whether someone was depressed enough to be considered psychotic. If they didn't have enough insight into their illness they were psychotic. If they didn't want to talk to you, that was paranoid, and they were considered psychotic. If the patient stopped in the middle of recounting their story, that was thought blocking, this was also psychotic. Otherwise they were just neurotic and long-term psychoanalysis was the treatment of choice.

Psychoanalysis held the key to the cure even though the goal of analysis was insight not symptom reduction. Increases in symptoms and patients suffering in the process of gaining insight were part of the process of doing intensive therapy. Through intensive analysis of one's early childhood, the therapist could find the root conflict that caused and sustained the patient's symptoms. Through the therapeutic relationship, the therapist could re-parent and create a new self, free of conflict. Analogies were made to a surgeon cutting out the source of the problem and then doing reconstructive surgery. Pain was part of any effective analysis as of any surgery. The only difference was, if the patient didn't get better it wasn't the fault of the analyst, it was either the patient's resistance to change or the patient covering up the severity of their illness. This is highlighted in the "how many psychiatrists does it take to change a light bulb" joke. The answer obviously is only one, but it has to want to be changed.

    It seemed so straight forward, except for the tricky patients in the middle. There were patients on the borderline between neurotic and psychotic. They were given the wonderfully named diagnosis of pseudo-neurotic schizophrenia. They looked like they were neurotic, just like you and me, but if you put them on the couch they would act "crazy" just like patients with schizophrenia. They were the ones who didn't get better. It was important to identify these patients to prevent this catastrophe. More importantly, the therapist had to identify them early and modify the treatment, so that they wouldn't track them down and ruin their month-long August vacations on Cape Cod.

    Psychotherapy was thought of as beneficial for everyone and psychoanalysis was the Cadillac of psychotherapy. Psychoanalytic techniques were modified to even reach people with psychotic disorders. Although it wasn't clear if any of these actually helped the patient, they did make the therapist feel better about the time they spent with seemingly hopeless patients. The chairmen of almost every psychiatry department in the country were analytically trained and this set the stage for the perpetuity of this treatment, it seemed forever. As long as the funding was available, it was the ideal balance, the glory days for psychiatry. "The neurotics built castles in the sky, the psychotics lived there and the psychiatrists collected the rent."

I said things seemed simple, if you were neurotic you got psychoanalysis or at least some cheaper, shortened version of it. If you were psychotic that got tricky. If you had a lot of money, you might have the luxury to spend several years in one of the premier psychiatric facilities like the Institute of Living (formerly the Hartford Retreat). Away from the stressors of the world, taken by private limousine on excursions through the countryside, and participating in private individual psychotherapy sessions several times per week, sometimes this gave time to heal psychic wounds. If you didn't have money, you might end up in a large, state run hospital. The treatment there was mixed. Some of the less ill patients may have gotten to work on the farms on these large hospital campuses or participate in a variety of group activities. Others suffered in back wards receiving treatment that might vary from restraints, seclusion, shock treatments or treatments one might still get now in spas, such as cold wet body wraps. Psychoanalysis generally was not practiced in these facilities. Psychiatrists here were looking for medications that actually reduced symptoms; they were more realistic about not being able to cure patients.

I had the opportunity to visit Connecticut Valley Hospital in Middletown, CT and see some of the old hospital wards. There were rooms full of bathtubs for hot and cold baths treatments. There were massage tables that you would find in high-class spas for cold wraps to calm the nerves. Most fascinating were the drug treatment logs from the 1920's. These were filled with the names you'd find in a well-stocked health food store, St. John's Wort, Valerian, and many others. Despite all of these herbal medications, the ranks of the state hospitals grew exponentially until the 1950's. Neither an extensive pharmacopoeia of herbal tinctures and spa treatments nor psychotherapy helped these severely ill individuals enough to re-enter the outside world. It seemed as if the size of these long-term hospitals would have to grow indefinitely. That was until the introduction of some very interesting new medications.

Psychiatric illnesses were called "functional" disorders. This distinguished them from the brain diseases in neurology. Neurological disorders could be seen in brain dissections, presumably after the death of the patient, which for most neurological patients was an untimely inevitability. No such defects were found in most psychiatric patients with the crude assessment methods available at the time. When defects were found, it couldn't be proven that these weren't incidental findings, since patients lived longer after diagnosis than neurological patients. Therefore, finding medications to treat functional illness was not a major thrust of psychiatric research. Research, instead, focused on finding new therapies and therapeutic environments to re-educate and retrain patients to function more normally.

In the mid 1950's the first antipsychotic, chlorpromazine (Thorazine), was serendipitously discovered in the pursuit of a new antihistamine. Antihistamines were used to boost opiate anesthetics and Thorazine shared their sedating and calming properties. Prior medications used in psychiatry were just sedating, like barbiturates and bromides. Reports came that Thorazine actually stopped hallucinations and paranoid symptoms. Analysts were suspicious; this medication was just masking the symptoms. We recall that, analysts weren't interested in mere symptom reduction, and only psychoanalysis could offer a cure. When newer versions of antipsychotic medications emerged in the 1960's that were not very sedating, the skeptics became fewer.

Also in the 1950s, observations in the treatment of tuberculosis patients, that an anti-tuberculosis drug was elevating patients' moods led to the discovery of monoamine oxidase inhibitor (MAOIs) antidepressants. The MAOIs were very dangerous medications that occasionally resulted in heart attacks, strokes and even the death of the patient. It wasn't until the 1960's that it was realized by avoiding certain foods, and certain medications, which interacted with MAOIs, it was possible to prevent this catastrophic rise in blood pressure. Meanwhile, newer and safer tricyclic antidepressants (TCAs like Elavil and Tofranil) had come out. These medications were modifications of the antipsychotic medications and suffered from some of the same side effects: sedation, dry mouth, constipation, weight gain, and cardiac irregularities, but were still easier to use than MAOIs.

With the introduction of medications to treat severe depression and psychosis the ability to separate these two diagnoses was becoming essential. Since the side effects of the medications were troubling, you wanted to be able to reliably diagnose patients who might benefit from a medication, while excluding others who wouldn't. The analysts, who were still dominant in psychiatry, resisted changes to diagnoses that might have assisted in matching patients to new treatments. They remained skeptical of these medications that provided "merely symptomatic relief." Medications didn't address the underlying causes of the illnesses, which clearly have deep roots in poor parenting. One of my teachers at Yale, Stephen Fleck, wrote extensively and persuasively that the roots of schizophrenia lie in multiple generations of family dysfunction. His work led to the notion of the "schizophrenogenic" mother. He claimed it took three generations of dysfunctional parenting to produce a schizophrenic child. Current knowledge confirms that schizophrenia does run in families and is a result of an interaction between the environment and genes. However, the environmental factor is most likely viral and not poor parenting.

Advances in psychiatry would not be deterred. In 1971, medication containing the element, lithium, was introduced to the US from Europe. Lithium carbonate was the salt of lithium, the third element on the periodic table of the elements. It was a compound known since the 1800's to have a calming effect and purported to be in the original formula for the soft drink, 7-Up. It was tried as a sodium salt substitute in the early 1900's for cardiac patients. The only problem was that too many of these individuals died from it. Death was a significant deterrent for American psychiatrists to take a serious look at this element until the European psychiatrists had worked out a system of checking blood levels of the drug and finding a safe dosage range. Lithium was a miracle medication for patients with manic-depression psychosis (what we now call bipolar disorder). Patients, who were hospitalized annually for months with "psychotic breaks," showed dramatic improvement within weeks when given lithium, and never needed another hospitalization.

The only problem was identifying who had the "manic depressive" diagnosis which lithium helped. Under DSMII anyone who had hallucinations or delusions was considered to have schizophrenia, not an indication for lithium. In 1970, American psychiatrists diagnosed schizophrenia at 10 times the rate of their English counterparts. Our diagnostic system, based upon psychoanalytic theory of causality, was now really impeding not only research but also clinical care by failing to recognize who would benefit from new treatments. Researchers in the burgeoning field of psychopharmacology research were getting fed up with the analysts and devised their own diagnostic criteria, the Research Diagnostic Criteria or RDC.

The RDC was to be entirely empirically based. There were no theoretical preconceived notions of what caused the problem, just clustering of symptoms. No Freudian theories of oral fixations, or oedipal conflicts would bias these criteria. They were to be clustered first by clinical observation and then adjusted by statistical means. For example, major depression would have a list of symptoms that if the individual had 5 of 10 for a specified period that would qualify for the diagnosis. Surveys of patient populations helped to validate the criteria and multiple investigators would rate the same individual to see if the criteria reliably led to the same diagnosis. The result was a set of criteria that if five psychiatrists examined the same patient at least 4 would come up with the same diagnosis and usually the fifth could be persuaded to change his mind. The system worked so well that the American Psychiatric Association in 1980 used almost all of the RDC criteria in its new diagnostic manual, DSMIII. All was not so rosy for the analysts.

The analysts balked at such a cold and anti-theoretical diagnostic system. This was "just a cookbook with lists of symptoms," they complained. "It was a mindless volume that threw out decades of theory." A more hidden fear was that many of their patients would not meet criteria for a diagnosis, meaning that insurers may not cover their treatments for long-term reconstructive therapy. What would they do with their patients? How would they pay for their children's college educations? Have no fear; compromise was here, here in the formation of a multi-axial diagnostic system. DSMIII went so far as to create five of them. Axis I had the a-theoretical, symptom-based, checklist-made diagnoses that reflected presumably biologically based disease states. These included the reliability-tested diagnoses based upon the RDC. Axis II included the personality disorders that were developmentally based, i.e. due to failures of parenting that could be benefited by long-term psychotherapy. This concession to the analysts was most evident in the placement of mental retardation on Axis I instead of Axis II with the other developmental disorders, since no analyst would rightfully use their skill on such a cognitively impaired individual. This inconsistency was corrected in subsequently revised editions when psychoanalytic concepts began to be worked out of Axis II as well. By this time the analysts' fears were realized, insurers stopped paying for any treatment that wasn't on Axis I, and psychoanalysis was not covered at all.

(Second edition note: In the most recent DSM V, the multi-axial system was eliminated. The axis II disorders with the strongest validity were able to join the big boys of axis I. However, I do regret the loss of the axes III, IV and V explained below.)

What about the other three Axes you may ask? Axis III was straightforward. On it any medical diagnosis was recorded. This reflected psychiatry's efforts to rejoin the medical community, which it had temporarily left. There was a brief period in the late 1970's when a six-month internship in internal medicine was eliminated as a requirement for taking the psychiatry certification boards. Why did a psychiatrist need to know any medicine since they wouldn't have to examine or touch patients? They were to be versed in the "talking cure." Samuel Shem's 1978 classic interns must read book, "House of God" included psychiatry as a NPC (no patient contact) specialty. Unfortunately, lack of medical training for psychiatrists proved to be a disaster after only a few years and was reintroduced. Psychiatric hospitals needed the limited medical expertise of their residents to identify a multitude of physical problems that occurred in the psychiatric patients. Medical problems were no less prevalent in outpatients. Psychiatrists were moving back to a "mind body connection," understanding patients from a "bio-psycho-social" perspective. Today, the awareness that knowledge of medicine is essential to safe and effective use of psychotropic medication is used as a justification to limit psychologists, who have no medical training requirement, from obtaining medication-prescribing privileges.

(Second edition note: I can see why axis III was eliminated since it implied a difference between medical and psychiatric disorders. I did like that psychiatric disorders were placed higher on the list as axis I and II, while medical diagnoses came in a distant third.)

Axis IV was where stressors are coded. This allowed for recognition that some patients got ill only under extreme stress. Two patients might both have the same depressive or anxious symptoms but one may have only gotten them after some extreme stress while the other happened spontaneously. Under a bio-psycho-social model these two patients may have quite different conditions. Recent gene research has supported this. A gene has been identified which correlated with the ability to handle stress. Individuals with two copies of the weaker variant become depressed with minimal stress while those with two copies of the stronger variant don't seem to become depressed at all. Individuals with one of each copy fall in the middle in their ability to cope with stress.

Finally, Axis V reflected an individual's level of function. This is a quite helpful axis since determining who should get medication or treatment has all to do with how much the condition affects one's ability to function. This axis has been turned into a rating scale that allows the psychiatrist to note improvement or worsening over time. With this new multi-axial system, insurers started to ask therapists to make treatment plans that included goals to reduce symptoms that now could be more easily measured. The psychoanalytically oriented therapists became outraged; their goal was "insight" not symptom reduction. Symptom reduction came as a consequence of insight that really couldn't be measured. One by one they dropped out of accepting insurance payments.

Not long after the introduction of DSMIII, the field of psychiatry boomed. New medications were being developed at a rapid pace. Many of these medications worked in new ways and were not just "me-too" drugs. Large surveys of the general population were done with the new diagnostic criteria that gave our best estimates of the prevalence of mental disorders in the US and around the world. The rest of the world started using DSMIII, instead of ICD9; allowing epidemiologists to see that the rates of major psychiatric conditions like schizophrenia and Bipolar disorder (the new name for manic depression) didn't vary much around the world. This gave indirect evidence for the biologic basis of these disorders since rates didn't vary despite different parenting and societal environments. Reliability is the statistical term used to mean that multiple assessments would come up with the same conclusion. DSMIII proved to be a very reliable tool to make diagnoses. However, there were some hidden problems in this effort to gain reliability that may have affected validity.

Validity means that the conclusion or diagnosis that one comes up with is correct. With validity comes an ability to make predictions about course of illness and treatment outcome. Valid diagnoses are likely to have minimal overlap especially when a biologic or genetic marker is found. DSMIII and subsequent DSM IV started to show some cracks in its validity as more treatments became available and genetic markers were found. For example, the criteria for major depression were made fairly broad. In requiring 5 of a list of criteria, it included about 6% of the general population. This was a cut off that made statistical sense, but didn't correlate with any biologic markers, course of illness or treatment. Requiring fewer criteria would have included up to 20% of the population while requiring more didn't change the prevalence of the diagnosis much. This meant that if you had 5 of the symptoms, you likely had many more symptoms, which gave a semblance of internal validity to the diagnosis.

However, these symptoms were still broad because they had to be reliably understood by clinicians and less reliable symptoms were excluded from the criteria. For example, in the original DSMIII melancholic subtype of depression there was a criterion, "distinct quality of mood," which meant that the patient could distinguish this depression from ordinary sadness. This criterion was replaced by the circular, "prior response to medication," in DSMIIIR, because of the difficulty in clinicians being able to agree on whether a patient's depression had "distinct quality" to it. Remember, if several clinicians couldn't agree on a symptom, this would hurt its reliability. It was a very valid or helpful symptom despite its low reliability and was reintroduced in DSMIV.

When clinical trials of medications are done for FDA approval, they use the broad categories and not any subtype. Two patients may meet the minimal criteria for a disorder but not have much symptom overlap. This is similar to two people going out to eat, one orders lo Mein from a Chinese restaurant and the other orders spaghetti from an Italian restaurant, are they eating the same or different categories of food? In psychiatry the analogy may be distinguishing the depressed anxious patient from the anxious depressed patient. In being so broad, medication trials with a variety of medications that work very differently, all demonstrate a similar 50-70% response rate which is only about 10% better than a placebo. This has led to criticisms that these medications offer very little over doing nothing, which is flat out wrong. It is more likely that lack of diagnostic precision serves to dilute the study population of good responders with patients who have a different disorder that is less responsive to the study medication.

Efforts to define subcategories of major depression that may respond preferentially to one class of antidepressant over the other hasn't been successfully done since the 1980's when MAOIs were shown to be more effective than TCAs for a subtype called atypical depression. The reasons for this failure is not clear to me, since I and many other clinicians seem to be able to identify clusters of symptoms that respond preferentially to different medications. I partly blame the pharmaceutical companies that fund close to 90% of the drug research and would rather have a 60% response rate for 6% of the population than a 90% response rate for less than 1%. (One recent exception is the approval of Wellbutrin for seasonal mood disorder.) It is also very difficult to recruit patients into a drug trial especially if the criteria become very narrow. In my conversations with leading researchers, they talk about the difficulty in finding these subtypes in their samples and have put their hopes on genetic markers. These markers are still many years away and may not work either because an illness may change over time. As a person stays ill or has recurrences, more or different neurotransmitter systems may be affected. This means that two individuals with the same gene may need different treatments. This same problem exists with other conditions like diabetes and epilepsy that may worsen with time requiring more or different medications at more advanced stages. For example, a young person with type 2 diabetes might be initially able to control their illness with diet alone. Over time as the disease progresses multiple medications might be necessary. After many years complications such as retinopathy or neuropathy may require additional medications.

The same SSRI medication can treat a variety of conditions including: major depression, panic disorder, obsessive-compulsive disorder, generalized anxiety, and social anxiety disorder. Does this mean they are the same condition? If a patient's depression responds to a medication indicated for bipolar disorder even though they have never had mania, does that patient have bipolar disorder? What if they respond to the addition of an antipsychotic medication, are they psychotic? This starts to sound like the arguments that the analysts had about whether someone was neurotic or psychotic. Fortunately I have never heard anyone call such a patient a "pseudo-bipolar depressive" or a "pseudo-psychotic depressive." But I have used the unofficial diagnostic term bipolar 2 ½ or cyclical mood disorder to describe depressed patients who respond better to medications approved for bipolar disorder than to medications approved for depression.

Psychiatry is in a new phase not dissimilar to the 1970s when the advent of new and effective treatments advanced faster than our diagnoses. This failure of diagnoses to keep up with available treatments may be holding back researchers from making new discoveries in treatments and identification of biologic markers. For example, certain gene markers for bipolar disorder only seem apparent when family members with psychiatric illness not meeting criteria for bipolar disorder are included. Researchers have taken to use terms like, "sub syndromal" depression or bipolar to include family members who don't meet criteria for the illness but may carry the marker genes and have some of the same symptoms but not enough to be diagnosed with the index disorder. A recent study of depressed patients revealed that 40% of them had symptoms of "sub-syndromal" hypomania; meaning that they were within one or two criteria for bipolar disorder. (By the way, medical diagnoses face the same dilemma. For example, many patients with symptoms of Lyme disease have fewer than the 5 markers on a Western Blot test needed to meet criteria for Lyme disease. Does this mean they shouldn't be treated for the illness? Patients with risk factors for diabetes have been given the label "metabolic syndrome" and given treatment indicated for diabetes treatment. We don't have the same labels in psychiatry that encourage treatment of sub-syndromal conditions.)

Fortunately, astute psychiatrists have used their clinical experience to better match patients with effective treatments. This is why it would be devastating for patients if they could not receive medications for "off-label" indications. All medications approved by the FDA must be proven safe and effective for a specific indication or diagnosis. If our diagnoses have flaws or limitations, we are restricting some medications where they may be helpful or using them where they might not work. This is also why patients should not put too much emphasis on their DSM diagnosis and the indication label for medications. If it is helping, who cares what the medication is called? Patients often ask why I prescribed an antidepressant for their anxiety, when they just wanted an anxiety medication. "I'm not depressed." They say. I say, "Be glad that its working, not addicting and you'd probably get depressed if we didn't treat your anxiety now." If you are improving, ask for the most benign label the doctor is willing to give. Sometimes the best medication for your DSM diagnosis is a medication approved for a different diagnosis that may not even be psychiatric.

(Second edition note: A recent large study out of Canada reported that patients treated with high doses of benzodiazepines for long periods of time had an increased risk for dementia. Realizing that

many patients will refuse to take an antidepressant for their anxiety because they "are not depressed," I speculate that high dose benzodiazepine use is a proxy for patients who should be on an antidepressant. Both Alzheimer's disease and depression are associated with low brain derived neurotrophic factor (BDNF) which protects the brain from deterioration. Antidepressants but not benzodiazepines have been shown to increase BDNF. Connect the dots.)

⌘⌘⌘⌘⌘

CONFESSIONS OF A REFORMED BIPOLAR OVER-DIAGNOSER AND HOW TO SEE RESIDUAL ADHD

In my early years on the faculty at the University of Connecticut I got the reputation of Mr. Bipolar. If a resident had a suspicion that a patient had bipolar disorder and wanted to convince the attending, I was called in as the case conference consultant. Granted, patients were pre-selected and were hospitalized with severe symptoms, but I can't recall an instance when I didn't entertain the bipolar diagnosis. The older attendings were more likely to consider a diagnosis of schizophrenia, borderline personality, or even attribute most of the symptoms to substance abuse. But I liked to err on the side of a diagnosis that I felt had a better prognosis and course of treatment. I had seen lithium perform miracles for the right patient and it wasn't always apparent who that right patient was. Lithium wasn't given to patients who didn't have a mood disorder, so giving one of the above labels would mean the patient would suffer with antipsychotic medication, drug and alcohol rehab or long-term psychotherapy and be doomed to years of relapses. Drug and alcohol rehabilitation programs at that time were opposed to using any psychotropic medications, which were deemed to be crutches. A trial of lithium could be therapeutic in a mere two to four weeks. If it didn't work, not much time was lost.

It wasn't long before I started getting a flood of referrals of patients with bipolar disorder. I got so many one month that I decided to start a bipolar group. I learned so much from this group because all the patients were bright and insightful, if not into their own illness, then they at least saw the symptoms in the others. One of my first realizations was that patients with bipolar disorder, who were purported to lack insight, were able to see other people's weaknesses exquisitely well. One young woman patient with schizoaffective disorder eagerly wanted to be in a group, so I decided to see if she would fit in and if the others would accept her. Schizoaffective disorder meant the person suffered from symptoms of both bipolar disorder and schizophrenia (with hallucinations and delusions that persisted even after mood symptoms resolved). Not long after entering the group, she innocently asked the others how they had dealt with their hallucinations and delusions. I was concerned about her question because none of the others in the group revealed that they ever experienced such symptoms. To my surprise, all but one of the patients in the group admitted that they had been able to hide the fact that they had psychotic symptoms of delusions, paranoia and even hallucinations. If they had admitted these symptoms they would, in certain settings, have been diagnosed with schizophrenia or schizoaffective disorder too. These patients were high functioning doctors, lawyers, teachers and other professionals. Fortunately, these symptoms responded fairly quickly to medications, but some symptoms took much longer to improve.

When I was in my last year of psychiatry residency, I worked in the outpatient clinic at Yale New Haven Hospital. The clinic had a special lithium clinic where I had the opportunity to see a variety of miracle patients. There were a number who had been hospitalized every year with psychotic delusions. They were diagnosed with schizophrenia but hated the side effects of the antipsychotic medication so they would discontinue them as soon as they could. This cycle was repeated for one of my patients annually for 16 years until 1971 when he was re-diagnosed with manic depression and was placed on lithium. He didn't have a hospitalization for the next 14 years prior to my seeing him and didn't seem likely to relapse again. He had gone back to school and finished his law degree, remaining diligent with his lithium prescription.

One of the newly diagnosed and lithium treated patients I worked with was a 45-year-old married man. I began to treat him and his wife with couple's counseling a few weeks after discharge from the hospital and beginning lithium. He had been severely depressed for a couple of years. He had lost his job and spent days in bed. His wife held the family together, continuing to work, shop, cook, clean, and watch after the needs of the kids. After several failed antidepressant trials he became manic. When he was manic, he began going out all-night spending a lot of money. He didn't see anything wrong with his behavior as he was making up for lost time. He was verbally abusive to his wife and family. After starting lithium, his mood normalized, he was no longer depressed or manic, but he was still difficult to live with. He complained that his family didn't understand what he went through when he was so depressed and why he needed to enjoy his improved wellbeing. He was doing more, spending was contained, but his activities were mostly for his benefit. Never did he consider what he had put his wife and family through. Therapy with him was like beating your head up against a wall. He couldn't see where he had done anything wrong and resented his wife's anger at his persistent disengagement from the family. This time it was worse, though, since he was enjoying himself. I sympathized with the wife and wondered why she stood by him. Then, suddenly, after six months on lithium, in one of our couple's sessions, he showed remorse. He apologized for his being inconsiderate and thanked his wife for all she had done for him and the family. I was shocked. Was I such a good therapist that I was able to break through that thick head of his? I was a mere resident; I didn't believe I was that good a therapist. His wife noted that this was his old self come back. That is why she stayed with him.

    I have come to appreciate this phenomenon in almost all of my bipolar patients. This is particularly true of those who have experienced severe mania or bipolar type I disorder. Six to twelve months after beginning lithium they gain insight into their behavior and seem to have a personality change. I have seen it with some other mood stabilizer treatments but much less often with the new atypical antipsychotic medications used now to treat bipolar disorder. It is such a predictable response that I like to tell family members about it so they know what to expect and try to hold on during those turbulent six months when the patient seems to not have any major mood symptoms but is still behaving like an "asshole." I like to use this "technical" term because everyone seems to understand what I am saying and acknowledge his or her behavior.

Psychotherapy oriented psychiatrists have termed this the hyperthymic personality. The implication is that medication won't change it since it is a personality trait. My observations of a personality change after adequate treatment belies this assertion. I have seen this change most consistently with lithium. Therefore, I strongly encourage patients who continue to have these seemingly personality symptoms to try lithium. So many physicians and patients are frightened by lithium's potential side effects that they use other medications first. The reality is that if carefully monitored and used in lower than recommended dosages, lithium has fewer side effects than most of the newer medications indicated for bipolar disorder, except perhaps Lamictal (lamotrigine).

Recent studies of the MRI brain scans of patients presenting with bipolar disorder demonstrate that certain parts of the brain seem smaller or atrophied. This is true at the onset of diagnosis implying that this atrophy is occurring prior to the onset of symptoms and is not an effect of medications. It may take years for this deterioration to result in symptoms. Patients with bipolar symptoms who don't get treated until later in life seem to complain more of memory problems. Fortunately, certain medications, especially lithium, seem to possess properties that encourage brain regeneration through a compound called BDNF, or brain derived neurotrophic factor. Lithium may be working in multiple ways, not the least being encouraging re-growth of lost brain tissue. This may be why it takes six months or more to see more subtle personality changes.

I have had patients who have been unsuccessfully treated with a multitude of medications approved for bipolar disorder, but refused to try lithium. Many of my patients have only responded to lithium. Some have suffered for years because of fears of deteriorating kidney function. I have only had two patients need dialysis or kidney transplant and both had taken overdoses of the drug and had other medical conditions, such as diabetes, autoimmune disease and hypertension. Patients can become toxic on lithium if they aren't careful about their use of anti-inflammatory medications like ibuprofen and naproxen (which have become over the counter) and certain blood pressure medications. Dosage of lithium is a major factor in side effects. Lithium doses and any side effects can be kept low, while using newer antimanic medications to manage acute and residual symptoms. I believe that lithium's major benefits are long term and can be gotten at doses lower than recommended (probably at doses producing blood levels of 0.4-0.6 mmol/L or even lower).

In the early 1990's an influential research study was done to determine what was the best level of lithium to use for maintenance treatment. Prior studies on acute treatment lead to recommended levels of 0.8 to 1.2 or even 1.5 mmol/L. The researchers did a seemingly well-designed double blind controlled study. They entered bipolar patients stabilized for at least several months on lithium and randomly assigned them to receive lithium doses that lead to levels of either 0.4 to 0.6 or 0.8 to 1.0. The results were dramatic. Half of the patients assigned to the lower level relapsed within six months. The conclusion seemed obvious that the lower dose was ineffective and all patients should be maintained with the higher levels. This was front-page news.

Several years later, at a small conference, a new analysis of this same study was reported. Prior to randomization, patients entered the study with a variety of blood levels. It seemed that all of the patients who relapsed in the group assigned to the lower blood level had entered the study with lithium levels in the higher range. The relapse rate among the patients entering the study with initial lower lithium levels and assigned to stay on a lower level was no different than the rate among those who entered and stayed on a higher level. The side effects were much higher in the higher blood level group. The conclusion of this reanalysis of the same study was that rapid dosage reduction of lithium is associated with relapse. Also, the higher doses are associated with more side effects and may not be needed for a significant portion of stable patients. Unfortunately, like most corrections, this did not make front-page news.

One study revealed that it often took 7to 8 years for a patient with bipolar disorder to be correctly diagnosed. My bias towards making this diagnosis came from an awareness of the negative consequences of delayed and inappropriate treatment. Multiple failed antidepressant trials, interspersed with failed marriages and lost jobs were routine for individuals for whom the diagnosis of bipolar is missed. This also doesn't take into account the theoretical worsening of brain atrophy. Patients rarely present to treatment because they are feeling too good; so many highs go unreported. The typical patient comes in the autumn distraught about financial ruin, lost job and relationships that occurred over the preceding months. The characteristic bipolar pattern of response to antidepressants is one where the same medication works for several months to years then fails at another time. If there is a relapse several months later, the antidepressant worsens the feelings of agitation and irritability. Alternatively, the patient fails to respond to multiple medications with different mechanisms of action. The addition of a medication approved for bipolar disorder, such as lithium, valproic acid, lamotrigine or an antipsychotic medication, often leads to a fairly rapid response. These medications aren't thought of because they are not labeled as antidepressants.

While working at the University outpatient psychiatry clinic, I got referred patient after patient responding to this strategy. My success rate was impressive. Then I encountered a college professor who complained of chronic insomnia. He was full of energy, spoke fast, complained of mind racing and couldn't sleep; all of these are classic bipolar symptoms. He didn't respond to a variety of sleeping aids so I tried him on bipolar medications. We went through multiple trials all causing terrible side effects and an inability to function. He did manage to sleep with some of them, but he couldn't wake up even with small dosages. After almost a year of trying different medications, I realized that his symptoms never changed throughout the year. All patients with bipolar cycled with highs and lows or normal periods. He was hyper all year long. He did tell me this early on, but I was taught to be skeptical of what bipolar patients told you. The diagnosis of chronic mania doesn't exist, or if it does, I've never seen it. Since he was hyper all the time, this must be some type of attention deficit disorder. The diagnosis of attention deficit hyperactivity disorder (ADHD) didn't appear evident since he never complained of poor attention. He had managed to do well in school and was successful in earning a PhD. It was a surprise to him when I proposed giving him a stimulant to help him sleep. I explained my rationale and carefully began Ritalin just in case it might make him worse. He improved with each increase in dose up to 80mg. He was able to sleep now without any sleeping medications. Ritalin was supposed to cause insomnia, but for him it stopped his mind racing so he could sleep. Besides helping with his sleep, he noted that everything that he did became easier. The following year, his students voted him teacher of the year.

After seeing the dramatic effect of a stimulant on someone who appeared to have bipolar symptoms, I started to see ADHD more frequently. Most child psychiatrists at the time diagnosed most children with ADHD and now are being accused of over diagnosing bipolar disorder. For me, it was the opposite. I was at a meeting with a prominent child psychiatrist and asked him how he differentiated these disorders since the symptoms overlapped so much. He scoffed at my question and finally said quickly that people with ADHD didn't have mood symptoms. Even he didn't really believe this because a book he published identified 6 types of "ADHD," which included a bipolar type. This is like being a minister who only preaches to Lutherans who somehow decides that there are different types of Lutherans, Methodist-Lutherans, Jewish-Lutherans and Muslim-Lutherans, and all you have to do is give them slightly different sermons. My experience suggested that ADHD and bipolar disorder were very different conditions requiring different treatments but with very similar presentations. The most reliable difference is that ADHD remained stable over time, while bipolar symptoms cycled throughout the year. This time element is not one of the diagnostic criteria for either condition.

One presentation that is particularly confusing diagnostically is the combination of ADHD with anxiety and depressive symptoms. I have had quite a few patients present like this. The typical patient is Jon Combo III. He was a high functioning executive at a large company who faced increasing responsibility as he advanced in the company. He was married with 2 young children who were placing increasing demands on his time, as he wanted to be an active parent who attended their various activities. He was very compulsive, which helped him organize his multiple tasks. As the workload increased and home life became more of a distraction, he started having to recheck his work. Fears of the children's health resulted in his checking the electric switches, stove and appliances to avoid the risk of a fire starting. This behavior, which looks like OCD (obsessive compulsive disorder), worsened and his functioning deteriorated. It got more and more difficult to get out of the house on time for work and to leave work because of his rechecking. He got increasingly depressed as failure approached. My initial diagnosis was OCD so I began him on Zoloft (sertraline), a selective serotonin reuptake inhibitor (SSRI) antidepressant FDA approved for OCD. Initially he seemed to be relieved from some of the anxiety, but as the dosage was increased he got worse. He had a hard time explaining how he was worse but it seemed he was more tired and was having trouble concentrating, which was making him angry, irritable and frustrated. The initial positive response followed by irritability made me think that he had bipolar disorder that was being made worse by the antidepressant. So I tried several mood stabilizers, first Depakote, then lithium and finally Risperidal (an antipsychotic medication). Each of these medications seemed worse than the preceding one. The patient's energy level, thinking and concentration worsened, leading to more anger and dysfunction even after one or two low dosages. The enigma of Jon Combo III was solved when I paradoxically gave him a stimulant with the low dose SSRI and his thinking cleared and he was suddenly able to function again. The primary diagnosis was ADHD.

Mr. Combo always had ADHD but compensated for the inattention and distractibility by developing compulsive behaviors to make sure he didn't forget to do things. When the tasks got too great, the compulsiveness went into overdrive and started to interfere more than it was helping. When the SSRI reduced the checking behavior, he made even more mistakes and couldn't concentrate. Most SSRIs and bipolar medications reduce dopamine function in the brain, which is the opposite effect of stimulants that help concentration. His inability to think and function properly made him upset and agitated. Effective treatment is tricky and requires recognition of this complex set of symptoms and seemingly paradoxical response to medications. It is very easy to misdiagnosis Mr. Combo as bipolar disorder because there is a mix of mood, anxiety and concentration symptoms that seem to get worse with antidepressants, but it also gets worse with mood stabilizers. Stimulants alone also worsen the anxiety and don't help the depression. I have found the best treatment is a low dose of antidepressant begun first (preferably sertraline which has a significant dopamine effect) followed by the careful titration of a stimulant (usually an amphetamine over a methylphenidate preparation). An alternative treatment is with Trileptal and a stimulant. Trileptal is a medication used for bipolar disorder. Although not FDA approved for this, it doesn't seem to have the same cognitive dulling effects of other bipolar medications for this patient type. The dosage of Trileptal is also lower than I use in bipolar patients.

This condition that I call a "decompensated ADHD" turns out to be more common than I ever thought. I think I misdiagnosed most of them as bipolar and some as OCD. Now I am a reformed over-diagnoser of bipolar. I have to give partial credit to my psychodynamic training for eventually seeing this diagnostic dilemma. In psychoanalytic theory, a symptom serves as a defense mechanism against a conflict between two seemingly bad alternatives. In this situation, the obsessive behavior serves as a defense against errors made due to distractibility. The agitation that emerges from taking away one defense mechanism is an attempt to alert the individual to the urgency to prevent failure in the face of persistent poor concentration by removal of obsession as a coping tool. Treatment of the underlying inattention with medication, and psychotherapy to help teach better coping skills,(including setting priorities,) will help reduce the need for compulsive behavior and frustration. Patients need to be active participants to find the right balance of anxiety reducing SSRI and concentration enhancing stimulant.

  I confess that I used to over diagnose bipolar disorder at a time when others under diagnosed it. However, it is important to recognize that it is better to err on the side of recognizing and treating a more dangerous diagnosis first. But if the treatment doesn't seem to be working or is producing worse consequences, a reassessment needs to be made of both the treatment and the working diagnosis. Two individuals may appear alike on the surface but have very different underlying conditions.

⌘⌘⌘⌘⌘

YOU CAN'T TEACH OLD DOGS OR NEURONS NEW TRICKS-WHEN UNDESIRABLE MEDICATION COMBINATIONS MAYBE BEST

I was working as an attending psychiatrist at a local community hospital. While making my morning rounds on my inpatients, I received a page from one of the local primary care physicians. It was with a fair degree of urgency that he called. He told me the story of his patient whom he inherited from another physician who had retired. This was not the first time I received a call like this from a relatively young physician, fresh with up to date knowledge of evidence based medical protocols. They diligently try to update their patients' treatments to conform to the latest standards of care. They are young, idealistic and fully invested in their university-instilled knowledge about the right way to treat patients. Tragically, they become disconcerted when confronted with patients whose treatment includes medications that are either old or they never learned about. If they dare to keep these archaic treatments they might turn into the provider most mocked by all who teach in the Ivy Tower University Hospital, that provider who clearly hasn't learned a thing since their training half a century ago, the LMD or local medical doctor.

His patient was a 78-year-old woman who spoke only Polish. She was now in the emergency department extremely agitated. He had been trying to manage her for several weeks. She might be hallucinating and he tried her on some antipsychotic medication, which did not seem to be working. "Would you please see her as soon as possible, and admit her to your psychiatry service." In my first year of medical internship my senior resident would have referred to her as a "GOMER," which was the euphemism from Samuel Shem's classic tale of medical training, *House of God*. It stands for "get out of my emergency room." I have since completed my psychiatry residency during which I learned of the importance of empathy and calling someone a GOMER did not convey that sentiment. Her attending too had gotten sensitivity training that might not have been part of residency training in the time of Dr. Shem. This young attending was truly interested in helping this elderly woman. So much so that it became evident to me that his efforts to help her were what was wrong with her.

When I arrived in the emergency room Mrs. M was lying restlessly on a stretcher with a family member holding her hand. She spoke rapidly in Polish, stopping when it became apparent that I didn't understand a word. She didn't understand a word of what I said either. Her daughter was with her and told me the story. She had come for the winter from Poland with her husband, which they had been doing for a couple of years. She had a chronic anxiety problem for which she had taken Valium (diazepam) 10mg for as long as anyone could remember. She was a strong farmwoman. Her hands were coarse from manual labor and her face full of deep wrinkles from excessive sun exposure. She had managed through many rough economic times and now had little to worry about. Her physician in Poland continued to prescribe the Valium, as did the Polish-speaking physician she had in the United States. Her new doctor, the one who placed the desperate call to me, who took over from the now retired Polish doctor, felt that she had been on Valium too long and should come off. He tried to replace it with newer medications, Ativan and then Xanax. Then he tried a variety of others, each worse than the previous.

Valium and Librium were the first of a class of medications called benzodiazepines that came out in the early 1960's. These medications help with mild anxiety and difficulty sleeping and they have anticonvulsant and muscle relaxant effects. More importantly they were significantly safer in overdose than their predecessor medications, barbiturates and meprobamate (Miltown). The lethality of overdose of barbiturates was well known from the deaths of Marylyn Monroe and Elvis Presley. Valium became the standard treatment for all types of anxiety. It was given intravenously to stop seizures. It was used to relieve back spasms. It became so popular, that it became a joke in Woody Allen's movies. When Allen asked in a crowded store, "Does anyone have a Valium?" seemingly everyone had one.

Valium's popularity hid for a while its addicting properties. Newer agents came out in the 1970's and 80's, most notably Xanax (alprazolam). Xanax was marketed as a non-benzodiazepine because of some minor differences in its chemical structure. But its actions were still on the same site in the brain, the benzodiazepine receptor. The manufacturer, Upjohn, exploited this difference claiming it was more similar to an antidepressant and therefore not habit forming like other benzodiazepines. They sponsored studies in depression and the new diagnosis of panic disorder. These studies were able to show reduction in a depression rating scale presumably because a significant number of items on the rating scale were symptoms of anxiety. When studying panic disorder large dosages were used and they never reported the efforts to reduce or discontinue the medication. When I began working at the Veterans Administration Hospital, it seemed as if the entire clinic of Veterans, struggling with anxiety from Post Traumatic Stress Disorder (PTSD), was hooked on the drug. I recall the drug rep wheeling her cart of Xanax literature telling me that there was no addiction from Xanax. I had to yell at her about the atrocity her advertising had done to my clinic as I now tried to manage a clinic with hundreds of Xanax addicts.

Xanax is now clearly labeled as a benzodiazepine. The various benzodiazepines mainly differ in how long they last and how quickly they get into the brain. The quicker the medication gets into the brain, the more quickly the individual feels its effect and the more likely to find this taking of the medication reinforcing. One feature of addiction is the reinforcing effects of the drug. Drugs taken by inhaling, smoking or injecting get to the brain faster than oral drugs and are more likely to cause rapid addiction because they give a more rapid reward to the user. Valium and Xanax both get into the brain quickly, even by oral route, rapidly rewarding the user with its euphoric relaxant effect.

Contrary to Upjohn's marketing literature, the shorter acting benzodiazepines are more addicting because the patient is more likely to notice the effect wearing off and need to take more. When used at higher doses, actual withdrawal symptoms may be felt in is little as 3 to 6 hours after taking Xanax. Valium on the other hand lasts closer to 24 hours. In this sense Xanax is more addictive than Valium. By comparison, heroin has a very short half-life and users have to imbibe several times per day in order to maintain a high and prevent withdrawal symptoms. Methadone, which is used to treat heroin addicts, lasts over 24 hours reducing some of the addict's behaviors in constantly needing to take more. Within the class of benzodiazepines, Klonopin (clonazepam) has the most favorable profile since it lasts almost 20 hours and is slow to get into the brain. It still can be habit forming, but patients are less likely to take it as frequently and thereby increase the daily dose unnecessarily.

So what happened to Mrs. M? She had been on Valium for so many years that she was used to the effects of the medication. She had a physical dependence on it but did not have any abuse or over use of the drug. She took it only once per day and rarely took more. As noted above, Valium lasts over 24 hours so the once per day dosing kept her free from withdrawal. She never abused the medication even though it had a rapid onset. Over the years, she had learned its effects and how to use it effectively. The switch to Ativan and then Xanax on a once daily basis was inadequate to prevent her from going through benzodiazepine withdrawal. Neither she nor her physician ever made the connection that her agitation was evidence of Valium withdrawal. The use of antipsychotic medication only exacerbated the situation by introducing the very unpleasant side effect of akathisia, or extreme restlessness.

In the emergency department, I had her take one dose of Valium and in less than an hour she was fine and able to go home. She smiled at me and gladly agreed to follow-up with me. The following week, when I saw her in my office, it was apparent that she had also become depressed and was prescribed an antidepressant in addition to the Valium. I was able to take her off the antidepressant after six months but never the Valium, which she stayed on for many years that I followed her. The lesson for the young physician was that if a treatment is working, even if it may not be the most up to date, be careful before you consider altering it. The lesson for the rest of us is that newer isn't always better and the lowly LMD may be savvier than he is given credit for.

When I start working with a patient I follow some simple methodical rules in my search to find the best medications.

Start one medication at a time so as to learn its effect and side effects.

Limit potentially addicting doses of medications and avoid them in patients with addiction histories.

Don't stop a medication that had partial benefit until it is clear that a new medication has some benefit.

Be cautious about the effect of one medication on another, adjusting dosages to take into account metabolic interactions.

Don't stop a medication combination started by other doctors if it is clearly working, even if it doesn't make sense. Try to find out if it is causing side effects and nibble away at potentially unnecessary medications.

Newer isn't always better. Sometimes the best medications are old medications.

Don't be afraid of potential side effects. What may be a side effect in one person, for example constipation, may be a beneficial effect in another, e.g. treatment for irritable bowel.

When a patient doesn't follow my suggestions either by mistake or deliberately I don't admonish but try to learn from the experience. Sometimes a patient's "non-compliance" is the right move. Treatment, after all, is a collaborative experiment.

It's hard to teach old dogs or neurons new tricks. Some patients have become so used to a particular medication, that changing it is fraught with peril. ⌘⌘⌘⌘⌘

THE RAM HYPOTHESIS AND WHY REMEMBERING EVERYTHING MAY MAKE YOU DEPRESSED

In my years of psychiatric practice one of the most common complaints of my patients *after* they have gotten well is difficulty remembering things. This has always been a curious complaint since when they were depressed and anxious they clearly functioned quite poorly. Poor concentration is one of the major symptoms of anxiety and depression. In the midst of an episode individuals are so overtaken by anxiety that they can't make decisions, worry about everything and eventually shut down. This may involve missing work, avoiding chores and not going to social activities with a retreat to the bedroom. The memory complaints during depression usually involve important things and affect functioning at work and home. Trivial things take on paramount importance, while important things are neglected. The boss not saying hello that day may signify a major snub. Preoccupation with this may lead to obsessing about all past rejections. Obsessing then leads to reduced efficiency with task completion. This in turn leads to poor work performance, which leads to actual reprimands from the boss, reinforcing the original perception that the boss must not like you.

Treatment for the anxiety and depression results in a return of function. The individual returns to social activities and work, taking back responsibilities and starting to enjoy life again. Yet, this is the time that I hear complaints about forgetting names of people, trouble finding words and a variety of other short-term memory problems. The salesman, who bragged about quickly remembering the names of every client, is struggling to recall a familiar contact. The mother confuses the names of her child's friends or their parents. However, they tend not to forget to pick up their children. They don't forget to do important things.

I try to change medication. The SSRIs (serotonin reuptake inhibitors such as Prozac, Zoloft, Paxil, Celexa and Lexapro) are noted to effect memory. Try to switch to another type of medication and either the depression and anxiety returns or the memory problem doesn't improve. A patient who responds well to a norepinephrine medication (Wellbutrin or desipramine) has the same memory complaint. A patient who responds to a mood stabilizer such as lithium or Depakote also has the complaint. Patients haven't reported any improvement in the symptom with the newer medication, Trintellex (vortioxetine), even though it touts enhanced cognition. Electroconvulsive therapy (ECT) is most noted to have memory complaints. Most revealing is when I discontinue the medication. If the patient remains well, the memory complaint persists. If the memory complaint improves, I know a relapse is imminent.

I didn't, at first, believe these memory complaints, since more formal memory testing doesn't reveal a deficit. However, after running several therapy groups and hearing the complaint universally, I started to believe. I tried to find an answer.

The patients who complained the most of memory problems were the ones who worried the most. The worrying took on an obsessive quality. It was as if by repeating the fear in their mind they could prevent the occurrence of something feared. "Maybe I would forget to bring my son to his practice," the obsessive would think. "Did I shut off the light switch...unplug the toaster...?" Some of the worries were based on reality, "my sick mother could die any day..." or irrational, "if I don't chew my food 15 times on each side, I might choke..." It seemed as if these worries were swirling around in the patient's mind until all other thoughts became thwarted. The ability to plan and carry out tasks came to a halt. Anything that involves the possibility of adding additional worry had to be avoided. As things escalate, even going out of the house to work or do chores was too much. The system shut down.

I have been interested in computers for many years. I remember my first PC running Windows 3.01. This was a major advance over the DOS operating system because you didn't have to remember non-intuitive commands. The computer somehow remembered this for you and gave you a simple menu of options to initiate. You could start a program to type a letter. Then you could open another program where you had some data to look at and go back to the original letter you were working on. (This was something my original Macintosh computer could do but was much more expensive than a PC). Then I would get another program to put a fancy screen saver picture on my computer when I stopped working on it for a few minutes, boom, the computer would freeze up. Not a key would operate, and you would get the "blue screen of death" with a bunch of gibberish. You couldn't do anything. All I could do was turn off the computer. Sometimes, before freezing up, I would get an error message that said "out of memory." Although the system was designed to allow the user to run multiple programs simultaneously, it had a limited capacity to manage these multiple tasks.

Windows 95 edition managed to correct some of this problem. When the computer gave you an out of memory message, you could sometimes close one of the programs so it would not crash. You could run one or two of the programs. This out of memory message was referring to the computer's RAM or rapid access memory. RAM was very expensive then. I remember spending $200 for 8 MB of RAM. Thieves were going into offices to steal the RAM from company computers—more expensive than gold. Windows 95 reduced the frequency of system crashes, but it required more memory to prevent out of memory messages and freeze-ups.

Then technology advanced and the price of RAM began to fall. Increased RAM in the computer and changes to the operating system prevented crashes and I no longer see out of memory messages on my computer. But, I do see the equivalent of out of memory messages in my patients.

Excessive worrying is an activity that fills up our RAM. In vulnerable individuals this results in a "system crash," a "breakdown."

Depression and anxiety is the consequence of the mind running out of memory such that it can't think or function correctly. This is usually more due to a system malfunction than exposure to overwhelming stress. Although, overwhelming stress can be a trigger, it is the individual elevating the significance of certain thoughts, feelings or events to a much greater level than is justified. This may be due to prior traumas or experiences that suggest a need to be on heightened alert or some other biologic phenomenon.

Obsessing is the paradigm for this effect. In obsessing, the individual over values a particular thought and speculates on catastrophic consequences of not worrying about it or doing some ritual to ward it off. A patient with depression is like a computer running Windows 3.01, but trying to run too many programs at once until the system crashes—you get "the blue screen of death." This was your out of memory message. Often, it occurred without warning, when the last straw was lifted onto the camel's back, the final stressor that put the individual over the top.

Taking an antidepressant is like getting an upgrade to Windows 95 without a RAM upgrade. The system doesn't crash so easily but you still can't run any more programs. The antidepressant forces you to prioritize. You can't obsess or worry about everything as before and you won't crash. If you try to overload your memory, something has to give. The antidepressant serves like a filter allowing only more important things to be put in RAM. Things of less importance (and yes people's names, and word finding are of less importance than most other things) are given a lower priority.

Another way of looking at this is that in anxiety and depression, people are overly sensitive to things. They worry about everything and the result is reduced functioning. Medications (particularly the SSRIs) make people care less about these problems. Problems become less overwhelming. Critiques become simple comments. Obsessions melt into the background.

The majority of patients I see complain that their antidepressants cause the side effect of short-term memory loss. This is particularly true of high functioning individuals who multi-task. I tell them that this is not a side effect of the medication. It is a side effect of getting well.

The medication makes you care less about minor problems. Take too much of the antidepressant and you become careless. You don't care about anything. Without paying attention, you can't remember things. This is particularly true of serotonin enhancing medications. These medications are particularly good at reducing obsessing. However, obsessing is one of the processes of keeping a thought in our short-term memory. If this is blocked too much, memory and concentration suffer. Individuals with ADHD have the opposite problem and don't obsess enough, being distracted easily and not caring enough. They need a norepinephrine medication to improve concentration. Their attention worsens with SSRI medication that inhibits obsessing.

So what are the implications of this RAM hypothesis? For starters, medication dosages need to be kept to the minimal effective amount. Sometimes a low dose of a norepinephrine enhancing medication may help concentration but not memory. You want to prevent obsessing but not impair concentration. But what can you do when you have so much to remember and can get easily overwhelmed?

Psychotherapy can be utilized to set priorities for things to do and reassess the power of stressors. Some things may seem of utmost importance but with careful introspection may not be of much consequence. The criticism from the boss about not having done a specific task may remind you of when you got fired from the last job, but this boss might be helping you to set priorities. Maybe you need to tell the boss your limits and ask to prioritize tasks or get additional help.

You have too much to remember: Work assignments, children's' projects and activities. How many different passwords do you have: e-mail, bankcards, lockers, computer logons, website and store codes, on and on. You are told to change them regularly. You can upgrade your computers memory, but what about yours? This calls for data compression.

What does data compression mean for a human being? Instead of trying to remember 20 things to do each day, you keep a list and remember only one thing- the list. But you'll forget the list somewhere. You'll lose the list. This is where habits come into play. We don't forget to get dressed and brush our teeth in the morning because it has become a habit. Habits are done without much thought and therefore don't consume our RAM. So the list formation must become a habit. The list is always placed in the same location, e.g. in your wallet, shirt pocket, a planner or palm device. Recent studies have shown that different parts of the brain are involved with rote practices than with recently acquired knowledge.

I once went to a special memory seminar offered as a bonus lecture for physicians. The speaker was a real showman. He had the audience put together a random story with at least twenty items and some numbers. He then repeated this elaborate story, including the numbers, back to the audience. He told us his technique. He made word associations with the random items so that they had more coherence and were linked to other items in his stored memory. It looked impressive, but this was a lot of work for what was a random list of items. I could have put it all on a piece of paper and put it in my special place. Remembering everyone's name is not important to me. Knowing their stories and other details is more critical. I make notes for important things so that I don't have to fill my RAM. This allows me to keep my mind clear at the end of the day.

Having an adequate amount of free RAM is necessary to facilitate retrieval of memories from the longer-term memory. With data compression, you are not trying to keep a lot of things in short-term memory and you find that your recall of things actually improves dramatically. There isn't the battle between what is ridiculously floating in your mind and efforts to retrieve from longer-term memory. No need for tricks or gimmicks to remember trivial items. You don't even try to remember these things. You have made a list and know where it is because of your habit.

So, the next time you face the embarrassment of not remembering someone's name, think that you must be too well to be concerned with such trivialities. Don't try to remember things of little significance, write them down. Protect your RAM from intruders wanting to steal or tie it up. Follow these simple rules of data compression, and you might be pleasantly surprised when you correctly remember your own child's name.

*(Second edition bonus: **The File Draw Effect**.*

As I have gotten older and wiser, I have another explanation or corollary to the RAM hypothesis for the progressive difficulty with retrieval of which most of my older patients complain. When we were very young all of our knowledge could fit in a manila folder. By the time you reach my age my knowledge and experiences fill boxes and boxes of files. When asked to recall the name of a movie or actor or some other piece of trivia, we have to sort through all of these boxes of data. Sometimes this might take minutes, hours or even days, then eureka, it comes to you and you blurt it out as a non sequitur. Google has solved this by searching the internet day and night uploading all of this data into its vast memory banks. We don't need to do this, nor do we have to worry about this memory retrieval issue since we can access Google on a multitude of devices that we carry with us. The boxes and boxes of data are now available to us in digital format with an efficient search engine. I don't worry anymore about keeping all this knowledge on the tip of my tongue. This only takes up my RAM causing more problems with recalling the important passwords so I can access my devices. I also use the computer as my accessory brain, making lists of vacations, packing items, and finance and calendar reminders. I just need to be logical with my file system and use bookmarks for important computer sites so I know how to find where I put everything.)

⌘⌘⌘⌘⌘

Origins of panic

Anxiety is a normal part of life. Without anxiety very little would get done. Why study for a test if we don't worry about the results? Why go to the doctor for a physical if we don't care about our health? Why take cholesterol-lowering medications when we have no overt symptoms unless we worried about our having a heart attack or stroke? These are examples of anxiety leading to our own well-being. However, fear can be used to intimidate, hurt or manipulate. Politicians use fear to motivate people to go out and vote. Dictators and tyrants use terror to subjugate the masses. Extremist groups use random acts of violence such as suicide bombings to scare the masses for unclear gains except to create chaos that allows lawlessness to flourish.

Anxiety comes in many varieties. There is rational worry about real issues for which we need to make decisions. If there is a lack of mental clarity due to a concentration problem or conflicting goals, anxiety may increase and lead to indecisiveness. Some worry is totally irrational based upon false premises or superstitious notions. "Step on the crack and you'll break your mother's back." In obsessive-compulsive disorder, the patient seems to be lacking a sense of completeness. "Did I do that? Maybe not, let me check. Did I check it right? Maybe not, let me check again." Irrational worries usually take the form, if I don't do this, something bad will happen.

Panic is the most extreme and concentrated form of anxiety with many symptoms flooding at once. It occurs when a person feels life or limb is in jeopardy. It is the activation of our bodies' alarm system or fight or flight response. It is a primitive reminder of our jungle origins when man had to face danger at every turn. It too had an adaptive function. All of its symptoms have functions that relate to preparation to fight or flee.

Panic attacks come on quickly and have peak symptoms within ten minutes or less. Adrenaline surge causes heart rate and breathing rates to go up, bringing in more oxygen and pumping more blood to large muscle groups in our arms and legs that will be needed to fight or flee. This adrenaline rush gives a sense of warmth leading to sweating to reduce overheating. Blood volume shifts from areas that can wait to areas to areas where it is needed in case of our need to run or fight. Blood leaving the gut gives a sense of nausea due to slowing digestion of food. Blood leaves the fingers, toes and lips resulting in a numb and tingling sensation. The pupils dilate to change focus to distance causing blurred vision for anything close up. The rapidly shifting blood supply may cause a sense of wooziness or faintness. In preparation for battle with potential of physical pain, the mind goes into a dissociated state of detachment that may outlast the other physiological symptoms described. This helps us to ignore pain sensations that may result from battle.

What if this reaction occurs when there is no apparent danger or cause? The body is telling you there is something seriously wrong but you don't know what it is. You panic. You worry that you might be dying or "going crazy." Patients often go to the emergency room with these symptoms and after an extensive work-up they are told nothing is wrong. But their body has told them something is seriously wrong. They have to explain it in some way. The explanation usually takes the form of an association with whatever is happening externally or with a contemporaneous stream of thoughts. Maybe it occurred while driving on the highway, so the highway is avoided. Maybe in the store, so stores are avoided. Eventually, the individual is constricted from going many places developing agoraphobia. If the panic occurred while having a bad thought, any bad thought might trigger anxiety.

In our jungle days if we encountered a tiger peeking out of the woods near a particular clearing, we might avoid that area in the future. In behavioral terms seeing the tiger was our stimulus for our panic response. The particular clearing became paired with this stimulus such that seeing the clearing elicited the same response as seeing the tiger. This is called classical conditioning as described in Pavlov's famous dog experiment. Pavlov rang a bell while presenting the dogs with meat. The dog's normal response to the meat was to salivate. After several presentations the dogs salivated in response to hearing the bell even when no meat was present. In the jungle example, the person became conditioned to have a panic response when they saw the clearing even in the absence of seeing a tiger. In classical conditioning a physiologic response, such as fight or flight response, becomes paired with an external unrelated stimulus, in this case the clearing.

The dogs took several tries to learn this response. Humans are "smarter" and learn to make the connection in one exposure. In addition, we readily do stimulus generalization. This means we learn so well from a particular experience that we generalize to any similar circumstance. So if we have a panic attack in a particular store, we might avoid all stores. Worse yet we have a hard time forgetting or breaking these connections. So one can see that people who develop agoraphobia in response to panic attacks are actually our best learners and not "crazy" or "stupid" as many others might accuse them of being. Their problem is that they learned the wrong lesson in response to a false alarm. Just as the Department of Homeland security sometimes heightens its warnings on false "chatter," after a patient's panic alarm goes off it becomes more sensitive, increasing the likelihood of subsequent false alarms. Patients with panic have to reset the alarm to be less sensitive and be retrained to extinguish this inappropriate response.

Undoing a conditioned response is very difficult. While one exposure to a situation during a panic attack conditions our avoidance, it takes multiple exposures to the same situation without having a panic attack to extinguish the pairing. There are two opposing camps on treatment for panic disorder. One advocates for heavy use of medication to rapidly squelch the attacks and the other argues that exposure without medication but using cognitive behavioral therapy can be more effective. In studies comparing these treatments, the group that advocated their form of treatment showed that they performed better. I advocate for both interventions done together. If you try to expose a patient to the avoided situation and they panic, you can actually reinforce the avoidance. If you give them too much medication they lack the drive and motivation to challenge themselves to do what they have learned to avoid. Sedating medications might stop the panic attacks, but you might not have helped the patient much if they are still disabled by the agoraphobia and too drugged to initiate efforts to overcome avoidance behaviors.

Sherri was a 54 year old married woman who had panic attacks and severe agoraphobia most of her life. She limited herself to local traveling and still experienced panic attacks despite treatment with high doses of benzodiazepines initially prescribed by a psychiatrist but continued by her primary care doctor. Her husband was thinking of retiring soon and was upset that Sherri would not travel. She avoided high bridges and wouldn't go on a plane or train. She finally presented to me after her husband decided to separate from her, feeling she was dragging him down. I explained the nature of panic attacks and agoraphobia to her. I added an antidepressant and switched her benzodiazepine to Klonopin. I slowly reduced her Klonopin down to just 0.5mg and referred her to a therapist. She improved rapidly. Although separated, she continued to see her husband who felt skeptical of her changes. She wanted to go out now and do things that she was restricted from doing in the past. After several months she realized that she didn't need her husband and his skepticism about her progress was bringing her down. Enjoying her new freedom, she planned and took plane flights to visit her children in Europe and the West Coast.

Klonopin is a medication commonly used to treat panic attacks. So is Xanax. Both have been FDA approved to treat panic disorder. Xanax or alprazolam is a fairly short acting medication, which if not given 3 to 4 times per day can cause inter-dosing withdrawal symptoms. As the medication is wearing off the patient is likely to be more prone to panic attacks. This is especially evident when a patient wakes up with panic, which I rarely see in un-medicated patients. Patients try to compensate by using more than is needed; only exacerbating these peaks and valleys of medication effect. I have helped more patients by taking them off their Xanax than by putting them on it. Klonopin or clonazepam is a much longer acting benzodiazepine which means twice daily dosing is all that is needed to prevent panic attacks. Previously used as an anti-seizure medication, it was approved to treat panic attacks only just before it went generic and knowledge of its appropriate use was not widely disseminated. The PDR (Physician's Desk Reference) that has the FDA approved information reports two studies of Klonopin in panic disorder which very few physicians seem to be aware of. In one study patients were given either a placebo or 5 different dosages of Klonopin, 0.5, 1, 2, 3 or 4 mg per day. Interestingly only the group receiving 1mg per day did better than placebo with 74% being panic free compared to 54% on placebo. In the second study, doctors were able to titrate the dose of Klonopin as needed. Klonopin did better than placebo but the average dose taken was 2.3 mg and the response rate was lower than in the study with Klonopin 1mg. These studies may seem contradictory but my clinical experience reinforces the findings. Patients do better on a lower dose of Klonopin than a higher dose. Why would this be?

Patients with panic want immediate relief for their panic attacks. But panic attacks are brief and time limited. If allowed to self medicate they take more than they need. Once a panic attack starts the medication doesn't abort it but may prevent the next attack. So if a patient takes too much medication during a panic attack they are just going to feel over medicated and sedated. This wooziness feels like a symptom of the attack. Being overmedicated they can't think clearly which is necessary to overcome their irrational fears. Finally, after being over medicated they are more likely to experience withdrawal symptoms from the medication leading to more panic just as in the case of Xanax. How do you convince a patient not to use too much of the medication when they are still symptomatic?

Not all patients with panic attacks will respond to low dose of Klonopin. This doesn't mean they should have more. I advocate for adding alternative medications to get a more complete response. Panic patients have irrational worries very similar to what is seen in obsessive-compulsive disorder. More than half of patients with panic disorder will have depression at some time in their life. If a low dose of benzodiazepine is not adequate a serotonin antidepressant (SSRI) should be added. If this strategy fails patients should be re-evaluated for either attention deficit disorder (ADHD) or bipolar disorder. Panic attacks are a common complaint in patients with bipolar disorder and occur in both manic and depressed phases.

Jeff was a 36-year-old married man who was struggling with panic attacks for several years. He was a tough guy who did body building and felt he should be able to control this without medications. He went to several different therapists and spent hundreds of dollars on an advertised treatment program on audiotapes. He listened to the tapes religiously and did all of the exercises but still felt terrible with panic attacks. He forced himself to resist impulses to avoid situations yet he still felt trapped by panic. I explained the value of medication to reset his panic alarm to be less sensitive. He began on a low dose of Klonopin to which I added Zoloft. Within a couple of months he was cured. Once on the medication, all that he had learned with the tapes and therapy fell into place. Over the course of a year he came off the Klonopin and weaned off the Zoloft. Within a few months off of the medications the panic returned. He was disappointed and despaired that it took higher dosages of medication and took longer to improve. He did improve and again was able to come off the Klonopin but chose to stay on a low dose of Zoloft to prevent relapse.

Agoraphobia is like gangrene. If you let one avoidance fester untreated it spreads and leads to other avoidances. Gangrene may start in the toes but eventually the whole leg is infected and must be removed restricting ambulation. I have had patients who let their agoraphobia go untreated so long that they can't leave their neighborhood or even their house. Ironically, the situations avoided often make no sense. One elderly patient of mine loves to travel but won't fly. She will take a Titanic-like boat across to Europe, at great expense, but won't fly. She has taken Amtrak across the country and has been in two train wrecks and will continue to use the train but not fly. She feels she is too old to change. Therefore I strongly encourage tackling all fears systematically when one is young. Also the earlier one gets treatment the less opportunity for avoidances to develop, and maladaptive relationships have not become ingrained.

Medication alone is never adequate to treat panic disorder. Some form of cognitive behavioral therapy with exposure needs to be given in addition. For some highly motivated patients just reading self-help books or tapes (bibliotherapy) may be enough when added on to medications. But most patients need an active therapist to guide and motivate them to overcome their fears. For some couples the dependency needs of the agoraphobic partner match the nurturing needs of the spouse. Steve presented with fairly new onset panic attacks after an incident at work. He responded quickly to medications and counseling. His dramatic improvement was incentive for him to refer his wife who had lifelong panic and agoraphobia. She took longer to improve but as she did she needed her husband less and less. She eventually decided to leave her husband as she felt she had missed out on a good part of her life and didn't want to be trapped in a relationship. When she was agoraphobic she needed her husband to do things for her. This enabling came at the expense of his making decisions for her. She came to see this original support of her as controlling behavior. He had a hard time letting go of his parental role. Steve eventually remarried. I don't know what happened to his wife.

It is evident that while anxiety can be a normal part of life, excess anxiety can lead to many negative consequences. These can greatly limit an individual's potential in life. It can also affect their interpersonal lives and may lead to inappropriate choices in relationships. Fortunately there are very good treatments that involve both judicious use of medications and psychotherapy.

⌘⌘⌘⌘⌘

LIFE, LIBERTY AND THE PURSUIT OF HAPPINESS; ASSESSING RISKS AND BENEFITS

Accounts of mental illness go back to recorded history. If an individual suffered from a mental illness it was believed that they were being punished by higher powers for some wrong doing or possessed by spirits. This meant that they deserved their fate and were burdened by guilt and shame. When no reason could be identified convoluted thinking suggested transgressions in a prior life or failure to atone for original sin. Blaming the victim helped others worry less about their fate, if they behaved well they most certainly would be protected. The mentally ill were feared and ostracized lest they spread their evil onto innocents. They were banished or put in some form of institutional isolation from the rest of society. Lacking the ability to feel happiness would thereby result in loss of a person's liberty and eventual life.

Treatment for psychiatric conditions has always been mired in controversy. Dating back to shackling in prisons and burning people at the stake as witches, acceptance of individuals with mental illness has been fraught with fear, prejudice and horror. One of Freud's most helpful contributions was popularizing the notion that mental illness was something real and could be understood. Even if many or most of his theories of causation have turned out to be wrong, he helped de-stigmatize mental illness and gave hope for understanding and perhaps curing it. However, Freud retreated into a "blame the patient" mentality with his disbelief of patient accounts of early sexual abuse (abandoning his seduction theory) and instead proposed a theory that the young patients fantasized these seductions by their elders.

Psychoanalytical concepts permeated popular culture in movies and art. Surrealism was a representation of the unconscious mind or dream states open to interpretation. Novels also included ideas of unconscious motivation and dream symbolism. Yet mental illness was still something feared because, if so identified, a person could be hospitalized seemingly indefinitely.

Freud was at first a neurologist, a physician who was looking for a biologic basis of mental illness. The diagnostic methods at the time were limited to gross anatomy and the physical examination. Laboratory testing was very limited and X-ray was not invented let alone more sophisticated brain scans. Neurological diseases had observable signs on physical examination, and on autopsy had clearly visible lesions in the brain or central nervous system, such as dead tissue in strokes or obvious tumors. Mental illness had no clearly visible lesions but brain function was nevertheless impaired. They were thus deemed "functional" illnesses. Epilepsy was one condition that crossed over this boundary. In some epilepsy cases physical signs or lesions were evident but not in others. Since nothing could be clearly seen as abnormal in psychiatric illness the treatment was presumed to be psychological and behavioral with the assumption that a medical intervention would be unwarranted. This resulted in treatments that were either religious, such as faith healing, or non-treatment consisting of protection of society by incarceration of the individual in asylums. The fact that some individuals improved by removal of stressors and compassionate care gave encouragement that non-medical treatment might be developed.

We all fear what we don't understand. Is it contagious? What do we need to protect ourselves from being victimized by it? Freud and others at his time helped develop theories of causation that told us it was not contagious and we didn't need to fear it. It also gave hope to develop psychotherapies that might cure mentally ill patients. Unfortunately, the treatments were far from successful for most patients even after years of treatment. There were spontaneous remissions and mildly ill patients learned to cope better. Those with severe mental illness like manic depression (now called Bipolar disorder) and schizophrenia deteriorated in their ability to function despite the outward appearance of good physical health. Ironically, as in ancient times, many modern therapies blamed lack of improvement on the weakness and resistances of the patient rather than failure of the basic theory of the treatment.

It was near the end of my second year working at the Veterans Administration Hospital when I agreed to change positions from Chief of the Mental Hygiene Clinic to become Chief of the Inpatient Psychiatric Unit. After two years working as director of the outpatient clinic, I managed to keep all but a few patients out of the hospital by aggressive use of medications and therapy. When I did need to hospitalize someone that often meant they would need even more aggressive treatment. ECT (electroconvulsive therapy) is the most powerful treatment for the most severely ill. As a condition of my accepting the position, I requested and was approved for special one-week training in ECT from the most prominent expert in the field at the time, Max Fink. I knew Dr. Fink from my medical school training as he taught our psychopharmacology lectures at Stony Brook. We used to joke that they were building the Shoreham nuclear power plant on Long Island just for him. However, both ECT and nuclear power became foci of protest. Environmental concerns prevented the power plant from ever being completed and Dr. Fink had to keep a low profile to evade protestors, including Scientologists.

     Max Fink's ECT certification course was enlightening. He gave a historical prospective of how ECT was discovered. Treatments were based upon chance findings and astute observations. One observation that patients with epilepsy rarely suffered from psychosis led to the notion that inducing seizures could act as a treatment for psychosis. The concept of giving one illness to treat another was common with treatments such as using leeches and bloodletting. In the 1800's patients with tertiary syphilis were infected with malaria to induce high fevers with some improvement in the syphilis. Camphor was given to induce convulsions to cure insanity in the 1700's. Passing electric currents through animals prior to slaughter was used as a humane form of anesthesia and observers noted it caused seizures. Using electricity was a safer and more controllable method of inducing a seizure than using toxic compounds like camphor. The account of the first time ECT was used clinically was of a homeless catatonic man in Italy. There was no family and no informed consent at the time. The patient had not spoken for months that he was in the hospital and was at risk of withering away. The psychiatric team didn't know what dose of current to use and started low. Nothing happened. They increased the current.

This time the patient spoke for the first time stating something to the effect, "the first one was nothing but with second one you're going to kill me." They increased the current; he had a seizure and began talking afterward. He eventually was discharged from the hospital. What we know now is that catatonia is more likely a form of bipolar depression that is very responsive to ECT.

When general anesthesia was introduced to ECT you could put the patient asleep and paralyze him so that no convulsion occurred and the patients still improved. This gave evidence that it was the seizure activity in the brain and not the muscular convulsions throughout the body that relieved the depressive state. Unfortunately for psychiatry, images of ECT given without anesthesia are what were popularized in *One Flew Over the Cuckoo's Nest*, leading to its widespread fear and opposition to this life saving procedure. Several states and individual cities tried and several succeeded in banning the use of ECT treatments claiming them to be cruel and barbaric treatments. I would agree that ECT is more invasive than other treatments as it involves the use of general anesthesia and often leaves memory gaps. Is it any more barbaric than surgical interventions or chemotherapy or radiation treatments, all of which can be life saving? The major real side effect of memory gaps occurs for the periods when the patient was severely depressed, which may be merciful. Yet to ban a life saving treatment is like banning cesarean sections because they leave scars on the mother. In many cases it is the safest and only effective treatment for a severely ill patient who might kill him or herself or die of wasting away.

All treatments have potential side effects that must be weighed against the potential benefits. Psychotherapy has side effects. It might re-traumatize a patient by bringing up repressed traumas. The attention paid by the therapist to a narcissistic patient may reinforce his or her sense of entitlement. Cognitive behavioral exposure therapy may heighten anxiety and reinforce avoidant behavior if not completed effectively. Even exercise, which is a good treatment for depression and anxiety, can lead to physical injury.

Joe was a 26-year-old man who presented with severe recurrent depressions. He had a chronic sense of despair and thought of suicide regularly. The only relief occurred when he smoked marijuana and drank. He had a couple of DUI (driving while intoxicated) arrests and had to keep sober to avoid jail time. Having no relief now, he presented to me for help. When he told me his story he was adamant about not taking any medications. I told him that he had been using drugs for most of his adult life but didn't want to take medications?

Jill was a 30-year-old woman also chronically and severely depressed. Her drug of choice was marijuana, which she smoked several times per day. She complained of no motivation or drive. She couldn't sleep without smoking a joint. She would get irritable and angry if she didn't smoke. She would accept medications but wouldn't stop marijuana use. I told her that I couldn't help her unless she quit.

Drugs that are abused are more potent than most psychotropic medications. This means that the therapeutic effects of psychotropic medications are greatly diminished or reversed by the recreational drugs. Drugs of abuse work rapidly producing their desirable effects almost immediately, but the brain adapts to this initial effect leading to tolerance and a need for more drug. This tolerance then leads to an eventual loss of beneficial effect and withdrawal when stopped. This dramatic worsening of symptoms in the face of withdrawal leads to continued abuse of the drug even in the absence of a positive effect. This is the very essence of addiction. Medications on the other hand usually don't produce their desired effect for days or weeks, and side effects occur first. The body develops tolerance to the side effects while the brain's adaptation to the medication moves it to a healthier state.

I find it amazing that patients are distressed by the lists of side effects that pharmaceutical manufacturers are mandated to list in their ads but they never think about what side effects they are having from commonly abused substances such as alcohol, tobacco and caffeine. If these substances were new drugs they would never have been approved. Alcohol causes sedation, poor coordination, confusion, nausea, vomiting, diarrhea, blurred vision, ataxia, memory lapses, liver failure, excessive urination, and dehydration, seizures, tremors, hallucinations and possible death. Tobacco causes anxiety, depression, tremors, carbon monoxide poisoning, asthma, emphysema, frequent colds, chronic bronchitis, pneumonia, irritability, insomnia, lung cancer and death. Caffeine is a relative of cocaine and causes anxiety, panic attacks, insomnia, fatigue, tremors, bladder irritability, headaches, cardiac arrhythmias, seizures and possible death.

Many of the over the counter remedies cause equally distressing side effects and herbal remedies are totally unregulated. The supplement industry managed to lobby congress so that they have no obligations to test the safety or efficacy of their products as long as they don't make claims that it treats any illness. I like to remind people that natural doesn't mean safe. Cocaine, opium, marijuana, strychnine, and many others are totally natural and not safe. Many pharmaceuticals are totally natural like lithium, and can be used safely because regulation has led to studies that assure purity, standardization and guidelines for safe use.

Fear traps and alienates us. It interferes with our better judgment. Fear can be a symptom of mental illness that keeps us from getting the help that we need. Psychiatric treatments have improved dramatically over the last fifty years. Any treatment must be evaluated for its relative risks and benefits. More importantly we must consider the risks of not treating. Not treating means total loss of happiness, leaves us trapped without liberty, and risks death of the patient either by his own hand or by increased rates of physical illness. In the pursuit of life, liberty and happiness we have to go beyond our fears and prejudice about psychiatric illness and accept the risks and benefits of treatments as we do for any other medical condition. We are fortunate that patients don't have to suffer without hope for relief as in years' past. Risks have to be taken in order to have the hope of any gains.

⌘⌘⌘⌘⌘

"I MUST BE THE WORST PATIENT YOU'VE EVER SEEN": MY THEORY OF RELATIVITY

It was the second half of my second year in residency, the first year of Psychiatry training when I returned to work at a Veteran's Administration Hospital for the first time since medical school. In medical school I learned psychiatric interviewing techniques in the back wards of a large VA Hospital on Long Island. The hospital grounds were beautiful. Located on green bucolic rolling hills overlooking the Long Island Sound, the hospital buildings were surrounded by a golf course, which no one seemed to use. Our professor took four medical students each Thursday afternoon to interview patients in different back wards. These were the chronic patients who were unlikely to ever leave their barrack style wards, let alone the hospital grounds.

There was Henry who told us about the government's secret experiments carried out on him. They had taken him to a secret location, anesthetized him and implanted two-way transmitters in his temples. They could read his thoughts with these devices as well as send him messages. The purpose of this elaborate plot eluded him, but after many years of dealing with its consequences, Henry had accepted the burdens. The medications he was given at least tamed his fears and anger. We never asked him how the batteries could have lasted so long on the transmitters or why there were no scars near the implants. He was one among several patients with schizophrenia we had seen that day. The ones who were better off we saw wandering the grounds talking to themselves and feeding the pigeons. We learned that it didn't matter if we pointed out the contradictions in Henry's beliefs since delusions were fixed beliefs that were held despite evidence to the contrary. We were told the story of a psychiatrist confronting his patient who believed that he was dead. The psychiatrist asked him if dead men bleed and the patient responded, "No." The psychiatrist then took a needle and pricked the patient's finger until it bled. The patient's response was, "I guess dead men do bleed."

The following week we attempted to interview the severely demented patients in another back ward. I say attempted, since we were lucky to get them to tell us a date, let alone one that was within 20 years of the correct one. In the same ward was Ray, who seemed perfectly normal in our interview. He ranted about the incompetence of the president, the sad state of the economy and other various things. He became hostile only if asked what day it was, responding with, "who cares what day it is in this place?" Or when asked to remember three words he said, "They're only words, words." Only after some careful questioning by our preceptor did he reveal that the last president he recalled was Truman. After many years of heavy drinking and poor nutrition, he had totally lost his ability to make new memories. He covered up his deficits with platitudes and angry diversionary tangential remarks. He had a condition called Korsakoff syndrome that is due to alcohol consuming all the thiamine in the brain resulting in permanent brain damage.

After six afternoons interviewing patients at this VA it was hard seeing anything hopeful. The beauty of the grounds hid the fetid odors and cries of despair in the back wards. If this were my only exposure to psychiatry, I would have changed specialties. Fortunately, I had a more positive and intensive psychiatry rotation at Long Island Jewish Hillside Hospital the following year. I avoided any other clinical rotations at the VA Hospital during medical school and retained an apprehension towards VA Hospitals in general until this required rotation in my Yale psychiatry residency.

My second psychiatry rotation was as a junior resident on the VA intake unit in which patients were evaluated and begun on treatments. Patients stayed there for one to two weeks and were discharged to a variety of outpatient treatments or transferred to one of three longer stay inpatient units. My supervisors were amazing and the hospital provided a full range of compassionate and effective treatment programs. The overwhelming majority of patients was appreciative and showed remarkable improvement. There were no back wards like I had seen in my medical school experience. This is not to say that we didn't have very ill patients with very serious psychiatric problems. My rotation began in January, which I quickly learned was the beginning of what I termed "manic season."

Patients with bipolar disorder, which used to be called manic depression, have cycles of illness. It was Emile Kraepelin at the beginning of the twentieth century, who first connected these alternating cycles of depression and elation or mania with the same illness. Previously, these episodes were considered separate illnesses instead of two phases of the same condition. By February, my caseload included 5 manic patients, two of whom were frequently in the isolation room in and out of restraints. Then came Tim.

Tim was a young, good-looking man of 22. He was brought to the emergency room by his family for manic symptoms of not sleeping, being more talkative, and behaving strangely. The event that led to his hospitalization was when he ran into the street shouting for people to "get undercover." When police were called he surrendered a gun he possessed. He was fearful that the CIA was after him for "knowing too much." When I got to evaluate him, his speech was pressured as he told his war stories. He claimed to have been in the Marines Special Forces stationed in secret operations in Laos, after the end of the Vietnam War, fighting remaining communist guerrilla fighters. He was later in the Middle East in another secret operation. He showed me a copy of his DD214, military discharge papers describing his special operations trainings. He had photos of himself in camouflage fatigues in jungle-like settings. I became engrossed in his elaborate tales of exploits. Just when I would seem to express some doubt in the veracity of his story, he would give greater elaborations with technical details that only a military person would know, or claim that the government would deny his accounts because they were top secret and without Congressional approval. This played into the spirit of distrust of government after Watergate, and the release of the Pentagon papers following Richard Nixon's' resignation.

Meanwhile, he sought to convince me that he was fine now, that his behavior was just due to flashbacks of his military experience. He needed to leave the hospital, as soon as possible, so that he could return to law school for his mid-term exams. His girlfriend of just 3 months had accepted his proposal of marriage and called concerned about his hospitalization. I informed him of his need to stay in the hospital since he was involuntarily committed on an emergency certificate, which got him out of any charges for his inappropriate public behavior. I offered to call his law school Dean to inform him of his hospitalization without telling the nature of his illness.

Over the next few days, I got several calls from a friend of the family. He told me he had known Tim since he was in a youth military organization. As Tim had predicted, sources in the military, that his friend was connected to, refuted that Tim was ever stationed out of the country. More importantly, based upon his military background he had no doubt that Tim's DD214 was forged and that he would have been too young to be in locations that he claimed, even if the government were keeping secrets. He explained that the format for the DD214 was not according to protocol. I told him how Tim would say that the government would cover-up his involvement in secret operations. I was baffled. Then I called the Dean of the law school.

The Dean had heard of Tim but not because he was a student there. He stated that he knew the names of all the students over the years and was surprised when a young woman came into his office to inform him that Tim was in the hospital with a broken leg and would miss mid-term exams. The Dean was curious and looked through the applications for the law school over the past several years and Tim was not among them. In fact he had never applied or been a student at the University in any program.

A few days later his fiancée came to the unit to visit and wanted to meet with me. She told me that they had met on the college campus. He was always carrying law books between classes. She loved him and his military background helped her to better connect with her detached father, a retired military officer. As I tried to explain to her the contradictory information I received, she became increasingly upset. She repeated some of Tim's paranoid notions of the government covering up his military service and was becoming agitated with each challenge to his stories. I left the room to let her calm down. She stormed out of my office to find Tim. When I returned to my office, I noticed that my notes on him were missing. I confronted her about the missing notes and she became outraged. A quick glance at her cloth bag, revealed the manila folder sticking out of it, she had taken it from my desk.

What I had witnessed was the rare phenomenon of a "folie a deux" or in proper psychiatric parlance, shared delusional disorder. This is when a non-psychotic individual believes the delusion of a partner despite evidence of it being untrue. His fiancée needed to believe Tim's stories. They brought approval from her critical father and a sense of importance to her. To accept that the stories were not true would have meant that she was a fool to have been duped. How could her judgment have been so wrong? I could see Tim's charm. His stories were fascinating with just enough detail to be convincing to naive individuals, me among them. Who doesn't believe that the government does secret operations? I thought of Henry with his implanted two-way radios, but after over twenty years the batteries would have worn out. In retrospect, I should have been more skeptical when such a young man came in telling tales of exploits most wouldn't have in a lifetime. I can't tell you what happened to him as he escaped the hospital unit, presumably with his fiancées' help.

I can't count the number of times a patient told me that they must be the worst patient I ever saw. They never are. Just by their awareness of their problem and their desire to get help they are far from the worst. Most of these individuals have an anxiety disorder and have been scared to try medications long enough to get better from them. The difficult patients are the ones who are deceitful about their behaviors, who resist taking medication while abusing drugs and alcohol, and who don't show for appointments and then complain about my not helping them. Thankfully, these are rare patients.

My general philosophy is to help the patient to understand their condition and rationale for treatment. I try to be realistic about how long it might take to see benefits and what likely side effects will occur.

I point out what symptoms might respond to medications and what issues are more likely to need psychotherapy. I find that patients are better able to tolerate a side effect if they know what to expect than if it is a surprise. They are more inclined to become engaged in psychotherapy earlier when they are informed of problems that are not likely to respond to medications. I try to educate the patient to make them a collaborator in the medical decision making process. The potentially difficult patient abdicates his responsibility in the medical decision making process and says, "You're the doctor. You tell me what to do." The implied message is that the patient isn't taking any responsibility in their treatment and if anything goes wrong it is the doctor's fault. I don't accept that unless the patient is truly incapable of making a decision. Otherwise, I can narrow down the choices to the two best that I think of and help the patient decide given the pluses and minuses of each. This makes the patient prepared for any potential adverse effects and aware that if something goes wrong that there is an alternative. If an adverse event occurs that I informed them of, they can decide if it is severe enough to stop the trial or if they can endure longer to see if it resolves. Knowing that there are alternatives helps reduce hopelessness that leads to suicidal thinking. Since there are so many treatments available and almost an infinite number of complementary combinations, I have never run out of ideas. Hope is often the only thing a patient has to hold on to and some medications, if given enough time, help the brain heal.

Patients who think they are "the worst" have a distorted and exaggerated sense of what is normal. Bruce, an accountant in a medium sized company, was increasingly overwhelmed by his workload. His wife needed a breast biopsy, which fortunately turned out to be benign. While calculating his son's financial needs for college he was becoming ill in the stomach. His bowel symptoms led him to see his internist who referred him to a gastroenterologist who performed an endoscopy and colonoscopy. The results were benign except some minor gastric irritation for which he began him on antibiotic for a presumed infection and an acid blocker. He subsequently developed chest pains and thought he was having a heart attack. He went to the emergency room where he got blood work and an EKG that were normal. However, because of his age and high blood pressure, he was sent to a cardiologist who gave him a stress test. He became short of breath due to another panic attack during the stress test so was unable to complete it. This caused the cardiologist to order a nuclear scan, which was normal. By this time, Bruce was experiencing daily panic attacks with chest pains and was convinced the physicians were not telling him about a serious medical finding. Why else would he still be so symptomatic? His continued obsessing on his physical health and lack of any findings on thousands of dollars worth of tests, finally led his internist to recommend seeing me. Referral to the psychiatrist is the punishment for bad patients who fail to get better after having exhausted all reimbursable procedures.

      Bruce told me he was the worst patient anyone had seen, since no one could find out what he had. It took less than five minutes for me to see that Bruce suffered from panic disorder and after months of extensive testing, never received treatment for this very responsive condition. Yes, it was all in his head, but it was his brain chemistry that was awry. I spent the remaining hour explaining that panic disorder was a real condition and it didn't mean he had an incurable illness. I taught him the fundamentals of cognitive behavioral treatment (CBT) and began a combination of a low dose of Klonopin and a serotonin antidepressant (SSRI). I explained how he would likely have some worsening of his anxiety for the first two weeks before he got better. Knowing what to expect was reassuring after all he had been through. I referred him to a counselor for more CBT. After one month he returned 80% better. The panic attacks did briefly get worse for a few days in the first two weeks, but were not nearly as bad as he anticipated. More importantly he hadn't had a panic attack in the last two weeks. He was still unsure of himself and had work to do on his self-confidence. This would improve over the next several months of treatment. This "worst patient" was one of the easiest to treat. The biggest obstacle was overcoming the stigma of a psychiatric label for what seemed to be a purely medical symptom. I have treated hundreds of Bruces in my practice. What are the "worst patients" for many specialty physicians are what psychiatrists help routinely.

Unfortunately, once a patient gets a psychiatric label, their medical physicians often discount most of their symptoms as psychiatric in origin and limit further evaluations. I thus become their de facto primary care doctor as well as psychiatrist. I have several patients who had panic disorder who after years of successful treatment present with symptoms of numbness, tingling or weakness or chest pains. Careful questioning reveals that the symptoms are more localized than prior panic symptoms or have a different time course. Panic symptoms tend to be bilateral (on both sides of the body) and simultaneous. They also tend to come on quickly in ten minutes or less and slowly fade over an hour or less. An individual may have a second attack, giving the impression of a longer duration but then there is a waxing and waning time course. This has allowed me to suggest further medical work-ups for selective patients who sometimes discover more serious conditions such as multiple sclerosis, tumors or heart disease. There has been only one time that I mistook a serious medical symptom for a psychiatric symptom. This patient continued to worsen and realized on her own that more evaluation was in order. Panic disorder symptoms have a fairly consistent pattern to a trained clinician and have minimal overlap with more serious disorders. Ordering of unnecessary medical tests can have a negative impact on the patient and create greater fear. The worst thing a physician can tell a panic patient is that nothing is wrong, because they know something is! What they mean is that they have ruled out a serious, life threatening physical illness and you are having panic attacks.

Perceptions of being the worst patient can manifest in the apparent fading of response to treatment. Many of my patients recall the first time they tried Prozac and felt great. This great feeling was never sustained despite multiple medication trials and retrials of Prozac. Some of these patients turned out to have bipolar disorder and were cycling in and out of depression. Some needed a dual action antidepressant that acted on norepinephrine as well as serotonin. But many were experiencing a phenomenon I refer to as the theory of relativity or to quote the Richard Farina novel title, *"Been down so long it looks like up to me."* Individuals who have been chronically depressed and finally try a medication that actually works are so thrilled and surprised by the improvements, they overlook other symptoms or aspects of their depression that have not improved. Only after a few months of enjoying the change, do they realize that they may not be all better. But instead of realizing that they may not have been as good as they thought, they begin to focus on what is not better and feel that they have relapsed.

We are more perceptive of relative changes in our environment and ourselves than absolute measures. This is true of sensations as well as depression. In several science museums there are demonstrations of this phenomenon with a cool stone plate next to a warm plate. Touch each separately and one is on the cool side and the other lukewarm. When both hands are placed simultaneously on the plates one feels cold and the other hot as the relative difference is more significant than their absolute temperatures. This theory of relativity also applies to the perception of time. Someone who has been depressed for months or years may forget that they ever felt good. Many patients will not report a past manic episode or minimize its severity while in the midst of a depressive episode causing the clinician to miss the bipolar disorder diagnosis. In a European study where national health records were available, up to a third of patients who had a documented manic episode, failed to report this when evaluated for their current depressive episode. On the prevention side, fading memory of the depressive episodes when the patient gets better often leads to premature discontinuation of medications in the false belief that they never had anything wrong in the first place.

I don't see this as deliberate deception or non-compliance but a problem with perception that needs to be countered by accurate retelling of known historical events. When my patients get better, they often ask why they still need to see me. The most important aspect of quarterly medication visits may be to remind patients of the risks of discontinuing prophylactic medications. I don't see treatment non-compliance as necessarily indicative of a bad patient, but it represents an incomplete acceptance of their illness. The best remedy for this is education and negotiation. If there has not been violence during an episode, I will negotiate with the patient to allow a gradual taper of medication, even if I know relapse is inevitable. If the taper is slow enough, not only are withdrawal symptoms avoided, but if a relapse occurs it might be more gradual and less severe in a partially medicated patient. Also, the patient has an excuse to stay in treatment during a more vulnerable period. The key is to predict the relapse and help the patient to see the early signs of recurrent symptoms. Bringing in a significant other or family member to watch for signs of relapse adds another layer of protection.

     Some psychiatrists have advocated for what has been labeled a "Ulysses contract." In Homer's *The Odyssey*," Ulysses knew that sailors who listened to the Sirens of Titan crashed their ships into the rocks, but he wanted to hear them. He instructed his crew to put wax in their ears whist tying Ulysses to the mast and instructed them to not pay attention to anything that he told them when he was listening to the Sirens. In psychiatry, we ask the patient to obey our advice lest they be influenced by internal voices or misguided notions associated with a relapse of their illness. We ask them when they are well and rational to trust us when we believe that they are in harms way and may need to be coerced into appropriate treatment.

     While patients view "the worst" in terms of severity, clinicians view "the worst" in terms of cooperation, acceptance of illness and compliance with treatment recommendations. Paradoxically, severity of illness is often an indicator of a more robust response to medication. Milder forms of depressive symptoms may be less responsive to medications and require more intensive and lengthy psychotherapy. When someone tells me that they must be the worst patient that I have ever treated, I view this as an indicator of the patient's insight into their illness and a positive predictor of their willingness to do what is necessary to get better. It may be a long hall to getting better, but having a motivated partner in treatment is half the battle.

⌘⌘⌘⌘⌘

Suicide and the Need for Hope

The threat or prospect of suicide by a patient is often the 800 lb gorilla in the room. Critics of psychiatry who trivialize mental illness don't realize that mental illness kills. Suicide is the leading cause of death in some young age groups and has become a major problem for the armed forces. Mental illness is the only illness that has resistance to getting well as one of its symptoms. The symptoms of paranoia towards people trying to help them and nihilistic feelings of hopelessness fight against attempts to treat depression. Patients in despair often misuse the very treatments given them to assist in their own demise. For the many years the only antidepressant medications that were available had a high potential to kill a patient in overdose. Hospital intensive care units (ICUs) seemed to always have a few patients who made suicide attempts with their prescribed antidepressants. For this reason, physicians often paradoxically prescribed lower doses of the antidepressants for the most depressed patients fearing that they would use them in overdose. In fact the doses were often too low to treat the depression but would activate the patient enough that they would be more likely to overdose. The more appropriate action would be to hospitalize the patient long enough for the medication to take effect. As newer antidepressants have come out that are much safer in overdose, more patients are given antidepressants readily but released from hospital too early when they are still very symptomatic.

Several studies of biologic markers have identified low serotonin function in patients who commit or attempt suicide. Certain medications such as lithium and clozapine have been demonstrated to reduce suicidal ideation. But this doesn't mean they are indicated for all patients who are suicidal. Appropriate treatment with psychotropic medication and psychotherapy can have the same beneficial effect. A seriously depressed and suicidal patient might be best treated with ECT because of its more rapid response.

Suicide attempts don't necessarily reflect the severity of a patient's depression. Studies have demonstrated that certain religious groups are much less likely to attempt suicide irrespective of the severity of illness. Other patients with personality disorders and milder reactive depressions may make frequent suicidal gestures to gain attention for their suffering even when it is temporary. Although they don't want to die they can make miscalculations in their attempts and their threats need to be taken seriously. Drug and alcohol use may disinhibit a patient enough such that they act on negative feelings that they would not have done otherwise.

I have found a commonality among all patients who attempt suicide whether they intended to die or not. Whether or not it was an impulsive or carefully planned act the individual believed that suicide was the best option that they had at the time. This is true even if the thought processes were irrational or rational. Accepting this commonality in all suicide attempts, the solution is the same, to help the patient see alternatives that make more sense or give a better outcome. Treatment must include an attempt to convince the patient that suicide is far from the best solution. Sometimes this involves giving hope for finding of a new, more effective medication regimen. At other times it is helping to find solutions to economic and social dilemmas. In all cases it calls for forbearance in acting on suicidal impulses until they can be thought through with a caring professional.

Jack was a middle aged mid-level executive in a large insurance company. He had a severe agitated depression and came to see me after discharge from the hospital. He didn't feel any better after several weeks in the hospital and was placed on disability from work. He told me on the first day that his insurance policy only covered psychiatric disability for two years. When it ran out he intended to kill himself. I felt like Mr. Phelps in the television show *Mission Impossible*, you have two years to cure this man. If you fail he will die and you will forever be responsible. I agreed to take on the mission and he promised to give me two years. Jack was a former military man who was always devoted and loyal to everyone he was responsible for, his troops, his company division, staff and most of all his family. His employer was doing massive layoffs and he had to identify who would be cut. Prior to disability leave, he was boss of over 100 employees and most had to be laid off. It was devastating for him and he knew eventually he would be laid off as well. His wife was ill and he had young children to support. His only reason to live was so that his family could collect his disability payments. After that would run out, he figured the payout of a life insurance policy, after he killed himself, would be the best he could do to for his family.

Jack was so depressed that he would often spend 23 hours a day in bed. He tried multiple medications at doses that were higher than approved to minimal avail. Looking through literature on treatment refractory depression, I tried everything including combining TCA and MAOI antidepressants, which is technically contraindicated. I told him that this combination might kill him and he said. "Then give me double doses." He never tried to kill himself and was always compliant with appointments. He knew I was trying hard and appreciated my efforts. As the two-year mark was approaching, I encouraged another course of ECT. It had limited benefit. The social workers in the hospital helped him realize that after two years he would become eligible for early retirement benefits, which combined with his social security disability payments were about the same as his current disability income. So he would still be worth more to his family alive than dead. My deadline had been extended but he was still depressed.

I never lost hope and projected this to him. As new medications came out I prescribed them for him. As I thought of complementary combinations I recommended them. I had him see several therapists while I gave him extended and more frequent sessions. He did several day treatment programs. He remained severely depressed. Then one winter he did some of his own research and decided to try some nutritional supplements. I concurred since his meals consisted of once daily frozen dinners; I had concern about his diet. He bought a variety of pill supplements. Miraculously, one session he came in stating he was feeling better. I had him on about six medications including lithium for several years. New evidence for neuro-degeneration in depression was coming out as well as the brain regenerative powers of several medications. I believe that these combined with the supplements began to heal his damaged brain. Also, I felt that his taking the initiative to find his own remedies empowered him to take control of his life. He had been depressed for over 10 years and now was getting better. Unfortunately, the years of inactivity and poor nutrition led to development of heart disease. Despite eating only once per day he gained over 50 lbs from inactivity and poor food selection. He suffered a heart attack as he began to fix up the neglected house. This time he wanted to live and underwent a coronary artery bypass. He lived another ten years with only mild depressive symptoms mostly due to his physical limitations. This was long enough to see his children marry and have their own children.

The story of Jack's depression reinforced my belief that no one is hopeless. It may take years to recover for some patients. It is the rare patient with depression who doesn't eventually improve. Patients do best when they actively participate in their recovery overcoming learned helplessness. I also believe in the theory that depression is associated with degeneration of the brain that may be worse in more chronic conditions. The healing powers of medications, therapy, exercise, diet and vitamins still need to be honed. Sometimes the only advantage to changing medications is giving the patient hope for something new while still staying in treatment. I have quite a few patients who have taken a long time to recover. One chronically depressed woman cynically called me a hopeless optimist. That may be true but it has kept many patient alive long enough for them to get better.

Whenever I begin a new treatment for a patient who has failed previous trials, I always inform them of my next idea if the current one fails. This makes it clear that I haven't run out of options and the patient shouldn't give up hope. Combining medications may benefit in two ways; first, the second medication may augment the first. Second, adding another medication allows the patient to remain on the first medication longer without being discouraged by the long delay and giving up hope.

Joan was a 40-year-old woman with chronic depression. She was in a bad marriage with her husband constantly berating her. She was abused as a child and felt economically trapped in her marriage. She had made frequent suicide attempts whenever she felt she couldn't deal with her husband. In therapy she had come to realize that these were attempts at demonstrating the seriousness of her depression to her husband. He only seemed to be caring when she was in the hospital and had to take care of the children by himself. Medications and ECT only provided temporary relief of her depression. She relapsed within a few weeks of returning home to the old regimen. I had a serious talk to Joan about her frequent suicide attempts. I told her that she could never get better until she eliminated suicide as an option. Suicide was too easy an out that interfered with doing the hard work necessary to solve her problems. Besides, I told her, she wasn't proving herself to be very good at killing herself and should redirect her efforts in a more constructive way.

I had the opportunity to evaluate a young man in the Yale emergency room. He had tried to kill himself with a gunshot to the head the prior year. You could see his scalp pulsating presumably where the bullet shattered his skull. He survived and now had physical disabilities in addition to persistent depression. This reminded me that no suicide plan is fool proof. I tell patients who think that they have a fool proof plan to kill themselves about this man and several others who failed and had made their lives worse than they ever could have imagined.

One night on-call during my internship I was sitting with a fellow resident and a young attractive nurse started up a conversation in a back room of the ICU. While her affect was bubbly she seemed to be jokingly bringing up the topic of ways to kill oneself. We joked for about 30 minutes about various methods and their relative merits such as leaving a mess or not. We were horrified the next week when we found out that she had killed herself by one of the methods that we described. We later found out that she had gotten pregnant by a married man. If only she had asked for help with her real problem. If only we explored more fully why she was asking about methods of killing oneself. Now I never talk about ways to kill oneself to anyone. I never joke about it even to friends or family. You never know when someone is going down this dark path.

When suicide is an option, the patient doesn't try hard enough to discover other approaches. Patients, for a variety of reasons, may have developed maladaptive coping mechanisms that affect their interpersonal relationships. Fear of rejection leads to testing and challenging the partner until the partner actually leaves in frustration and anger. Suicide shouldn't be an out from making hard choices. It is hard work to learn new strategies to improve relationships and make them more rewarding. A relatively new therapy treatment called Dialectical Behavior Therapy (DBT) has been designed for this purpose. As opposed to traditional psychoanalytical psychotherapy where the therapist hopes to have the patient gain insight into their problems and hopes the patient changes or is changed by a more positive relationship with the therapist, DBT is an active treatment focused on problem solving. DBT is an active therapy with homework assignments and goal setting. There are workbooks and learning tools. The therapist helps guide the patient to discover alternative coping strategies and methods of defining and finding solutions to problems.

As Joan learned new coping skills, she began to reach out more to others. She got involved with her church, left her husband and moved into a small-subsidized apartment. Her mood and self-esteem improved and she went from volunteer work to a paid part-time job. She has been able to survive by herself with her disability and small salary. She has not thought seriously of suicide in many years. *(Second edition update: She subsequently remarried and has remained happy in her new marriage. She maintains a good relationship with her children. Her depression has not returned while remaining on the medications that I continue to prescribe.)*

Suicide is a traumatic event for friends, family and mental health providers. It leaves a terrible legacy with the message that one can escape one's problems avoiding the hard work necessary to solve them. Surviving siblings and children are more likely to attempt suicide themselves or feel guilt and anger at the deceased. Patients often use the excuse that others would be better off without them since they feel they are a burden to the family. The alternative is worse. Fortunately, with appropriate treatment, almost all the patients improve given enough time, effort, support and hope.

⌘⌘⌘⌘⌘

A DANGER TO OTHERS

I often hear people report to me about the terrible crime some "crazy person" committed. News reports talk about some "deranged" individual who assaulted or hurt some stranger. This leads to fears of people with mental illness. The truth is individuals with mental illness are much more likely to be victims of violence than to commit any. When I hear about some act of violence on the TV or radio it is usually a sociopathic person committing the act for personal gain not someone with a mental illness. Sociopathy is not a mental illness but a personality flaw where the individual has no concern for others and has no difficulty hurting another for personal gain. Sociopathy is not treated by psychiatric interventions. Never the less, some patients do commit acts of violence but more often for bizarre reasons.

I was a medical student doing an outpatient psychiatry rotation at the new Stony Brook University Hospital. I was alone taking an intake history from a new potential outpatient, Greg. The clinic was on a lower floor of the all glass hospital building. The hospital was part of a medical complex with two 20-story towers and one 8-story tower standing on stilts above a 5-acre base. The towers on select floors are connected by bridges, making it look like a spaceship tethered to its launch pad. As the tallest structure on Long Island, it shines like a beacon of dramatic proportions. The new shiny building with all new futuristic interior and furnishings must have inspired hope to Greg that it offered some modern cures.

As I took his history, he told me of his long-standing depression and difficulties in relationships. He was articulate and composed in his history telling. He had multiple hospitalizations at almost all the facilities in a 40-mile radius, all except Stony Brook Hospital. He longed to experience the inside of the psychiatric ward and believed they could help him. But his symptoms didn't seem acute enough to merit a hospital stay. As I expressed doubt about his need for hospitalization his tone of voice escalated. Finally, he leaped up and grabbed the back of the modern metal and fabric chair waving it at the all glass enclosure and shouted, "If I threw this chair through this glass, you'd have me admitted in no time with a shot of Haldol in my butt!" I calmly stood up and worked my way to the glass door and told him that I would be right back. He calmly put the chair back and sat down while I brought in my supervising resident physician. Greg repeated his performance as he had done for me to the resident. However, the resident was more experienced and informed Greg that if he did as he threatened we would have security put him in restraints and have him committed to the State Hospital. Realizing that his performance would not gain his acceptance to the glass Mecca, he stormed out of the office without further threat.

    I learned that this was a manipulation by a person with borderline personality disorder. They often do things for dramatic effect in order to gain attention for their distress. Unfortunately, like an acting-out child, it is often the wrong kind of attention that rarely leads to anything positive. Instead they suffer from an empty sense of self and chronic despair. When the despair and loneliness become too intense to bear they make suicide threats or deceits such as another patient of mine, Jane. Jane was married to a man who suffered from progressive multiple sclerosis. Experimental treatment with chemotherapy left him sterile and he had a tendency to drown his sorrows in alcohol while neglecting his wife. Jane acted out her anger with her husband and loneliness by sleeping with a neighbor, Jim. When Jim didn't call her for over a week, she decided to tell a mutual friend that she was pregnant. She wanted Jim to call her and say their sex meant something to him but he never called her after their encounter. She knew the mutual friend would reveal her secret to Jim and hoped that he would call her to express his affection for her. Instead of expressing his affection he wanted to help pay and take her for an abortion for this fake pregnancy. All she really wanted was attention from her husband but everything got so complicated and now she just felt rejected by both men. After several days of this ruse she pretended to have a miscarriage for her false pregnancy and I helped her to express her feelings to her husband in order to obtain genuine loving attention.

Threats of violence not only come as attempts at manipulation. I was working my 24-hour call shift in the Yale Psychiatric emergency room. All six beds were full and I was busy trying to decide who needed hospitalization and who could be discharged home. Bruno was a large 20-year-old man with a diagnosis of paranoid schizophrenia who was brought to the emergency room after assaulting his mother. They had argued about his not wanting to take his antipsychotic medication, Thorazine. He spent a lot of time at the gym but complained that with Thorazine he couldn't bench press more than 300 lbs. I told him that I thought that was very good and that he needed to take his medications in order to continue to live at home. Both parents were at his bedside with his father offering to take him back home while his mother looked at me with a terrifying look, unable to speak. "Oh c'mon ma', dad says I can come home." He repeated several times, clearly not expressing remorse or insight as to why his mother was scared. His tone became angrier and focused upon his mother's silence, implying she didn't want to allow him home now. I became increasingly concerned that she would be forever blamed for his needing to go to the hospital, which might endanger her in the future.

So I looked at him with resolution and told him that hospitalization was my decision and not his mother's. As I repeated the word, "My…," I saw him lifting himself off the bed towards me. Fortunately for me I always wore sneakers and old clothes when on call at the emergency room and never a tie. He managed to grab hold of my flannel shirt while I turned away hearing the rip, rip of my old shirt. I sprinted out of the psychiatry section through the surgical section and eventually locked myself in a bathroom. As he chased after me through the surgical ward, a former football player turned surgical resident tackled him so that security could bring him back to psychiatry and place him securely in four point restraints. I remained locked in the bathroom until I received the all-clear page. I returned to see Bruno's horrified parents. I stood in front of them, seemingly calm on the outside but with my shirt tattered at both sleeves and across the back.

"Don't worry," I told them. "I always bring a change of clothes. I guess you can see why he needs to be in the hospital," I said looking at his father. It is useful to have a reflexive response, to seem calm on the outside while in crisis.

     A number of years later, I was working at a private outpatient clinic and didn't realize that the facility would be closed on Good Friday. I had scheduled several patients who seemed in crisis but there was no other staff in the facility. I was meeting with a young woman and her mother. The daughter was suffering from panic attacks and I was explaining the symptoms of panic, how they were the body's false alarm. Suddenly we heard screams coming from outside of the office. I excused myself to see what was going on. There was my next patient, Tom, with his wife. She had called for the emergency appointment as he was becoming paranoid and manic. Her feet were dangling while her back was cantilevered across the railing to the suite entry door with Tom's hands wrapped around her neck. I shouted at Tom to let go and told his wife to leave immediately. I ran back to the office with my patient and her mother, calmly telling them to hold on while I made a phone call to 911. My voice was so calm that I was afraid that the 911 operator wouldn't take me seriously, but I didn't want my patient with panic to panic. "Hello, this is Doctor Liebowitz. I have a bit of a crisis. One of my patients is out of control. Would you send someone as soon as possible?" As I tried to get back to my discussion of panic disorder, we heard a loud commotion in the waiting area. I peeked out the office door. Tom was standing naked from the waist up, arms stretched like Tarzan, bookcase knocked on the floor and coffee table and chairs up ended. I closed and locked the office door waiting for the police. Our session lasted longer than scheduled as we awaited the police and recalled 911 to give them my phone number so they could call when the coast was clear. I suspect our session was akin to intensive exposure therapy as they walked through the rubble of the office on their way out. Tom was caught down the street and brought to the hospital.

I've learned the importance of interior locks on all office doors and having telephone access. More important is being calm and clear headed in the face of crisis. I was not going to confront someone who was not thinking clearly as I did Bruno. No one was hurt. I don't schedule patients that I don't know after hours or when I will be alone. I don't put myself into the line of fire to stop a confrontation but always have an escape route. If I receive a call from a family member suggestive of a psychotic relapse with the potential for loss of control, I advise going to the hospital. Mental health providers must realize that they are not being helpful by heroically trying to keep someone out of a level of care that they need. Crises with patients tend to be time limited and it is important to give de-escalation a chance first, often with the offer of a calming medication and "asylum" from ongoing stressors. Patients don't like being out of control and have often thanked me for directing them to the help that they need, even if it means me refusing to see them in my office to avoid a hospital visit.

One weekend on call at the Connecticut Mental Health Center a young man with schizophrenia came into our weekend crisis clinic. The secretary had received a message from his father instructing us to keep him but gave no further information. Dale was about 29 and I had seen him before in the walk-in clinic. He was jumpy and restless. He told me that he had just returned from a trip to Florida with his parents and his Prolixin injection (a long acting antipsychotic medication) felt like it was wearing off. Could I give him some additional pills? I was reading his chart and noted that the last time I had seen him he was having some trouble with a girlfriend. So I asked him about her. I was trying to keep him in the building, as his father had asked, while trying to get more information. He told me had broken up with her and hadn't seen her in awhile. "Can I get him his medication, now?" He nervously interrupted my questioning.

I continued to engage him. I smelled gasoline on him and asked about that. "I've been working on my car," he said. Unable to stall any longer I got his medication and suggested he sit in the waiting area to see its effect. As soon as he got his medication he bolted out the front door. There were two police officers ready to intercept him as he left the building. As I subsequently learned, he had just doused his girlfriend with gasoline but hadn't set fire to her. Ironically, had he remained in the building, the police couldn't have arrested him as he would have been a patient. I learned that my ability to predict violence is limited even after the fact. I can't tell whether someone is lying to me but it is important to confront incongruities to try to get closer to the truth.

There was one time I was fairly certain of the potential of harm. This was a patient, Mary, who I saw for only two occasions. She was frightened about a boyfriend that wanted to control every aspect of her life and limited her ability to see her family and friends. She had to keep her visit to me a secret for fear he would become violent. The level of her fear and degree of control of her boyfriend prompted me to call her family during the visit and tell her that she must not go back to the boyfriend and go to her parents instead. On the second visit she informed me that she went back to the boyfriend against my advice saying she was more frightened not to go back. Together with a therapist we tried to inform her of safe houses and restraining orders that might help her. We never saw her after that but read about her murder in the newspaper. I still can't think of how we could have saved her. She was not psychotic and she would not have accepted a hospital stay for protection. Her own trauma history made her minimize abusive behavior in her boyfriend. This demonstrates how the mentally ill can be more likely victimized by others. It can take years to build a patient's self confidence enough to leave an abusive relationship. Incredibly sometimes negative attention seems preferable to loneliness.

Large patients can seem more threatening especially if they talk loud and fast. One such patient was being seen by a slight female psychiatric resident at the clinic where I was in charge. He could be heard almost screaming through the closed door. One of the secretaries noted a large bulge in his pants pocket and thought it might be a gun. She ran to me out of concern for everyone's safety, especially the resident alone with this patient. We decided to call hospital security who also brought the local police. We evacuated everyone from the waiting room while four police officers took positions outside of the resident's office. We placed a call to the resident to provide an excuse for her to leave him alone in the room. She was frightened and had noticed the large bulge in his front pocket. With all the staff safely out of the area, the police stormed in to the office and took the patient down to the ground. The large bulge turned out to be a wallet. There were no weapons on him, but he consented to hospitalization due to his escalating agitated behavior. Everyone was afraid to ask him about the bulge which might have spared an overreaction. I suspect had he been a smaller man or a woman this might not have happened.

     My experience has been that most of these large men are gentle giants. But caution is always advised. As I was leaving the VA hospital canteen with a bag of red licorice I encountered one of my PTSD patients in the hallway. He was a large well-developed man with extensive tattoos on arms and neck. He had cowboy boots with his pant legs tucked in. "Hi Doc," he said. "Can I have some candy?" While I was struggling to open the bag, he quickly pulled out a 12 inch hunting knife to help me rip open the bag and just as quickly secured the knife back in his boot. "Here, take as much as you like." I wasn't going to set a limit with a large man with a 12-inch blade. He politely took only two pieces thanked me and wished me a good day. Rather than being scared after the encounter I had a sense that he would have protected me. We had bonded but it was disturbing that patients were walking around the hospital with weapons.

     Another patient who I had seen for several years was grateful for being able to see me privately after many years of going to clinics. He had paranoid schizophrenia and looked like someone you would see homeless on the street despite having a home and a girlfriend. He remained delusional about being Jesus but was able to contain talking about the delusion while taking his medication. He wouldn't hurt anyone and all the staff agreed. He faced a crisis after his father died and he couldn't afford to live in his home alone. He took in a boarder who cheated him out of rent and possibly felt he was meeting his obligation by providing marijuana to him. This only exacerbated the patient's psychosis. I was unable to engage any social service agencies to help the patient evict this boarder. Finally, I convinced the patient that he would be better serviced at a clinic that had access to these social services supports. He reluctantly took my advice. Unfortunately, he continued to decompensate and I soon learned that he was arrested for entering the capital building and threatening a major political figure. In interviews with the media he noted he was being treated at the new clinic. I'm sure he was protecting me from any embarrassment connected to his arrest. His threats were clearly a psychotic attempt to get help for his hopeless situation. Sorry to say, sometimes the only way for severely ill patients to get the help they need is to make threats or commit crimes.

Sometimes it is a symptom of the illness that is responsible for a violent act. I had seen a patient who was discharged from Whiting Forensic Institute for the criminally mentally ill. This man was released after about fifteen years for the crime of killing his wife and two children. He told me what had happened. He had became severely depressed and paranoid. He thought either aliens or gangsters were going to rape, torture and kill his family. In order to protect them from this horrible fate, he planned to kill them mercifully and then kill himself. He was unsuccessful in killing himself, so was arrested. In Connecticut, most patients pleading insanity do more time in jail than those who don't. His was such a clear-cut psychotic reaction that responded to medication. He had extreme guilt for what he had done and was accepting of side effects of his fairly high dose of medication. A psychiatric review board closely monitored his treatment and whereabouts. I wasn't about to reduce or change his medication with the knowledge that without medication he could do such violence.

Ironically as more and better medications have become available to treat mental illness over the last fifty years, there have been drastic cuts in psychiatric treatment facilities. The prospect of enhanced outpatient community services were supposed to replace large psychiatric hospitals. This noble goal was not met as states saw the cost savings from closing hospitals and didn't have the gumption to reallocate enough funds to outpatient services. In addition, the states were able to off load their traditional cost burden of treating the chronically mentally ill onto private and community facilities that could receive Medicare and Medicaid dollars. These entitlement programs wouldn't pay for state hospital stays. If a patient could be discharged to the community and re-hospitalized in another facility the federal government instead of the state would pay most of the cost. However, Medicare would only pay for brief stays, usually much less than is needed to adequately treat a psychotic individual. This has resulted in a revolving door of admissions for the chronically mentally ill. Many who are unable to care for themselves, even with modern medications, have ended up warehoused in nursing homes covered by Medicaid or in jail for petty crimes or random acts of violence. We all pay for this shortsightedness.

     I was an attending at a community hospital and admitted a clinic patient as part of my service to the hospital commitment. He was a patient with chronic mental illness. As I walked into the nurses' station, one of the nurses was near tears. This patient had cornered her in the parking garage and made a sexual pass at her a few days prior to admission. This patient was a regular on the unit with multiple hospitalizations for the brief Medicare covered stays. The recurrent nature of his behavior and relapses suggested to me he needed a longer stay than was possible in a community setting. We talked with the nurse to see if she would press charges against the patient to discourage his inappropriate behavior, but she was embarrassed and sympathetic to his mental illness. This led me to go through the extensive effort to have a commitment hearing to get him placed in a state hospital. The hearing was held with three psychiatrists and the judge all agreeing that he should be committed to the state hospital. We called the state hospital, which now had only about 600 beds for most of the state of Connecticut. They agreed that he should be hospitalized (it's hard to go against a probate judge's decision) but their policy was that the patient had to be rejected for admission from no less than six other facilities. As it turned out, the state's only for-profit hospital accepted him for admission. He was out of the hospital in a little over a week (the highest Medicare reimbursement). This for profit hospital no longer exists. That was the last year that I worked on an inpatient unit.

While we can't usually predict violence, we can appreciate that when it is part of a mental illness, effective treatment of that illness greatly reduces the risk of violence occurring. Society's stigma against substance abuse and mental illness has resulted in inadequate resources to prevent and treat. Every state in the union has discovered that they can reduce their treatment costs for the mentally ill by closing non-reimbursable state facilities and off-loading patients to private and community facilities able to receive federal dollars. Then we wonder why we have seen massive expansions of prison populations and growth of Medicare and Medicaid spending.

(Second edition update: Unfortunately, I have not observed much is any improvement in this access to longer term inpatient treatment. I have noticed that Connecticut has put more resources into mental health treatment in the prison system. This seems to have helped greatly reduce the prison population. In addition, after release from prison, individuals can receive up to a year's worth of Medicaid insurance which allows for treatment after prison release.)

⌘⌘⌘⌘⌘

STUDY CONCLUSIONS, LIES AND STATISTICS

Evidence-based medicine is the latest mantra in the academic community. It means that the best scientific evidence should guide treatment decisions. No one can argue that treatment decisions shouldn't be made using clinically proven treatments. But the reality is not so clear-cut. I have read many articles and editorials in the press accusing pharmaceutical companies of bribing physicians with tuna fish sandwiches and pens to prescribe expensive medications for off-label uses, i.e. not FDA approved uses. Pharmaceutical companies have paid multimillion-dollar fines for off-label marketing such that drug reps cringe at the mention of a non-approved use of their medication. Some states have banned free dinner meetings paid for by manufacturers to inform doctors of new treatments. The irony is that these very pharmaceutical companies pay for almost all of the research on new medications. The FDA reviews what they can say about medications and mandates all the warnings, but the original research is all designed and paid for by these private companies. This means that the source of the majority of evidence for evidence-based medicine comes from the manufacturers.

The FDA regulates the conduct of all these clinical trials and scientists peer review the reports. They also now require reporting of all trials at the onset before they know whether or not they support the medications efficacy or safety. However, despite this oversight, it is fairly easy for a company to bias these studies in their drugs' favor. This can be done by selection bias of patients and comparator agents, by deciding when to take measurements and how long to carry them out. Most importantly they don't do many head to head comparisons with old agents. The goal of a series of new drug registry trials is to prove that the medication is safe and effective for an indicated condition. It doesn't have to be proven better than existing treatments but in order to market the medication something should stand out. What they fear most is a trial that shows the older medication to be superior and will try to avoid doing a trial where this may happen.

The federal government is the major sponsor of research but it tends to favor more basic research. Occasionally, when pressed by a need, it will sponsor a large clinical trial. When government officials realized how much they were spending on new antipsychotic medications they decided to sponsor several large clinical studies to compare these expensive medications to older and much less expensive ones. One of these studies sponsored by the National Institute of Mental Health (NIMH) was done in children designed to compare two newer medications, Zyprexa (olanzapine) and Risperidal (risperidone) with an older medication, Moban (molindone). The result showed that all three medications seemed equally effective but the older medication was superior in not causing weight gain. The only manufacturer for Moban, Endo pharmaceuticals, decided to stop marketing this drug because they had sales of only $9 million per year. I asked several other pharmaceutical companies if they would take up this medication but all declined. The drug compound no longer had patent protection so there was not enough money to be made in marketing it. If a company decided to market it and was successful in increasing sales due to it's "evidence based" proven superiority, generic competition would just undermine the sales of the company that made the new investment in marketing it. So this is an example of evidence-based medicine being thwarted by market forces with the patient suffering.

(Second edition note: We are experiencing severe shortages of some of the older inexpensive generic medications. This has impacted many of my patients. I've had at least one hospitalization due to the inefficacy of substitute medications. Some of these patients have been stable for years on their medications but have to find substitutes when uncertain of the efficacy of different medications for their condition some of which are priced substantially higher. Market forces have not been effective in assuring the availability of inexpensive, safe generic medications.)

What really is the evidence in evidenced-based medicine? There are three levels of evidence from the least powerful observation of cases to the most powerful placebo controlled studies. In reporting of the efficacy of a treatment in a series of patient cases, it is probable that the observation is simply due to chance. Without a group to compare one treatment to another you don't know if the finding would have occurred on its own by chance. The next level of evidence is to try to match the patient cases given a treatment to another collection of patients getting another intervention or none at all (matched case controls). Since these two groups weren't selected at the same time and the treatments weren't assigned randomly you can have many problems with bias. For example the group getting the intervention may have been more ill than the group not getting treatment. The gold standard for evidence-based treatment is the double blind, randomly assigned, placebo-controlled with an active drug comparator study. Wow what a mouthful.

These double blind studies are complicated to design and incredibly more expensive to do than their description suggests. First you have to pick a target diagnosis to treat. You want this as pure as possible to minimize variability of having patients with other co-morbid or additional diagnoses. You then have to select what dosages of medications might be tried. At least one group will get the study drug. Another group would get a placebo because we know that in almost all psychiatric conditions at least a third of patients respond to placebo. You want to see that the study medication performs better than the placebo. The researchers evaluating the patients must not know what treatment the patients are getting so they don't bias the results. In addition, the patients must not know what they are getting so they don't bias the results. In other words both subjects and researchers are blind to the treatment (double-blind with placebo control). These researchers are getting paid the most for patients who complete the trial and positive results are likely to get them contracts for additional studies. So they may bias their ratings to look more positive. This would not be wise since the drug and placebo will look just as good, resulting in a failed trial (the active drug didn't do better than a placebo). Most good researchers are aware of this potential problem and are concerned by this type of bias leading to a failed trial. Critics have pointed out that in many antidepressant trials the drug had only a slight advantage over the placebo.

Aware of the potential for enhancing placebo effects, many researchers have overcompensated and been more cautious in their ratings of improvement. This has resulted in a bias in the opposite direction where the drug and placebo don't do very well. To evaluate for this kind of bias, many studies now put in an active comparator drug that is known to be effective. If this medication also fails to show a response better than placebo you know the study failed and this doesn't mean that the new drug doesn't work but something was wrong with the conduction of the trial.

As you can see data collection is very complicated and expensive to do. This results in many trials having only several hundred patients. The number of patients entered is usually a minimum to show a statistical effect. The results of many different studies are sometimes combined (pooled data in a meta-analysis) to give greater confidence in the outcomes. In the example of depression, studies have looked at response to treatment, which is usually defined as a fifty percent reduction in symptoms as measured by a standard rating scale. Some patients began these studies with such severe depressions, that a fifty percent reduction still means they are significantly depressed. Recently, researchers have realized the importance of looking at remission of symptoms, which is to say, the patient has improved such that they only have a minimum of symptoms.

In these meta-analyses of depression trials response rates for antidepressants are in the range of 50 to 70%. Remission rates for depression are only between 30 and 50%. This means that using evidenced-based data from state of the art double-blind placebo controlled studies leaves more than half of all patients significantly depressed! As you can see, the current state of evidence-based medicine leaves most psychiatric patients under-treated. And much of the data is tainted by source of payment and decisions that are based more on marketability of drugs than what might be best for an individual patient.

Towards the end of my last year in medical school, my very progressive medical school program brought the entire class back to the classroom to relearn how to interpret laboratory test results. We had already learned our basic and clinical sciences and experienced over a year and a half of seeing patients in hospitals and clinics. We had seen thousands of tests ordered by our mentors. This course was to demonstrate why ordering most of these tests were of little value and how dangerous it was to rely upon their results.

One of the major concepts was that sensitivity and specificity of the test was less important than how likely or probable the person being tested had the condition. For example, we screen patients in well physicals all the time for multiple organ functions. In a person who was asymptomatic for say kidney disease, his risk for having a problem is the same as the general population, which for a young healthy male is 4.7% according to a 2006 Norwegian study. If the test had a 95% chance of picking up a problem (sensitivity) and 95% change of being wrong (specificity) and you tested a million people you would identify 44,650 people with the disease (95% of the 4.7% of the 1 million people) but you would also pick up 47,768 people falsely who had no problem (5% of 1 million minus 44,650, because of the only 95% accuracy of the test). So a positive result in the test would have no better than a 50:50 chance of being right. Another way to look at this is that you had to screen 20 people to identify one person with the problem.

How do you deal with this problem? You don't test everyone randomly, but look for symptoms of the problem, or only screen a subpopulation of people who are more likely to have the disease. In the above example, if you only screened people over age 55 who had hypertension or diabetes, known risk factors for kidney problems you would only need to screen 6 people to find a positive result and this would be more likely to be a true positive. How does this relate to psychiatry where lab testing is lacking?

Part of the reason antidepressant trials may have such low response and remission rates may be failure to make the right diagnosis. In a recent study of depressed patients, 40% of the patients had symptoms of hypomania at some time in the past. These symptoms were not enough to meet criteria for bipolar disorder, but may represent a different subset of depression that responds to different types of medications. Our screening criteria may not be specific enough to identify who will respond preferentially to antidepressants leading to a washing out of therapeutic effect. This makes the medication look much less effective than it truly would be if the correct target population could be identified. Efforts to subcategorize depression go back to 1980 with DSM III melancholic subtype. The hope was to identify symptoms suggestive of who would respond to an antidepressant.

In 1980 we thought we had our first laboratory test for severe melancholic depression, the dexamethasone suppression test or DST. Psychiatrists were jubilant. Finally we would enter the world of real doctors and be able to send patients to a lab and confirm what was obvious to everyone, the person was depressed. In the test, the patient was given a pill of a high potency steroid, dexamethasone, in the evening and blood was drawn three times the next day. In people without depression, the next day, their naturally occurring steroid secretion of cortisol was suppressed by the artificial steroid dexamethasone as evident on all blood draws. In depressed patients about 50% of the time at least one of the cortisol levels was not suppressed. This was exciting from a research point of view as it demonstrated a clear biologic difference in depression but from a clinician's point of view it had no value. I could diagnose depression at better than 50% odds blindfolded with wax in my ears.

Still patients and clinicians, particularly in academic settings, did the test routinely. Some psychiatrist groups set up their own labs and made significant money from this useless testing. The party ended when it became clear that not only was the test not very sensitive to pick up disease (only 50% of the time), it wasn't very specific either. It was discovered that anyone who was sick with another medical problem, particularly one in which there was significant weight loss, tested positive on the DST. This did not predict who would benefit from antidepressants.

In writing this I just realized how depressing all of this must sound. The studies are flawed and biased, our labs are worthless and the treatments barely work. This is not my interpretation of all of this. I want to point out how complicated the process is in trying to identify the best way to treat patients. Fortunately, most psychiatrists are very astute and pragmatic in their approach. We're not afraid to use medications for indications that are not approved and readily combine treatments to enhance effects. The anti-psychiatry critics fail to appreciate this complexity and need for creative thinking to help our patients. I have left out the most important type of study that is relevant for treatment, the A-B-A designed study with a sample size of one.

Patients often complain to me that they feel like guinea pigs for the medications that I give them. Yes this is true, but that just may be the best way to figure out what they need. No other type of study is going to tell the specific patient what they need as an individual. As noted, we can start with the evidence and pick approved medications but this would be helpful only 50% of the time. Rational selection of subsequent medications has been the main theme of this book. The brain is so complex that we are only beginning to understand the many interactions of various hormones, neurotransmitters and small molecules and how they may influence mood. Humans have a relatively limited capacity to express how they feel. So the overt manifestation of depression may be a consequence of hundreds or thousands of types of abnormalities requiring different treatments. The best evidence we have now about what to give a particular patient is what worked for that person in the past. This is the nature of the A-B-A designed study. The first is to give the treatment A and see the result. In the B phase the treatment is either removed or substituted. Finally, we go back to the A treatment to confirm that it really works. In some of my sessions I feel like an eye doctor asking, is it better this way or that.

Unfortunately, there needs to be significant time for interventions to work that introduces some memory and time bias in the analysis, which is why the psychiatrist must take careful notes of target symptoms. The result might be influenced by what medication may have preceded the new treatment or the season during which a trial took place, or level of psychosocial stressors that may have influenced the outcome. But it is still specific to the patient and beats random selection based upon the most recent television ad watched or which manufacturer paid for lunch that day.

The next best predictor in selection of a treatment might be what a first degree relative responded to. Although, we need to assess the similarity of symptom profiles and other variables such as substance use and physical illnesses before we can assume the predictive value of this piece of data. After that, logical medication selection given one at a time and evaluated in a comprehensive fashion is the best course. This is supplemented by appropriate psychotherapy, hope and healthy lifestyle. Sometimes all this fails because our diagnosis is wrong.

I was working at a community hospital where I treated inpatients and outpatients in several day hospital programs and a clinic. I admitted a 40-year-old man, Roger, who had carried the diagnosis of schizophrenia since he was medically discharged from the Army at age 20. He lived a simple life, living at home with his 80-year-old father and supporting himself on disability. He was treated psychiatrically in the hospital clinic with a variety of antipsychotic medications. Once or twice per week he would get agitated and his father would bring him to the emergency room where they would see his agitation and assume a psychotic relapse. They would give him a shot of Haldol 5 to 10mg each time and send him out. One day, the emergency room doctor was fed up with his coming so often and decided to hospitalize him. I became his psychiatric attending in the hospital. Rather than just trusting the chart, I began to ask him questions about his symptoms over the years.

He was an odd appearing fellow. His body language expressed an insecurity and discomfort in social settings. He didn't speak spontaneously but didn't seem paranoid. He seemed just very socially awkward. I asked him if he ever experienced hearing voices or seeing things that others didn't. He denied all psychotic symptoms except for extreme anxiety. His description of symptoms was more consistent with panic attacks and social anxiety than with schizophrenia. I also thought that he had Asperger's Syndrome that is a mild form of autism. This made him seem odd and socially awkward. I had recently returned from a meeting at the World Health Organization in Geneva, Switzerland where John Wing, a prominent British psychiatrist, presented the significance of this new diagnosis that he and his wife had been researching. This was a new diagnosis that he hoped to have accepted into the next International Classification of Diseases (ICD 10). Recognition of Asperger's syndrome would reduce the number of patients misdiagnosed with schizophrenia and wrongly medicated. After diagnosing Roger with Asperger's, I decided to put him on an antidepressant for the panic and anxiety and wean the antipsychotic to a minimal dose. I referred him to a day treatment program where I was the attending. Interestingly, when we had to get authorization from the insurance company for his day treatment they said that they wouldn't pay for treatment of Asperger's or autism. I fudged and told them that he was also diagnosed with schizophrenia, which was true for 20 years.

After discharge, he resumed his pattern of frequent emergency room visits. Evaluation by the treatment team failed to find evidence for psychosis as cause for the ER visits. We asked him why he felt the need to go to the ER. His response was simple, "the fear, the fear." The antidepressant didn't have a chance yet to work on his panic, but we had to prevent these unnecessary ER visits. In each visit he would get Haldol that was causing a side effect called akathisia. Akathisia is an awful feeling of anxiety that feels as if you are crawling out of your skin. He didn't seem to understand our explanations of how to manage his anxiety and just wanted something for "the fear." I decided to have the pharmacy make a placebo with starch filled capsules. We labeled them "Fear-B-Gone." We gave him the bottle and told him he could take one per hour for up to 6 in a day. We told him that it was a safe and natural medication that he could take when he felt the fear.

Over the next two weeks he made no trips to the ER. His father came in for a family meeting with the treatment team. His father was a tall, thin, fit ex-military man. His voice was solid and resolute and it was difficult to know whether there was a hint of anger when he asked me point blank, "I want to know what medication you have given my son?"

I hesitated as my heart began to pound, wondering if I had done something wrong. My psychiatrist training and Jewish background took over and I responded to the question with another question. "Before I tell you, I want to know how you think your son is doing?"

His father said that in twenty years of coming to psychiatrists and various treatment facilities, "whatever medication that you have given my son it is the best medication that he has ever had." With a sigh of relief, I told his father that it was a placebo but that he also had other medications for his panic. I needed to prevent him from wrongly getting antipsychotic medication in the ER and this was the only way I could think of doing this safely. He didn't care what I was giving him; it was working. I continued him on Fear-b-gone for the six months that I saw him in the hospital clinic. Shortly after I stopped working in the clinic, I saw him back on the inpatient unit. He was again going to the ER for Haldol shots. I asked him why he wasn't taking his Fear-b-gone. They stopped it, he told me. I called the new attending in the clinic. She told me she thought that it was unethical to give a patient placebo. I told her it was unethical to take away a treatment that was working so that he ended up getting inappropriate treatment. But I wasn't his attending anymore.

I believe that the Fear-b-gone was more than a placebo. It was a transitional object that this concrete thinking man with Asperger's used to remind him of the comfort he received from his doctors and treatment team. It was a tangible object that was part of a behavioral intervention for anxiety reduction. I have another patient with Asperger's and anxiety who I have continued on placebo now for over five years without loss of efficacy. I have tried stopping it several times with worsening of her anxiety. With it I have prevented escalation of more side effect laden medications. It is cheap, safe and she knows that is a natural medication (I fill her bottles with gelatin capsules I buy at Wal-Mart.)

Placebos are the most studied drugs in the world. It is the medication that every other is compared to and routinely is effective in a third of cases. The multi-billion dollar supplement industry relies heavily on placebo effect. Few of these supplements are studied in placebo trials and the few that have been rarely demonstrate efficacy better than a placebo.

While seeming to tout the value of placebos, I am really calling attention to how difficult it is to beat the placebo effect. All of our available, FDA approved medications have been demonstrated to be more effective than a placebo in a majority of their clinical trials. In selecting medications multiple factors need to be taken into account. Evidence from carefully designed studies is just one of these factors.

Joanne was a woman in her mid- twenties who presented with symptoms of panic attacks, depression and obsessive-compulsive disorder (OCD). I began her on SSRI medication approved to treat these conditions. The OCD improved and so did some of the depression but she became more agitated. Over time things got worse and persistent symptoms of derealization or feeling detached and unreal proved very distressing. I tried higher doses of the SSRI but this caused intolerable side effects. Several different antidepressant medications similarly were not tolerated at high enough dosages to be adequately effective. Realizing that her symptoms seemed to wax and wane or cycle over time, I decided to try mood stabilizers. She went through several mood stabilizers including lithium, Depakote and Trileptal but all produced only partial benefit at low doses and she was unable to tolerate or worsened on increased doses that would have been considered therapeutic by controlled trials.

Standard protocol is to try a given medication and increase the dosage to therapeutic levels as determined by clinical trial studies. If the patient only gets a partial response the dose is raised to maximum approved or tolerated. But what if a patient doesn't tolerate or respond to maximum dosages? Drug manufacturers don't like to do trials where their medication is added to other medications and the FDA only recently even allowed medications to be approved as "add-on" treatments. Combining medications runs the risk of more potential side effects and drug interactions that may be wrongly connected to the manufacturers' medication. Also, if the base medication is that of another manufacturer, they may not want this potential adverse exposure with potential additional warnings applied to their drug. A clinical trial with multiple medications would also need a larger number of patients to be studied since as the number of variables increases there is more likely to be chance associations. You need a large enough "n" of subjects to reduce the risk that a finding is just a random occurrence. ("N" is the number of patients needed in the study to see a statistically significant result.) Joanne was in a therapeutic hinder zone with little evidence to support what to do.

Joanne did get partial responses to most of the medications given to her. So I decided to combine them one by one. I increased each new medication to its max-tolerated dose and waited until the response reached a plateau. Additional medications were added in a like fashion until 5 different medications, including three mood stabilizers and two antidepressants, were in the mix, all but one at sub therapeutic dosages per manufacturer studies. She was feeling very good now. After several months of doing well we tried to reduce or lower one medication. She got worse again. This happened with attempts to reduce any of the five medications. The evidence for her A-B-A designed trials suggested that all of her medications were essential to her well-being.

Rational poly pharmacology usually implies that the combination of medications that have complementary and different mechanisms of action can have a synergistic benefit. Psychiatry for years shunned this practice while it flourished in the treatment of cardiac disease, hypertension, diabetes and cancer treatments. Not until the FDA permitted an indication for Abilify, then Seroquel as add-ons to antidepressant medication did it give approval for the practice of poly pharmacy. Interestingly, the dosages recommended for add-on therapy are below what was recommended for their original indications. The FDA had approved two prior medications that were combination medication, Symbyax and Triavil. These two medications were approved as if they were a single agent. Nowhere is their support for combining medications of similar mechanism of action as I had done with Joanne.

What if medications with similar mechanisms of action had other actions that were responsible for different side effects? Would it be possible to stack these different medications together to get a high enough therapeutic effect, such as serotonin enhancement, while keeping side effects down because the side effect profiles were different? This may be what was benefiting Joanne. I don't advocate this approach often as it is difficult to manage and confusing but may be viable for some hard to treat patients. When I was in a university setting, patients would often come in with these seeming irrational combinations of medications and we scoffed at the LMD (local medical doctor's) lack of knowledge of evidence-based medicine. Instead, it was possible that the Ivy-tower doctors failed to appreciate the LMD's carefully done individualized clinical trial with an "n" of one?

(Second edition update: Genomic testing has been the new rage with companies and providers claiming with their genetic testing they can better select medications for patients. My experience to date has been less than positive and may end up the way of the dexamethasone suppression test. There are two main categories of gene testing being offered: metabolic and receptor gene variants. The metabolic genes are looking at a set of liver enzymes that metabolize various medications and food compounds. Variations occur when an individual either is a fast or slow metabolizer of a particular metabolic pathway. This may predict side effects but in practice a careful prescriber starts low and increases medication doses as needed. Medication responses are not necessarily correlated with blood levels and medications have active metabolites that maybe more important for recovery. The testing companies give a color coded report of green (use as directed), yellow (use with some caution), and red (try to avoid). My experience is that I have had patients do the best on medications that the testing company coded as red or yellow. If I had done the testing first, I would have missed using the best medication. I have not had the testing predict a medication better than my clinical judgment.

These metabolic gene tests don't identify diagnostic categories. They don't help to determine if someone has bipolar disorder, psychosis, OCD or PTSD which might be indication for different classes of medications. Also as we combine certain medications one medication might interfere with the metabolism of the other rendering the gene test irrelevant. As gene testing has advanced there has been expansion of the number of genes being tested that might lead to some diagnostic predictions in the future. They have tests for serotonin transporter genes and ones that affect other neurotransmitter expression or metabolism. The research has not yet given me enough guidance to justify the hundreds if not thousands of dollars of cost associated with these tests. I think that I have been better able to predict which medications to choose from a combination of symptoms, family history, past medication trials and carefully done future medication trials in the patient. I propose a system diagnosis and medication selection in later chapters.)

⌘⌘⌘⌘⌘

AFTERWARD-THE FUTURE

Early in my post-residency clinical work I admitted a young woman, Jill, with acute mania. She was agitated with mind racing and paranoia. I wanted to give her the antipsychotic medication, Haldol, as it would have calmed her mania more quickly than just mood stabilizers. She refused the medication telling me that Haldol and several other antipsychotic medications caused her to hallucinate. I argued with her briefly, trying to convince her that the medication was given to treat those symptoms and she may have misinterpreted a delayed response with exacerbation of her symptoms. She had seen hallucinations listed as one of the potential side effects in the package insert for the medication and knew that was her problem. I thought that I was smarter and better informed having done clinical trial research.

When a patient is being evaluated for side effects during a clinical trial, the researcher must report all complaints made by the patient, even if the purported side effect is actually a symptom of the underlying illness. This is why almost every medication will have listed as side effects the very same symptoms that are part of the condition it is approved to treat. I considered why Jill's psychosis might have gotten worse on antipsychotic medication, if her observations were correct. Most of the antipsychotic medications also have anticholinergic side effects. These are the same effects that many over the counter cold and allergy medications have that cause dryness. Many teens have learned that taking high doses of these medications can cause a drug high which may include hallucinations. Abuse of these over the counter decongestants has led government regulators to mandate that these medications be kept behind the pharmacists' counter. I didn't feel that an anticholinergic effect was the cause of this woman's worsening since Haldol has minimal anticholinergic effects. I gave her a different antipsychotic that she never had and she responded very well despite it having more anticholinergic effect than Haldol. I assumed she had been mistaken in her prior observations but remembered her comments.

Now I have learned a bit more about antipsychotic medications including the newer ones that have been labeled "atypical antipsychotics." What makes them "atypical" is somewhat controversial but generally is thought to be due to the medications blocking serotonin and dopamine receptors. This property is supposed to cause the patient to seem more animated and less zombie-like. These "negative" symptoms, which include social withdrawal and flat affect, are symptoms that the older medications didn't treat very well. As discussed in other chapters, dopamine is the "hue" or intensity neurotransmitter. Having too much dopamine leads to agitation and psychosis while blocking it too much causes a flattening. It also affects cognition or the ability to think clearly. Patients with ADHD focus better with dopamine enhancing medications.

As it turns out blocking a subgroup of serotonin receptors in part of the brain actually stimulates dopamine release in the front of the brain enhancing the patient's ability to think. In patients with schizophrenia this is thought to be a helpful effect in that it counteracts some of the dopamine blocking effects in the part of the brain necessary for higher cognitive processes. Interestingly, some of the older medications also seem to have this "atypical" action of blocking serotonin. Is it possible that Jill uniquely had more of this subgroup of serotonin receptors? If so, when she was given low doses of specific antipsychotic medications with anti-serotonin activity could this have resulted in more dopamine release than blockade causing a worsening of her psychosis? The anti-serotonin effects generally occur at lower dosages and she might not have received a high enough dose to block enough dopamine for an antipsychotic effect.

This dopamine enhancing effect of "atypical" antipsychotic medications may explain why they are useful for patients with major depression who haven't fully responded to antidepressant medication. The FDA so far has approved two antipsychotic medications for use as augmenting add-ons to antidepressants. The recommended dosages for their use are lower than that for treating psychosis or bipolar disorder. *(Second edition note: There are now four add on medications approved.)*

I have observed clinical evidence for a serotonin blocking effect from several antipsychotic medications. In several of my patients with schizophrenia they reported new onset of obsessive-compulsive (OCD) symptoms shortly after starting an antipsychotic medication. I've seen this with both old medications such as Haldol but often with newer agents including Zyprexa, Clozapine and Saphris (asenapine). These symptoms can be confused with worsening of psychosis but careful questioning reveals otherwise. The patient is distressed by the symptom and it is not part of an elaborate delusion. They are perceived as unwanted and intrusive and have included both intrusive thoughts and compulsive behaviors. One patient described a compulsion to repeat reassuring comments in his mind. Another found himself staring at others in a compulsive manner not out of any paranoid fear. Most of these symptoms resolved within a month of addition of low doses of selective serotonin reuptake inhibitors (SSRIs) such as Zoloft. OCD has been shown to improve with SSRI medications but usually require higher doses to respond. Increasing the dose of the antipsychotic medication usually made the obsessing worse or had no benefit.

Some of the older medications share this "atypical" property but these varied effects of older medications have not been fully studied or tested. Many of our older medications have effects that we didn't know they had, as we didn't even know what to look for. One example of a hidden effect is seen with the beta-blocking medication, pindolol. This is an old medication that was indicated for treating high blood pressure and heart problems. It was not widely used partly because it had some activating effects on the heart (this was called intrinsic sympathomimetic effect). Pindolol is relatively unique among beta-blockers because it also blocks a sub-set of serotonin receptors. These receptors can reduce the effect of serotonin antidepressants by shutting off the nerve cells' release of serotonin. The body is always trying to balance effects. So if one receptor turns on the release of a neurotransmitter another receptor is there to shut it down. Pindolol, by blocking this inhibitory effect, can enhance the effect of selective serotonin antidepressants. The theory of this action has been shown to be helpful for depressed patients in several studies.

So we can see that we can't always judge a medication by its label. We have beta-blockers that act on serotonin. Dopamine blocking antipsychotics also work on serotonin. In the 1980s a medication, trazodone was approved for treating depression. It failed to gain acceptance as an antidepressant since it was too sedating, but I began using it to help patients reduce their over dependence on addicting sedative medications. It has since become one of the most popular treatments for insomnia in depressed and anxious patients. There may be a gold mine of hidden benefits among many of our old medications but our current drug approval process doesn't reward their exploration or discovery. Since all of these older medications have already been approved, their relative safety tested by time and original clinical trials allows physicians to use them "off-label" despite lack of FDA approval. New studies need to be done to find the hidden talents that lie within these medications and to better guide clinicians. Unfortunately, when medications lose patent protection, drug companies no longer see profit in pursuing new FDA indications for these old medications. Another example of this is use of Trileptal (oxcarbazepine) for bipolar disorder. This also means that if new uses are found for older medications, this knowledge will have to be spread by word of mouth or be hidden in scientific journals. It won't have the powerful marketing power of large pharmaceutical companies. Patients and physicians might be reluctant to try these treatments tainted by the stigma of an "off-label" use.

Ongoing studies into brain function and dysfunction are identifying the multitude of interconnectedness between brain neurons and various regulators. New molecules and brain receptors are being identified. As their functions become known, we search for medications that can affect them. This gives hope to finding new medications to treat illnesses that have proven refractory and hope for medications that might work more specifically for a patient's problem thereby reducing side effects. But in this pursuit, I strongly advocate for not forsaking older remedies whose talents we may have missed for lack of knowledge about mechanism of action. A patient recently asked me if there were any new great medications for depression. I told him there have not been any miracle cures but we have learned to use some of our existing medications better especially in novel combinations. Some of these remedies may include nutrients and various supplements that need to be standardized and approved for purity and consistency.

(Second edition note: The resurrection of an old medication for depression use is best seen now with ketamine. This anesthetic agent has become popular due to purported rapid antidepressant effect. Private clinics have popped up all over to give this injection treatment. Pharmaceutical companies have scrambled to get in on the game by modifying the molecule so it can be patented and sold as a nasal spray. The results do look promising but most insurers are not covering the injections.)

⌘⌘⌘⌘⌘

APPENDIX: DEPRESSION TREATMENT PARADIGMS

This appendix is an attempt to outline and summarize my strategy for assessing and treating patients who present with the major symptom of depression. It is derived from my many readings of clinical trials, meetings with hundreds of clinicians and educators and my over 25 years of clinical experience. Although it does draw from many studies, I have not referenced or given credit for their work or ideas. I do appreciate the great works and thinking of these individuals but I have absorbed them into my practice and can't recall every source.

(Second edition note: I have left this section intact with minimal corrections as I still believe the recommendations. Some of these ideas have been expanded upon in the new chapters of the second edition which follow.)

When a person presents to me with the symptoms of depression I first obtain a detailed history from them. Everyone has a different way of expressing themselves and a personal way of describing the impact of their depression. Relatively few of my patients have not had contact with other health professionals and have tried a variety of remedies. Some are the children, parents or relatives of patients that I have seen. Some of them tried self-remedies including illicit drugs or legal medications obtained from friends, family or bought on the black market. While the DSM IV, the diagnostic manual used to make diagnoses, relies solely upon symptoms to make diagnoses, the reality is that past history, response to medications and family history may be more important in determining which treatment is best than the actual DSM diagnosis. Also, within a set of criteria for a specific diagnosis individuals may have different subsets of symptoms that may predict a preferential response to different treatments.

The complete initial assessment should include a longitudinal history of course of illness and symptom progression. When were medications initiated, and what was their response? Patients often don't recall the sequence of medications but this may be very important. Asking why a given medication was started or stopped may help the patient recall symptoms or side effects. A family history in the form of a genogram or family tree is very helpful in identifying heritable conditions and possible sources of trauma, such as untimely deaths or substance abuse. A detailed history of medication trials is as close to a battery of lab tests in psychiatry as we have. Knowledge of how each medication works and the effect on the patient becomes a pharmacologic probe of various neurotransmitter functions in the brain. So both positive and negative effects of medications can be enlightening.

A person presenting with depressive symptoms may not have major depressive disorder. People describe any negative mood state as depression even though psychiatrists have a different understanding of the term. Patients say they are depressed when they are disappointed. They may have an anxiety disorder, attention deficit disorder (ADHD) with negative consequences of their behavior, a grieving reaction or adjustment disorder to a difficult situation, or posttraumatic stress disorder (PTSD). Their symptoms can be part of the depressive phase of bipolar disorder or the prodrome to a schizophrenic disorder where all the diagnostic symptoms have yet to appear. They may have a secondary depressive disorder due to medical condition such as a stroke or negative reaction to medications such as steroids or alcohol. Each of these conditions may call for a different treatment recommendation. Some patients may have a combination of disorders for example PTSD with bipolar disorder or ADHD with an anxiety disorder making the assessment and treatment more complicated.

When multiple conditions may be the cause of the depression we need to rule out the most serious first. This implies that a serious medical condition should be ruled out first. All of the DSM disorders have this hierarchy built into the criteria that is often overlooked since it is further down the list as often lettered as D, E or F criteria. This criterion usually includes the phrase, "the symptoms are better described as part of another disorder...." If someone is using drugs or alcohol they must be stopped. I advise one month of abstinence for the "Pepsi challenge." If the person can't give up drugs or alcohol for one month to see if the depression improves this is evidence for a substance abuse problem. If treatment is successful, the patient may introduce small amounts of alcohol (up to 2 standard drinks for a woman and 4 for a man per occasion) to see if the alcohol reverses the benefits of the treatment. Sometimes offending medications can't be stopped for health reasons, then empirical treatment can be started to see if this is an obstacle to improvement.

There must be an assessment of the stressors and interpersonal relations and social supports. I offer psychotherapy to all of the patients. The focus of this intervention can change during the course of treatment. Initially, therapy may be just supportive in trying to cope with the wait for a medication response and side effects. Depression and anxiety often arises in the context of situations where the patient feels they are trapped or have no choice. This is akin to the learned helplessness models. The therapist may help the patient to see that they do have choices. For example, an abusive boss or spouse might be confronted despite the risk of loss of job or marriage. The patient may be guided in how to face the confrontation especially when they had prior bad experiences in confrontation. I often suggest a confrontation that is more of a statement of feeling, such as, "you've asked me to do many things; how do you want them prioritized?" Or to a spouse, "when you say those things it makes me feel...do you realize this?" Very often the depression is a way out of a difficult situation where the patient can't make a decision so getting ill becomes a way of maintaining the status quo or forcing a withdrawal from a conflict. Depression makes it impossible to think or act. Medications might give only a partial response in this situation but may improve thinking and concentration enough to work on a solution.

Below is an outline of some of my depression treatment paradigms

(Disclaimer: This is a strategy based upon the personal experience of Neil Liebowitz, M.D. and does not reflect the results of direct study. It does draw from communications with many clinicians and my interpretation of multiple studies, which I have not referenced. Many of the strategies have not been proven by clinical trial work and most might be considered "off-label" use of medications by FDA standards. They should be used for idea purposes with the guidance of a physician experienced in treating depression.)

(Second edition note: later chapters have been added to further describe my approach to obtaining a psychiatric history, doing medication trials and beginning of a treatment algorithm.)

Complete initial assessment- review:

Past response to medications and abused drugs

Family history of response to medication

Symptom profile

Stressors/ psychotherapy issues

Follow symptom hierarchy

Rule out bipolar, psychosis, organic causes-drugs, Lyme disease. These conditions alter choice of medications dramatically. Most common cause of treatment failure is drug and alcohol abuse. Give patient one-month challenge of abstinence while initiating medication. If patient can't comply, this is evidence for substance abuse disorder. If treatment is successful, patient can introduce small amounts of alcohol (up to 2 standard drinks for woman and up to 4 for a man per occasion).

Patient will learn if their tolerance is lower by next day's worsening of symptoms.

Look for treatment modifiers: OCD, panic, ADD/ADHD, eating disorders, abuse/PTSD. These conditions alter dosage of medications; psychotherapy needs, and may alter choice of medication if symptom signal is not strong.

Creating the color purple: Mix blue- serotonin, cool, calm, panic, obsessing with red- norepinephrine, energy, motivation, drive. Identify the "symptom signal."

The dopamine effect: DA changes the "intensity or hue of the color purple" Too little and patient feels flat, too much and patient is agitated. Raise the serotonin too high and you may indirectly reduce the DA resulting in too flat feeling. Too high and patient may develop psychotic symptoms e.g. cocaine, stimulants. Early studies of stimulants in depression produced mixed results with patients reporting intense unpleasant feelings. This leads to the dopamine dilemma.

The dopamine dilemma: The DA system is a fragile one. It adapts quickly in some people i.e. Rapid tolerance to the stimulant and antidepressant effects or has paradoxical effects in other patients, i.e. Calming effects in ADHD. On/off effects are noted in Parkinson's disease with Sinemet, the analogous super sensitivity effect of too much DA is seen with Tardive dyskinesia.

Patients are all assumed to meet criteria for major depression, dysthymia, or some anxiety disorder. The goal is to shorten the time for identification of the best medication combination for the individual patient. Choice of medications should follow a logical sequence based upon symptom profile and response to treatments and not be random or solely based upon avoidance of side effects or current FDA indication.

Treatment assumptions include:

Symptom remission is the goal, not just response. "Side effects" might be an indication of only partial symptom response (e.g. fatigue) instead of an adverse reaction to the medication.

Between 50-75% of patients will need a combination of medications for remission of symptoms. The current most popular strategy has been to select a medication based upon side effect profile and increase the dose to high levels to see if a more complete response can be had. My assumption is that this approach is not as good as carefully tailoring a combination of low dose medications towards individual needs. Lower doses result in fewer side effects, lower total medication costs (cutting pills may save on co-pays) and better overall response. Short-term efforts to get rapid response often lead to longer-term medication dissatisfaction and non-compliance due to side effects. (e.g. starting with a sedating SSRI to compensate for a transient increase in anxiety results in excess sedation a month later.) By using combinations of medications, troubling side effects can be reduced by careful adjustment of the medication mix.

Done carefully each medication trial serves as a "lab challenge test" (e.g. Medications are given one at a time to allow for observation of effect and side effects help identify which specific neurotransmitter systems need to be targeted.)

To make each challenge have maximum value, there should be a clear idea of the effect of each medication on various neurotransmitter systems. Since no antidepressant has conclusively shown superiority in response for the broad diagnosis of major depression, it is justified to select medications based upon "cleanness" of receptor selectivity or uniqueness of receptor mechanism of action spectrum. This reduces side effects, drug interactions and provides the most information as to neurotransmitter profile. (i.e. a medication with a more selective or well known receptor mechanism of action will provide more information about underlying pathology than a "broad spectrum" agent that affects multiple receptors.)

Differences within classes of antidepressants (e.g. SSRIs,) are not significant enough to justify switching within class unless the problem is of side effect tolerance. Since the clinician begins with the medication with the least side effects, switching is less common in the early stages, but may occur in the final "refinement" phase. For example, it might be easier to start an anxious patient on Paxil than Lexapro, but once a response is achieved you cannot remove the sedation from the Paxil. You can however, add a low dose of Klonopin to the Lexapro initially, and then remove the Klonopin as the Lexapro has taken effect.

The initial medication is continued if its symptom profile is remitted. The medication is increased if only a partial response to its expected symptom profile. If a fairly good partial response is obtained but effect has peaked and side effects inhibit any further increases, another same class medication may be tried.

The initial medication is augmented if residual symptoms are best treated with a different category of antidepressant. Generally, a medication dose is not increased to very high doses solely to "lose the selectivity" of the SSRI. This causes excessive side effect burden and has not saved on cost or drug interactions. In fact, P450 inhibition for some medications increasing drastically when to dose is elevated above a certain amount (e.g. Zoloft >150-200mg, Lexapro >20mg). Complementary augmenting strategies are the norm in a lot of medicine as in treatment of hypertension, cardiac disease, cancer and infection.

(Second edition note: refer to later chapter on how to do a medication trial.)

Symptom profiles-first pass evaluation- the following neurotransmitters are associated with these symptoms.

Low NE depression: Low energy is more pronounced in the early am and may improve by pm (think diurnal variation), low motivation, apathy, dysthymia- true lack of ability to enjoy anything, poor concentration (ADD-like), dwelling/ruminative anxiety about past issues, poor decision making (anxious dwelling is often a consequence of inability to think clearly enough to problem solve real problems), inability to cry; supporting features- cigarettes lift mood and calm, cocaine and stimulant preference but these often makes patient anxious and are done in combination with alcohol or opiates; Primary medications: Strattera first line, alternately, Wellbutrin or Desipramine. (Also screen for sleep apnea with this type of depression.)

Low NE/DA depression: chronic dysthymia, all of above features but less energy or contrarily, hyperactive with ADHD symptoms, inattention, distractibility, impulsivity, blah-tedium vitae; Supporting features: ADHD, tired when given SSRI or Strattera, calming effect from cocaine and stimulants-if abuses tends not to use large quantities e.g. self medicating, generally dislikes alcohol except to calm down to pass out. Primary medications: Wellbutrin, Desipramine (more for dysthymia), Stimulants-more for ADHD (Ritalin more DA, Adderall more balanced NE/DA). (Screen for sleep disorders.)

Low 5-HT depression: obsessive, anxiety about hypothetical future "what ifs"(in obsessing there is excessive focus on irrelevant details with resultant "catastrophizing"), depression is usually more an inability to anticipate pleasure- patient may enjoy situation once overcoming the anxious anticipation, sense of wellbeing/ "ill-being", generalized anxiety, if low energy-this is fatigue from worrying and is worse in the pm compared to am in low NE, negativity is of dwelling nature; true panic attacks, uncontrolled crying, rejection sensitivity (hypersensitivity to criticism). Supporting features: alcohol preference opiates sometimes-often reflective of pseudo psychotic symptoms with agitation. Primary medications: Lexapro, Zoloft (adds minor DA at 150+mg)

Combined 5-HT/ NE/DA: severe depression with melancholia, all of above symptoms combined; More likely to have co-morbid chronic pain, fibromyalgia, and migraine. Look for signs of latent psychosis such as agitation, severe obsessions that verge on delusional, erotomania. If present need atypical antipsychotic, lithium or anticonvulsant. Supporting features: severe recurrence, poop out of SSRI after several months (poop out of SNRI or combination therapy often reflective of bipolar depression). Primary medications: Effexor XR doses at least 150 but must try 225+mg or Cymbalta 60-120mg. (Watch for symptoms of psychosis or bipolar noted below.)

High DA symptoms (calls for antipsychotic medication): agitation, motor restlessness, psychomotor retardation, hallucinations, delusions, extreme rigidity or concrete thinking which is a change from baseline (i.e. not developmental as in Asperger's or intellectual disability.)

Special cases: opiate/ heavy marijuana users and borderline/ PTSD patients may do well on nefazodone; Elderly endogenously depressed and depressed with GERD may do well on Remeron; IBS patients may do well on TCA- nortriptyline or desipramine. Opiate abusers who report increased energy with opiates may benefit from Abilify 2.5-5mg q.o.d + Effexor or Wellbutrin or nefazodone. Depressed ADHD may benefit from nefazodone + Stimulant. *(Second edition note: the new antidepressants, Viibryd and Trintellex might work well in the subtype with co-morbid ADHD.)*

Second pass strategies- what to do next after partial and negative outcomes from above trials.

Fatigue on SSRI (Lexapro and initial Prozac not sedating- other SSRIs can be sedating in a dose related fashion): if good response, try lower dose or switch to non-sedating medication-Lexapro 5-10mg. If anxiety better but persistent low motivation, drive, energy, add Wellbutrin (if no history of panic and anxiety was mild to moderate prior) or Strattera (if had panic and more severe anxiety prior to SSRI or had poor tolerance of Wellbutrin or to doses of Effexor above 150mg).

Fatigue on Strattera: most likely ADHD, give in evening, consider stimulant or Wellbutrin.

Panic attacks with SSRI: add Klonopin 0.25-0.5mg bid- should be initiated 12 hours prior to SSRI in anyone presenting with panic. Patients with severe panic that persists beyond 2-3 weeks after starting an SSRI + Klonopin should be considered for an anticonvulsant or a low dose atypical antipsychotic and watched for bipolar (usually mixed type) or agitated depression.

Agitation on any antidepressant: same as above. (An interesting problem with DSM IV is that there is no diagnosis of agitated depression. These patients don't have the delusions or hallucinations to qualify for psychotic features, nor do they have hypomania to qualify for bipolar. They do respond to the addition of an antipsychotic and most closely fit the DSM II criteria for psychotic depression. Note that patients diagnosed in DSM IV with psychotic depression, in DSM II would be classified as schizophrenic.) DSM V has depression with anxiety but agitation is not the same as anxiety.

Poop out after successful remission first few months- augment with NE/DA, consider bipolar. Late poop-out after years- consider substance abuse esp. alcohol, severe life stressor requiring more psychotherapy- any med change would probably have placebo effect, modest increase in SSRI on temporary basis helps with stress tolerance.

Persistent generalized anxiety on higher dose SSRI-not panic and not agitation: augment with buspirone 7.5-30mg bid (higher dose in alcoholics, marijuana smokers like as well).

Insomnia with anxiety: augment with Trazodone 50-100mg HS

Refractory strategies

Always consider bipolar disorder for recurrent depressions, especially for patients who seem to have cycles of depression lasting less than one year. Cyclical depression can be viewed as bipolar with the mood curve shifted down (a type of bipolar III)

Severe melancholic depression requires most neurotransmitters to be hit hard. Most potent combination, Remeron + Effexor XR + atypical (Geodon 40-80 HS or Abilify 2.5- 5mg)

Medication pearls

Geodon (ziprasidone) doses below 60mg can be activating, above 80mg are usually sedating. For an agitated patient start with 80mg HS instead of 40mg bid and titrate up or down as needed. Geodon has TCA like antidepressant effects that may be responsible for this agitation at the lower dose before enough antipsychotic effect kicks in. Geodon binds tightly to DA receptor and I have seen more tardive dyskinesia with this medication.

Abilify has unique DA effects. Doses as low as 2.5mg q.o.d (has 70 hr half-life) may have dramatic energizing effects in certain patients. This has been noted in cocaine/opiate addicts who report being energized on opiates and some borderline patients.

All the antipsychotics make good augmenters for refractory conditions. Most refractory patients have concomitant agitation that is often worsened by the antidepressants. They all are different and patients have differential responses. The dosage makes a big difference- generally much lower than for psychosis. I have had good success with Risperidal 0.5-2mg for severe obsessing. Seroquel 25-400mg works well for bipolar patients who can't sleep who often get EPS on Risperidal. Geodon 20-40mg q.d. and Zyprexa 2.5-15mg may have unique antidepressant effects when others have failed- I reserve Zyprexa for refractory or acutely agitated patients close to hospitalization because of weight problem. Both Abilify and Seroquel XR have gotten FDA indications for augmenting antidepressants in unipolar depression. Low doses of Saphris 2.5 to 5mg may also help. Watch for emergence of OCD symptoms with Zyprexa, Haldol and Saphris.

Lithium augmentation: I use lithium as an augmenter instead of primary medication to avoid toxicities. Fewer than 25% will respond to lithium alone at the levels I recommend, but the risks are very low. Only lithium has a dual neurotrophic effect. Generally doses of 300-900mg are adequate for augmentation (keep level 0.6 or less to minimize side effects, can use up to 0.8 for bipolar but reduce after several years to reduce occult toxicity). Response to lithium is triphasic:

initial improvement in 1-2 weeks for major symptoms of mania/depression, then 6 months later improvement in "insight" with significant improved interpersonal relationships, finally sometime after 2-5years of stability many patients can safely taper off medication for brief periods e.g. For pregnancy.

Specific medication effects on neurotransmitters:

SSRIs Lexapro- cleanest 5-HT, inhibition 2D6 above 20mg (40%); Celexa-some antihistamine/Anticholinergic;

Zoloft-modest DA effect esp. above 150mg, but 2D6 inhibition at this level;

Paxil/ Prozac mild NE at higher dose, anticholinergic moderate, severe 2D6 all doses- avoid in most patients.

Prozac OK in young women.

Luvox (fluvoxamine)- most sedating, good for OCD, inhibits 3A4-eg Xanax. It is also relatively short acting and might not cause as much switch in bipolar depression.

Strattera most specific NE, some inhibition 2D6, mod anticholinergic

Wellbutrin- parent is mod DA, metabolite strong NE, mod 2D6

Remeron- direct acting 5-HT and NE, hits subsets of serotonin, 5HT3, in GI tract, strong antihistamine-increase weight

Effexor XR-XR is more potent antidepressant compared to IR which is too short acting requiring higher doses and bid dosing, at doses less than 150mg mostly SSRI, significant NE and some DA occurs at doses above 200mg.

Use of the weaker Venlafaxine (Effexor) IR preparation might be better for bipolar depression.

Cymbalta- dual action 5-ht/: NE about 2:1 as compared to Effexor 3-4:1. One approximate equivalent Cymbalta 60mg is close to Effexor 150 +Wellbutrin SR 150-300mg.

Fetzima (levomilnacipran) is a newer antidepressant that is has and NE: 5-ht that is close to 1:1. This might help with pain and be an alternate to combo therapy but is much more expensive than a combo.

The University of Indiana has maintained a very useful table of drug interactions predicted by liver enzyme metabolism that is available for free at: http://medicine.iupui.edu/clinpharm/ddis/. This table needs to be taken in the context of treatment needs. Just because there may be a drug interaction doesn't mean the medications can't be combined. Usually it means that a dosage adjustment may be needed.

(End of original first edition essays.)

(But wait, there's more, proceed forward. I decided against a foreword.)

⌘⌘⌘⌘⌘

HOW TO UNDERSTAND PSYCHOSIS-WE ALL CAN SPEAK SCHIZOPHRENAGEEZE

The prejudice against people with mental illness is most apparent towards people who have had psychotic symptoms. These are the people most referred to as "crazy." We might not be so prejudiced when we realize that almost all of us have had psychotic symptoms but don't label them as such. Psychosis is defined as being out of touch with reality. In our DSM terms we think of hallucinations and delusions as the hallmark of psychosis. These might be visual or auditory images that others don't experience or misinterpretations of signals leading to mild paranoia or more elaborate schemes that require extensive stretches of the imagination connecting far away dots of information. How many of us have had these experiences while asleep and woken up not sure if things that occurred in the dream actually happened? What about religious experiences many refer to as feeling the presence of God? What about the belief in an all knowing omnipresent being who may decide the fate of mankind? People have fought wars over beliefs that their invisible "Being" wanted others to die or convert to believing in their version of this invisible deity. How many have felt that their boss, parent or friends were out to get them when the support for this belief was thin? How can two individuals on opposite sides of the political spectrum have vastly divergent interpretations of the same facts presented to them? Depending on how strongly felt these beliefs are it might be difficult to find the border between strongly held beliefs or intuitions and psychotic delusions.

We experience the world through our five senses of sight, sound, smell, touch and taste. We have receptors to pick up these senses that send nerve impulses to the brain where they are interpreted. The body also has sensors in our internal organs that send signals of pain and discomfort which might alert the brain to address a concern about breathing, digestion or other physical issues. We, in addition, have thought processes which we engage in for interpretation of social interactions, dietary needs and future planning. Our brains must be able to sort out all of this data and determine its sources or origins. It must determine whether the signals are coming from one of the five external sensing organs or are images from a sleep state or an awake but contemplative state. We interpret these signals using knowledge obtained from past experiences or early learning. But what if we encounter new novel signals that we can't interpret having never experienced them before? Individuals who have certain types of seizures or migraines might experience auras during which sensations occur without an external stimulus. People who have lost limbs have phantom limb pain. After some surgeries or injuries where nerves have been damaged, this may lead to similar phantom sensations.

What would happen if the brain got flooded with too many inputs and could no longer determine if the data was coming from outside or inside the body? Those inputs might be from both external clues and thoughts or worries. We would lose touch with reality. We might misinterpret a thought as an external voice. Or we might over interpret an observation such that it coincided with a thought or fear that we had. If we were concerned that people didn't like us and thought about the many reasons for this, we could interpret a nose rub by a coworker as a signal that we must be putting off an offensive odor. If we thought that our job performance was subpar and we might hear a boss speaking loudly on the telephone we might think he is expressing discontent with your performance and discussing a plan to fire you.

Patients with psychosis usually report "racing thoughts." Many of us have had similar experiences of being overwhelmed with too many things to do or problems that need to be processed and decided upon. Racing thoughts in psychosis are often so fast that the patient can't keep up with them let alone articulate them verbally to someone. They may be going so fast that the individual may not even be able to talk coherently. If the thoughts are so rapid only bits and pieces of them might be articulated giving the appearance of a "flight of ideas" or jumping from one topic to another without apparent connection between them. Sometimes the thoughts are going so fast that the patient can't speak at all and may only gesticulate or freeze. This used to be called "thought blocking" where the individual might stop in mid sentence and jump to another topic. The freezing up in extreme form can result in catatonia where the individual becomes mute and immobile. It was recognized many years ago that patients with catatonia who seem shut down and non verbal are racing inside. They race so fast that they can't communicate with the outside. It would be like trying to enter a revolving door that was moving too fast for us to enter. Many creative individuals have flurries of ideas. Society values individuals who make new connections leading to discoveries or new insightful ways of thinking. Where is the border between extreme creativity and psychotic thought process? Kay Jamison, a noted psychologist with bipolar disorder, wrote about this in her book, Touched by fire. She documents many of our brilliant creative people having mania but they usually are only able to be productive during relatively well periods between episodes.

Individuals with psychosis are trying to make sense of their misperceptions. They are making hypotheses for the unusual stimuli and impart special meaning where one doesn't exist. This leads to extreme vulnerability which requires some form of self protection. If you feel vulnerable you might project this fear onto others. If unconsciously you know that your work performance has been deteriorating due to your difficulty thinking you might project this fear onto your boss or co-workers and think they are out to get you. If you hear voices, maybe god or the devil or dead relatives might be trying to communicate with you. As your function deteriorates from your inability to sort thoughts from outside conversation, it wouldn't be unreasonable to think that these outsiders are trying to control you. If your thoughts were so loud, you might think that others might be able to hear them. Schneider in 1959 wrote of schizophrenic first rank delusions of thought insertion, thought withdrawal, and belief that one's thoughts were being broadcast to the outside world. These symptoms, he wrote, were pathognomonic of schizophrenia, but it can be applied to almost any psychotic state.

When I was a resident on a research unit I had the rare opportunity to work with patients who came off all of their medications for up to several months while they participated in double blind placebo controlled studies. One of my patients was a middle aged woman whose depression was not being adequately treated as an outpatient. She was an executive secretary for a medium sized company. Over the course of several weeks she developed a Capgras syndrome. This is a rarely seen syndrome where the patient believes that individuals have been replaced by imposters. She thought that her bosses had set up the psychiatric unit to appear like a hospital but none of the people were really nurses, doctors or patients. I asked her what evidence she had for this. She noted that the nurses and doctors didn't wear uniforms and the patients didn't seem ill. She didn't see diplomas for the doctors either. I had her get up from her chair and look at my diplomas that were hanging on the wall behind her. She said, "Maybe you are a doctor, but no one else is." I tried to have her tell me why her employer would go through so much effort and spend so much money on setting this up. She didn't know why but believed she was such a poor worker over the past year that they must have been upset and wanted to humiliate her. I informed my attending of her emerging psychosis so that the study would be terminated and she could be put on appropriate antipsychotic medication. The delusions cleared fairly quickly and it was apparent that her prior medication, while not completely effective, had given her some relief.

The longer the psychosis is allowed to persist the more likely these delusional beliefs are to become fixed into one's memory. I had a woman who thought that she controlled a major company by her thoughts. This went on for many years and she never told anyone as she thought everyone already knew. When I gave her medications these telepathic communications stopped. Then I asked her why they had stopped she said, "The medications stopped the communications." But she quickly added, "You don't believe that I did that?" Just because the medications stopped the acute misinterpretation of sensations doesn't mean the past memory of these beliefs would be changed. After all they have become memories and to change these memories would have been a blow to her self esteem and required her to think of herself as "crazy" rather than superbly helpful. Unfortunately, many prescribers misinterpret the persistent memory of delusional ideas with continuing psychosis and try to increase antipsychotic medication to the detriment of the patient. The clinician must ask "do you think these phenomenon are still occurring?" and not ask "do you still think that these phenomenon occurred?"

    Over medicating a patient with psychosis can result in worsening cognition and other serious side effects. These side effects often lead to non compliance with taking the medications. The prescriber must realize that many of the delusions have become memories and are tied to the person's sense of self and self esteem. Asking the patient to deny these beliefs could result in lack of acceptance of illness or even worse, severe depression with suicidal ideation. Compassionate psychotherapy is needed to help the patient introduce doubt of their past beliefs or at least not to carry them forward and use these beliefs to misinterpret current events in such a way as to make poor decisions in the future. This is no easy task. I will tell family members that trying to convince someone that they were delusional would be like trying to convince the Catholic Pope that Jesus was not the son of God. You wouldn't even think of doing this. Many patients feel that their psychotic experiences brought them closer to god. Trying to do this is fraught with negative consequences.

    Most grandiose delusions on the one hand make the patient feel special but on the other it causes an extreme burden. I had a patient who came to the "New Haven" (Connecticut that is) because god told him to run for president of the United States. I pointed out that he was only 33 and the Constitution stated that one needed to be at least age 35. He told me that they would make an exception. No logic was able to convince him that this was a delusional idea for which he needed treatment. But then I thought about what it might feel like to be asked by god to travel down to DC and overcome extreme obstacles in order to run for president. "Wow," I told him, "that must put a tremendous burden on you." He began to cry after I said that. Here was a manic patient, who is grandiose and supposed to be in a state of euphoria, crying. The psychoanalysts viewed mania as a defense against underlying depression. But I think I did something else. It was the first time I spoke schizophrenageeze to a psychotic patient.

When speaking schizophrenageeze you respond to the emotion or feeling that you would anticipate having if you were experiencing the same delusion and thought of what consequences that would result if the delusional belief was true. For example, if the individual felt that the government had implanted electrodes in their brain and were listening to all their thoughts, I would want to also know if the government was also controlling him. This would lead to a discussion of how it felt to lose control of one's body and mind. You might feel angry and frightened. You want to know how to ignore what was happening to regain a sense of control. From there you find out if he was obligated to do something against his will and maybe encourage him to resist. Medications could be offered to help with the overwhelming anxiety associated with this loss of control. You could try to find out what things were going on in his life where he felt he was losing control. This might lead you to real things that were happening for which you could give appropriate advise.

A middle aged African American woman came to me upset because White men were following her everywhere. She didn't see them but they spoke to her. She couldn't take it and was refusing to take her medications and she saw the solution was to escape from these men. She decided to sell most of her possessions so she could buy a plane ticket to California to get as far away from them as possible. She returned several weeks later. She told me that the men had followed her to California and it took her several weeks to get enough money to pay for a bus ride back. I spoke to her about the fear she was experiencing and that medications could help her be less frightened. She agreed to take the medication. I never tried to convince her that the men in her head were not real as this would have ignored her reality. I used her logic that since the men would follow her wherever she went, it would be best to figure out how best to live with them. Medications would help her cope with this. Within a few weeks the "men" stopped talking to her but she had no explanation for this happening. I tried to reassure her that the medications would let her cope and may prevent their return. As she was improving she was able to articulate her fear of men in general and the fear she experienced when "white men" had taken her against her will to the hospital in the past.

There is usually a kernel of truth in every delusion. The individual has an exaggerated emotional response to this event which leads to an over interpretation of the event. As speculation occurs this leads to false beliefs in an attempt to explain the reason for the extreme emotional reaction. Anyone who has watched Fox News can see how they feed into people's fears and add to conspiracy theories. When four soldiers were killed in Benghazi Libya speculation flew as to inappropriate actions by the secretary of State, Hillary Clinton. Any tidbit of fact was twisted to fit into a conspiracy theory. Months of Congressional investigation found no conspiracy but by then Fox had made so many speculations and wove them into a seemingly coherent story that they had the force of delusions which became resistant to the facts. Many of their listeners became believers tainting her election.

It's fairly easy to see how a delusion can be formed by making distant connections based upon limited information in the context of highly charged emotions. Take someone's fear of harm, or unexplained depression or free floating anxiety and project the cause on outside forces. Introduce vaguely related details and connect dots that shouldn't be connected and you have the makings of a conspiracy. Have an individual whose thinking is impaired by overwhelming situational factors and the delusion becomes real. Think of all the parents afraid that their children may develop autism and introduce them to a discredited study linking autism to vaccines and you find delusions in individuals who do not have major psychotic disorder. You can't convince many of these parents that the study was flawed and retracted. Conspiracy theories prevented them from hearing the truth by introducing the notion that you can't trust the establishment including physicians, pharmaceutical companies and especially government. The only counter is to acknowledge the fears and provide support for how to cope with them. There have been outbreaks of preventable diseases now due to lack of vaccination and this fear is more real. The parents were presumably vaccinated and survived but they have since overestimated the risks of vaccination and underestimated the risks of not vaccinating. I have treated some of these individuals overwhelmed by one conspiracy theory or another and

I often have to resort to low dose antipsychotic medication. This usually reduces the intensity of the fear and slows their thinking enough to suggest they don't need to worry about the conspiracy. The medication won't eliminate or change their mind, just like a delusion, but they can move forward without adding new irrelevant data points to reinforce the belief. Also the medication may not be needed for more than several months similar to treatment of a brief reactive psychosis. I "sell" the medication as a way of reducing their anxiety and "not to treat psychosis." I point out that the dose prescribed is lower than that used to treat psychosis and that low dose antipsychotic medications have be helpful to treat depressions with severe anxiety. Remember that the patients didn't present to me because of their delusional beliefs but because they felt anxious, depressed and overwhelmed by their fears which they feel are justified by their beliefs. They didn't want me to argue against their beliefs and if I do, I may become part of the conspiracy to cover up "the truth" that they "know" is real.

      There needs to be a discussion of obsessions as distinct from delusions. Individuals suffering from obsessive compulsive disorder (OCD) don't speak schizophrenageeze. They are aware that their obsessions and compulsive rituals are irrational but feel too much anxiety to stop them. They haven't created elaborate conspiracy theories to justify their irrational behaviors and trying to give meaning to their actions only serves to give rationale to continue them. The person with OCD needs to just resist the compulsions and obsessions and learn to cope with the ensuing anxiety until it passes. The anxiety associated with delusions doesn't pass and logical reasoning often feeds in to paranoid ideation about the person trying to dissuade them. Telling the delusional person that their ideas are "crazy" only makes them distrust you because to them they are real. The feelings behind them are real and only compassionate acceptance of this fact will allow an outsider the ability to present more logical explanations to re-interpret the data upon which the delusions are built. The best that can be expected is to spread doubt on the delusional beliefs and encourage alternative interpretations of the facts. There are no logical explanations for OCD as the individual already is aware that they are irrational.

Contrary to psychosis, interpretation of the symptoms only reinforces OCD.

Thought processing for these two conditions is also different. In psychosis thoughts jump from one loosely connected thought to another like a discordant symphony. Obsessive thinking is more like a broken record skipping in the same groove unable to advance to the next track. The delusions flow too freely sweeping up ideas and events along the way like a funnel cloud only to pile the debris in a totally distant spot. The obsessive never leaves the spot where he started. Jane was a 40 year old married woman whose OCD got out of hand. She began checking the door locks 10 times but this didn't satisfy her needs. It spread to the garage doors, then the car doors, the stove, the faucets and furnace. The rituals ended up taking several hours per day such that she couldn't leave the house. If she had to leave, she instructed her husband to assist in her rituals to try to shorten the time but each instruction led to more time. She knew these were irrational and had no explanation for the need to do them except that it felt bad if she didn't do them. But it also it took more and more time to reach satisfaction. She was given medication to reduce her anxiety and instruction to limit each ritual. Her husband was discouraged from participating and to remind her that performing the rituals only led to worse anxiety. Eventually she reduced her time in ritual to under an hour and was able to participate in activities outside of the home again.

John worked for an IT company and was sent to do repair work on various computer equipment. He noted that some of the repair work was unnecessary and thought the customers were scheming to get new equipment. He began to get concerned that the customers were setting him up and he would be accused of defrauding the company. However, his bosses seemed content with his work and he was providing good customer service. His fears got so great that he began to suspect other coworkers of setting him up so they could take his job. He then wondered if this wasn't a money laundering operation for his company and he was being drawn into an elaborate illegal operation. He got depressed and panicked and came to see me. I began him on antipsychotic medication and his fear began to diminish. I was able to provide alternative interpretations for the events he observed. This included the notion that the company was willing to accept some losses to encourage good customer relations which might lead to more business. His delusions had only been present for a short while so they were not so impervious to re-interpretation. He was able to accept that he might have over interpreted the situation. But residual doubt persisted such that he chose to leave this company and take a different job. My work with him validated his feelings that things were not being managed the way he thought they should be but I was also able to provide reassurance that he would not get blamed for this. This allowed enough time for him to find a more suitable job that didn't compromise his integrity.

Some of my patients often ask me how they can deal with a psychotic family member. I tell them that first they can't argue with them over any delusional ideas. Then provide empathic support for any feelings that might be associated with the delusions. Try not to be sucked into the delusional net by doubting its reality but this doesn't mean you have to go along with it either. Remain neutral and provide sympathy for their plight. While medication may make the individual less prone to add to the delusion going forward they may not accept that they were wrong in the past. Medications may take weeks to months to soften delusions. Leave the past in the past and don't challenge what the patient felt happened. They have no way of knowing what really happened since their perceptions were distorted. You can only talk of the present and that the delusional ideas are not still happening. Have sympathy for the anxiety, fear and humiliation of not knowing what really happened in the psychotic state. Challenging the beliefs and actions may lead to defensive maneuvers and hostility. Provide support for having survived and moved forward despite overwhelming feelings. Remind them of the relief of agitation and anxiety provided by the medications. And that is how one speaks schizophrenageeze.

⌘⌘⌘⌘⌘

THE CLINICAL RELEVANCE OF DIFFERENTIATING OBSESSING AND DWELLING IN PATIENTS WITH ANXIETY AND DEPRESSION

The terms obsessing and dwelling (or ruminating) are often used interchangeably to describe types of worrying within the context of anxiety and depressive disorders. However, they are probably different constructs, which may involve two distinctly different brain neurotransmitter systems. It is plausible that nature teleologically designed two distinct reflective systems: one to process real events that have happened and another to predict future harmful events. Obsessing refers to worrying about things yet to happen or are only hypothetical and usually unlikely to happen. Dwelling or ruminating refers to worry or concern or preoccupation with things that have already happened or are realistic concerns. The importance of this distinction lies in its predictive value with respect to response to antidepressants with differing receptor specificity. I have observed that excessive obsessing is more responsive to serotonergic agents. Conversely dwelling / ruminating responds best to medications that have at least some noradrenergic effects. Patients suffering from both obsessing and ruminating may do better on a dual acting medication or combination of medications. The following brief case examples help to illustrate this.

Case report: BM was a 20 y/o male who had been treated successfully for classic and severe obsessive-compulsive disorder with fluoxetine 80mg (This theoretically provided mostly serotonergic effects but some noradrenergic effects due to the high dose). He was changed to escitalopram 40mg (presumably devoid of noradrenergic effects) because of side effects. He did well initially for a few months but he began to ruminate excessively about premature hair loss. This at first seemed like a return of his obsessing, but he indeed had significant male pattern balding over the prior few years. Since this was a realistic rumination about something that has happened, bupropion SR 150mg (a non-serotonergic, primarily noradrenergic medication) was added with a resultant robust reduction in this symptom.

Case report: JY was a 50 y/o woman who presented with depression, overeating, crying and emotional blunting. She had been on citalopram 20mg which "pooped-out" after several months. A change to escitalopram 10mg gave some improvement but her mood was still down. An initial elicitation of symptoms revealed emotional blunting, fatigue at the end of the day and well controlled anxiety. This symptom pattern would have led me to consider augmentation with a noradrenergic agent. However, more careful questioning noted that her depression was focused on her worrying about her future in view of her unhappy marriage and her self-described irrational thoughts of divorcing her husband. Rather than augmenting the escitalopram, I increased it to 20mg with dramatic improvement in mood and fatigue. The marital situation was unchanged but she was not worrying as much about her future. Instead she was agreeing to begin psychotherapy to work on realistic future goals and her unrealistically negative view of her husband.

Case report: GO was a 55 y/o woman presenting with panic and depression as well as arthritis and heart disease. Prior trials of paroxetine and escitalopram produced fatigue and worsening of depression. A trial of bupropion XL gave dramatic improvement in mood and anxiety. More careful questioning of her panic revealed that she did not have classic fear of dying or loss of control, but was dwelling on the realistic loss of function due to her medical problems. These "panic" attacks had a more gradual onset and lasted up to two hours.

Stahl proposed that serotonin might mediate symptoms of anxiety and obsessing, while norepinephrine (NE) might mediate energy, concentration and drive. However, anxiety has been successfully treated in some patients by SSRI's, SNRI's and in some cases just noradrenergic agents. I am proposing subdividing the worrying component of anxiety symptoms into two types that have predictive value in medication choice. This hypothesis would predict that patients who ruminate about real, past traumas or losses would respond preferentially to a medication that has some significant noradrenergic effect. On the other hand, patients who are fearful about imagined or hypothetical things that may happen to them or obsess unrealistically about their futures will need a serotonergic agent. Patients with OCD and panic obsess about calamities that will befall them if they don't take some irrational or excessive precaution. These patients respond well to SSRI's. Bupropion, a noradrenergic medication, has been effective in treating excessive grief associated with a real loss. Clearly there are patients who have both symptoms and they will need dual acting medications.

Patients with ruminations share some features with patients with ADHD in their difficulty concentrating enough to solve a real problem. The ruminative patient can't seem to organize their thinking and work out a logical solution. ADHD has been traditionally treated with NE medications such as stimulants, desipramine or atomoxetine. In obsessing there is a hyper focusing, albeit on irrelevant or irrational items. The obsessive patient is hyper organized to the extent of fantasizing too many scenarios that are illogical. Obsessive compulsive disorder usually calls for treatment with a serotonergic agent. It is interesting that the original Hamilton Depression Rating Scale had two separate items: one for rumination and guilt and another for obsessive anxiety. Newer versions of this scale may have removed this distinction.

(Note that the above essay was published in Psychiatry Online in 2005. I originally thought that this predictive hypothesis may not hold for patients who have bipolar disorder or psychosis. In fact when it doesn't seem to apply, I looked more carefully for a bipolar spectrum disorder. I have since come to realize this was partially due to the difference in duration of action of antidepressants. Since many patients with bipolar disorder respond rapidly to antidepressants and then lose that benefit, I thought of using shorter acting antidepressants. I wrote a letter to the editor that was published in JAMA Psychiatry July 2009 that elucidated my theory. Below is the content of my letter.)

TO THE EDITOR: In the February 2009 issue of the *Journal*, Mark A. Frye, M.D., et al. (1), and Joseph F. Goldberg, M.D., et al. (2) examined the predictors of treatment-emergent mania and mixed states in depressed bipolar patients. I would encourage both groups of investigators to review their data to examine two variables that have not been reported. The first is the diurnal variation of mood, which I find to be more extreme in patients who have bipolar depression and may be a predictor of a response to a mood stabilizer in unipolar patients. The second variable is the form of antidepressant given to patients. A convention in publishing is to use the generic names of medications, but this does not distinguish among the three preparations of bupropion (immediate release, 12-hour release, and 24-hour release) and two forms of venlafaxine (immediate- and time-release). Although time-release preparations technically have the same half-life of the underlying compound, their sustained presence keeps blood and brain levels more constant, resulting in differing side effects and efficacy profiles.

I have found that in bipolar patients with extreme diurnal variation of mood (characterized by severe a.m.-hour depression followed by significant brightening in the evening), the non-time-release preparations of medications, such as bupropion and venlafaxine, given in low doses in the a.m. hours only can be very helpful and less likely to cause manic switching. Conversely, the long acting preparations of the same medications tend to cause a reversal of diurnal variation, with improvement in the a.m. hours and agitation in the p.m. hours. It might turn out that short half-life reuptake inhibitors have a place in treating bipolar depression. Other relatively short-acting agents, such as atomoxetine, may also fall into this category.

With the above notions in mind, I have been able to use the shorter half-life antidepressants in some patients with bipolar depression using the same paradigm for medication selection on receptor binding. Bupropion in its original short duration form can be used for depressive symptoms that involve NE, such as low energy, fatigue and dwelling. Venlafaxine in its original tablet form can be used for bipolar depressions which have a serotonin associated symptom pattern such as obsessions. When used, I give the antidepressants only once per day in the am so as not to over activate and cause sleep disturbance. They might also be used on as needed basis for seasonal symptoms since patient with bipolar disorder cycle in ther symptoms and should be on concomitant mood stabilizers.

Baldwin et.al, proposed that anxiety and depression may exist on a continuum with disturbances in serotonin and norepinephrine. It is conceivable that some of the debate over the superiority of dual acting (SNRIs) versus single acting (SSRIs, NRI) may be confounded by the failure to separate these two types of worry when rating patients symptoms of anxiety and depression. Patients with only obsessive worry may find a medication with some NE effect less calming than a pure SSRI, whereas patients with some dwelling anxiety may need an SNRI for more complete remission of symptoms. The fact that some SSRI's may be less selective than others may also have obscured this distinction.

⌘⌘⌘⌘⌘

DYING IN BALANCE AND MY ORGAN IS MORE IMPORTANT THAN YOURS-MANAGING TREATMENTS FROM DIFFERENT SPECIALTIES

When I was an intern in Internal Medicine, my training director was highly influenced by *House of God* by Samuel Shem. His sense of humor was often not appropriate for patient consumption. He claimed that all patient problems could be summed up in two general categories, WTD1 and WTD2. WTD1 was short for "weak, tired and dizzy" while WTD2 was "waiting to die." The internist was successful when the patients' symptoms resolved or they "died in balance." The latter referred to all their lab values and numbers looking good just prior to the time of death. Samuel Shem became a psychiatrist and I believe he would agree with my goal, normalizing lab values is less important than the patient feeling better and if they happen to die, it is with a smile on their face for a life worth living.

I note the above because many efforts in modern medicine seem focused on "normalizing" numbers rather than treating the patient. Whenever a patient asks me the result of their lab tests, especially for medication blood levels, I always ask them "how are you doing?" The lab result is less important than the results of the treatment. Labs are for guidance. If the blood level of a medication is too high I might want to reduce the dose to prevent side effects. If the levels are too low and they are doing well, I don't care. I might ask if they are really taking the medication and if not, tell them that that's OK if you are doing well. I don't treat lab values, I treat patients. I don't get any satisfaction from patients being compliant with medications that are not helping them or are causing untoward effects.

Physicians have embraced using evidence-based treatments which on the surface is a noble aim. This means that physicians should prescribe the best treatments for each condition based upon the best scientific evidence. The best evidence is from large double blind studies in which active treatments are compared to each other and placebos. Unfortunately, these are very expensive studies to do, so most are funded by pharmaceutical companies who are able to design studies which can favor their medication by under or overdosing comparator medications or not enrolling enough patients to receive alternative medications so that true differences can't be proven. Additionally, it is difficult, if not impossible, to do statistical analyses of multiple variables in sub-populations of patients. For example, in studying a medication for high blood pressure they haven't differentiated patients with other conditions like depression or anxiety since the focus is on disease states associated with high blood pressure such as heart attack and stroke. Only recently was it demonstrated that depression was one of the greatest risk factors for heart attacks. This would suggest that additional studies should be done to look for the best anti-hypertension medications for the subpopulation of patients with depression and anxiety. Instead some of the most commonly used medications indicated by evidence based medicine to prevent heart attacks can worsen depression and interfere with antidepressants.

    Jill was a 45 year old married woman with a long history of anxiety and depression. She was treated by her primary care doctor with Cymbalta (duloxetine) for her depression and pain from arthritis. She was doing well for several years but had a panic attack when her teenage son got into a car accident while texting his new girlfriend. No one was hurt but she thought she was having a heart attack and went to the hospital emergency room. She was given an extensive work up including EKG, blood work and was referred to a cardiologist. He ordered an echocardiogram and stress tests which were all normal. Her blood pressure and pulse were high so the ER physicians began her on metoprolol and the cardiologist raised the dose. She continued to feel ill and in fact was feeling worse with fatigue and loss of drive. She couldn't concentrate. Now worrying that doctors had missed some serious problem she complained to her primary care doctor who told her that everything was normal and that the only thing he could suggest to her was to see a psychiatrist.

Reluctantly, after several weeks of resistance, she made her appointment to see me. I reviewed all of her symptoms and history. She was not the best student in school but managed to get by because most subjects seemed easy for her. Her son was similar and was recently diagnosed with attention deficit disorder but was refusing to take medications. She saw some of the same obstinacy in herself agreeing to the Cymbalta only because she didn't want to get addicted to pain medications for her arthritis. The improvement in her mood was an added bonus which she appreciated. Careful questioning revealed that the worsening of her fatigue began after going to the emergency room and worsened more after seeing the cardiologist. This correlated with her beginning the metoprolol and the subsequent dosage increase. I suggested that this medication should be changed but she didn't want to call her doctors about this. Knowing that her cardiac work-up was negative I told her that I could give her an alternate medication that was similar to the metoprolol but would not get into the brain as easily. I prescribed atenolol as a substitute. She called me a week later telling me she was back to her old self.

Metoprolol and atenolol are both medications of the class of beta blockers that are selective to the heart (Beta 1 selective). Metoprolol was approved more recently and the manufacturer did more studies to prove its superiority for certain heart conditions. My impression of some of the studies and experience switching people between these medications is that the dosage equivalencies used were not accurate. Most reports suggest that atenolol should be dosed about half as much as the equivalent dose of metoprolol. In my experience patients needed the same dosage of each medication to get an equivalent effect on blood pressure and heart rate. More importantly, metoprolol is lipophilic, which means it dissolves in fats and thereby may enter the brain more easily than atenolol. Beta blockers block the effects of adrenaline which is a hormone that in the body raises heart rate and blood pressure. In the brain this neurohormone helps concentration, drive and mood. Metoprolol blocks some of the effects of Cymbalta which raises adrenaline in the brain. We give medications that enhance adrenaline to patients with depression and attention deficit disorder so a beta blocker in the brain can reverse these benefits.

     Is metoprolol a more effective beta blocker than atenolol for preventing heart disease? Or would the depression worsening side effect of metoprolol make it less effective in patients with depression or for patients on antidepressants. As far as I know, no one has studied this. This leads me back to my internship. Do I follow evidence-based studies that call for metoprolol and have my patient "die in balance" having done everything by the book, or do I risk following a patient-centered approach that may cause my patient to die with a smile on her face? Having changed Jill's medication, she now can make a choice with personal evidence of her own trial comparing the effects and side effects of both medications. She can, with this firsthand knowledge, make a more informed decision about her own treatment.

     Feeling better, Jill decided to have her primary care physician continue to prescribe all of her medications including the new medication I started her on. Five years later she returned for another evaluation. She has gone through menopause and now has a number of new problems. She has to urinate frequently and often can't make it to the bathroom in time. She was referred to an urologist who diagnosed her with over active bladder and prescribed oxybutynin for her. The urinary urgency is better but she has gotten more forgetful and more tired again. She associates her memory problems with menopause. Sleep has been poor due to night sweats and hot flashes. All of this is making her more depressed and she is anxious that she might lose her job due to poor performance. She needs this job as her husband's business has not been well lately. She went to her gynecologist who advised against hormone replacement therapy due to a family history of breast cancer.

     Jill is typical in many ways and is a setup for bad pharmacology based upon evidence-based medicine. Oxybutynin is a standard medication for over active bladder that works as an anticholinergic medication. Many of our old antidepressant medications had anticholinergic side effects which included difficulty urinating, dry mouth, blurred vision, constipation and rapid heart rate. In the brain, anticholinergic medications cause memory loss and confusion. In Alzheimer's dementia the cholinergic system deteriorates. Several medications approved for Alzheimer's, such as Aricept work the opposite of Oxybutynin. Oxybutynin is another lipophilic medication that gets into the brain easily, worsening memory. I switched Jill's oxybutynin to trospium (Sanctura), which is also anticholinergic but is not lipophilic and can effectively treat overactive bladder without the cognitive side effects, but is not widely marketed. Some medications seemed to have flopped due to bad timing in their release when cheaper equally effective medications were available. Only later, after a medication has gone generic, did we appreciate certain differences that gave some medications an advantage. When a medication has gone generic there is no drug company who will want to spend the money to market it to prescribers. This knowledge has to be spread by word of mouth or through small case reports.

  Jill was happy with the change in medication. Her bladder symptoms were as well controlled on the trospium but she was still disturbed by her hot flashes and poor sleep. Sweating is another adrenaline symptom that can be helped by medications that block this hormone's action on the alpha receptor. Above we noted she was using a beta 1 adrenaline receptor blocker, atenolol, which controlled her rapid heart rate. There are several alpha blockers available and some psychiatric medications have this as a side effect. This mechanism was responsible for lowering patients' blood pressure causing dizziness. This may not be a problem if the dosage of the alpha blocker is low but might be a problem when combined with another blood pressure lowering medication like atenolol. There is a blood pressure medication, carvedilol, which has both alpha and beta adrenaline blocking activity so could help both sweating and rapid heart rate, but it gets into the brain more easily than atenolol. Terazocin (Hytrin) is an alpha blocker that is approved for both blood pressure and male urinary symptoms due to benign prostatic hypertrophy. At low doses it helps reduce sweating from multiple causes without lowering blood pressure significantly.

Blocking the alpha receptor in the brain doesn't seem to cause the same psychiatric problems as the beta receptor.

I didn't go over all of the possible treatments with Jill, but she might have noticed the smoke coming from my ears as I ran through the multitude of possibilities and drug interactions affecting multiple bodily systems. I settled on a simple one, trazodone. This is a medication that came out before Prozac (BP) which never hit it off as an antidepressant. Its sedating side effect was so strong that few patients were able to tolerate enough to get an antidepressant effect. I was working at a Veterans hospital when I began using it for depressed veterans with post traumatic stress disorder and substance abuse. The sedation allowed me to taper patients off their sedating addicting medications and I published an article on this. What I didn't realize at the time was that trazodone's alpha blockade effect might also help sleep, nightmares and night sweats as much as the sedation in these patients. So I decided on low dose trazodone for Jill as it could help both her night sweats and sleep. This improved her sleep but she still complained of night sweats and hot flashes. Adding one milligram of terazocin twice a day resolved them. She was so pleased with the results that she referred her husband, George, to me as he was sleeping poorly and disturbing her now.

George was 55 years old and has always been a hyperactive independent guy. He ran his own business which had its ups and downs until he hired Jill to do his bookkeeping. When she was not doing as well he became more aware of his short comings. This caused him to become increasingly anxious which led to troublesome urinary frequency. He drank a lot of coffee to keep up with his workload but felt his need to leave meetings with clients to urinate was unprofessional. His primary care doctor told him that his prostate was not enlarged so diagnosed him also with overactive bladder. He gave him some Myrbetriq to try since he had samples in his closet. George felt that this didn't work and maybe made him worse. He was hoping that I could help him as I had his wife.

I have sympathy for primary care physicians. They have so many disease states to learn about and treat. They get bombarded with drug reps peddling the latest, greatest medications for existing and sometime new seemingly made up conditions. It is impossible to keep up let alone learn the differences between treatments based upon mechanisms of action. The FDA approves medications for specific conditions defined by a set of symptoms and the medications clearly help these conditions. This is the definition of evidenced-based medicine. Several years ago with the new healthcare program, ACA, I was incentivized to start prescribing electronically instead of by paper prescription. This had two effects besides making my prescriptions more legible. I needed to get internet access for my prescribing and I was able to see what other physicians had ordered for my patients. Once I had the internet, the power of Google allowed me to look up details about all the medications I was prescribing as well as what other doctors had given my patients.

I looked up Myrbetriq. It is an interesting medication as it is not anticholinergic like most of the medications for over active bladder. It works on adrenaline, cool. I know adrenaline and its effects. It happens to target a different adrenaline receptor the beta-3 receptor which is focused in the bladder but instead of blocking it like the medications noted above, it stimulates them. Looking at the side effect profile in the package insert, it might not be as specific as it professes since it may raise blood pressure as you would expect for a drug that stimulates adrenaline. I learned from a drug rep (see chapter Marketing of a slightly better medication) that medications that stimulate adrenaline produce a "pseudo anticholinergic" effect. In other words like the anticholinergic medications they slow urination and cause dry mouth. But they do not cause the memory problems associated with true anticholinergic medications.

Obtaining more history from George suggested that like his son, he probably also suffered from attention deficit disorder since childhood. He compensated for this by drinking a lot of coffee and when he was younger he was very active in sports. He would always do things at the last minute and thrived on the anxiety that it produced. All of these things raise adrenaline. His urinary problem was not caused by too little adrenaline, but by too much causing a pseudo anticholinergic side effect such that he never fully emptied his bladder. He needed a medication that blocked his adrenaline in his bladder but not his head. Tamsulosin is such a medication. Also the excessive amounts of caffeine were irritating his bladder and causing sleep difficulty. I gave him atomoxetine (Strattera) a medication that stimulates adrenaline, for his ADHD symptoms so he could reduce his caffeine intake and be less anxious. Without the tamsulosin, the atomoxetine would have worsened his bladder problem. I was able to give him the adrenaline he needed in his brain for concentration with atomoxetine, while blocking its effect in his bladder with tamsulosin. If his blood pressure went up or he developed sweating from the excess adrenaline, I could switch his tamsulosin to terazocin which would block the adrenaline effect in the bladder, blood vessels, and sweat glands without impacting the brain. If instead he had tremors and increased heart rate, I could give nadolol which is a beta adrenergic blocker that doesn't get into the brain easily. Isn't pharmacology fun?

     In summary, I want to impress upon prescribers and patients that mechanism of actions as well as evidence-based studies comprise a starting point of medications that might be used to treat a specific problem. In order to find the best medications to treat individual patients we need to understand the pharmacology of each medication and how it might impact any concomitant medical or psychiatric conditions. Everyone is complicated by the fact that they have multiple conditions and different metabolisms which warrant individualized treatments. Medications have more than one action which can result in side effects, but sometimes these side effects can be used to benefit co-occurring problems. Alternatively, specific side effects might be ameliorated by other medications creating a cocktail of sorts. Specialists would be wise to consider co-occurring conditions when choosing medications rather than reflexively selecting the "best" "evidence-based" medication for the condition that they are called upon to fix or giving samples of the latest medication left by a pharmaceutical representative. When in doubt, Google is your friend that can help you rapidly find out all sorts of interesting facts not only about mechanism of action but also drug interactions, side effects, and duration of action which makes everyone a more informed prescriber.

And by the way, the brain is the most important organ!

Reference note:

(As a psychiatrist I must note that the worst beta blocker for patients with psychiatric conditions is metoprolol. It penetrates the brain easily (highly lipophilic) causing fatigue and reverses the norepinephrine benefits of many antidepressants and stimulants (i.e. causing depression and cognitive impairment). Two good alternatives are atenolol for beta 1 selectivity and nadolol for non selective use (e.g. tremors). These beta blockers are hydrophilic and don't cross bbb as easily). The original studies comparing atenolol with metoprolol were flawed in that they under dosed atenolol. The potency should be 1:1 published in 2012https://www.ncbi.nlm.nih.gov/pubmed/2891183 vs. earlier studies presumably paid for by manufacturer of Toprol in 1981 https://www.ncbi.nlm.nih.gov/pubmed/7308277 which dosed 2:1 metoprolol to atenolol.)

⌘⌘⌘⌘⌘

COMPLEX OR DIFFICULT CASES: ASSESSMENT STRATEGY

What is a difficult case? Any case where the patient doesn't respond favorably to multiple treatment trials might be considered a challenge for the clinician. This challenge is best met by reassessing both the diagnosis and the treatment process. The label "difficult" can have a negative connotation indicative of negative counter transference placing blame on the patient. It can also be associated with negative transference resulting in distrust on the part of the patient leading to withholding of information or noncompliance with treatment recommendations. In order to be non judgmental in our labeling, I propose to call them "complex" cases and would subdivide them into five main categories:

1. Psychiatric misdiagnosis

2. Medical misdiagnosis masquerading as psychiatric illness or affecting recovery

3. Psychosocial problems or conflicts not remedied by medication

4. Psychological resistance to treatment.

5. True refractory illness.

1. **Psychiatric misdiagnosis** is probably the most common cause of lack of response to treatment. The criteria of DSM don't take into account course of illness, stage of illness, family history or prior treatment response. Many patients who have been diagnosed with unipolar depression turn out to have bipolar disorder. Patients are unreliable in reporting past manic or hypo manic symptoms. Patients often receive multiple antidepressant trials unsuccessfully but are not tried on mood stabilizers. The advent of atypical antipsychotic augmentation may be capturing some of these misdiagnosed individuals. Look for bipolar "soft signs" such as: severe depression prior

to age 30, psychotic and/or agitation features, post partum depression, family history of bipolar or schizophrenia, migraines, and cycling of illness. One common element of cycling is late "poop-out" of medication. (See Multi modal assessment strategy for an alternative diagnostic strategy)

Poop-out of antidepressants is often talked about. I think that this is a misnomer as it reflects misdiagnosis. There are two types of medication loss of efficacy. The first is when an anxious depressed patient acknowledges a good response to an SSRI after one month. In the subsequent months they report a return of depression. Careful questioning will reveal that the anxiety symptoms are still controlled but the depression is now prominent with lack of drive and motivation reflecting an imbalance between the norepinephrine and serotonin systems. It is likely that some of these patients could have been identified earlier if they were questioned more for residual symptoms. These patients respond to addition of bupropion or atomoxetine or change to a SNRI.

The second scenario of medication "poop-out" occurs months to years after a good response and has features of agitation replacing the original anxiety. There may be reversal of diurnal variation of mood (i.e. originally mood was worse in am but now with antidepressant on board mood is worse in pm with agitation and poor sleep.) These patients are likely to have bipolar spectrum disorder and would benefit from a mood stabilizer with or without the antidepressant. If the mood stabilizer helps then a trial off the antidepressant should be considered.

The other most often missed diagnosis is co-morbid substance abuse particularly alcohol. Drinking more than 2 standard drinks for a woman or 4 for a man can inactivate the benefits of most antidepressants, in particular ones that work on serotonin. One effect of alcohol is to cause release of serotonin from the presynaptic granules giving a good feeling. This depletes serotonin availability for future use until it can be re-synthesized. SSRI medications work to enhance serotonin effects by receptor down regulation which reduces the number of receptors but enhances the sensitivity of remaining receptors. This effect is negated if serotonin has been depleted by alcohol. Encourage one month abstinence (my Pepsi challenge) with any medication trial combined with education about measures of standard drink size (e.g. 4-5 oz wine, 12 oz beer, 1 oz hard alcohol). Individuals notoriously under estimate the quantity of liquid in their glasses.

2. **Medical diagnosis affecting or mimicking psychiatric symptoms**. There are too many to report but here is a list of the most common ones that I have seen:

1. *Sleep apnea or other sleep disorders.* This causes fatigue, cognitive/memory problems, lack of motivation, and morning headaches. This can look like ADHD or depression. In addition, some patients wake up in a panic reflecting hypoxia. Waking up with panic is not that common except in some patients with PTSD. Screen patients claiming adult onset ADHD symptoms for am headaches and excessive daytime sleepiness. True ADHD has its onset in childhood even if it wasn't diagnosed at that age. Late onset of attention problems is reflective of another diathesis.

2. *Lyme disease.* This causes fatigue in afternoon, multiple joint aches; ask for history of tick exposure and inadequate antibiotic treatment.

3. *Medication side effect.* Metoprolol is a commonly prescribed beta blocker that is very lipophilic and counters norepinephrine medications and stimulants causing fatigue, depression and poor attention. Atenolol (beta 1 selective) and nadolol (non specific beta blocker) are alternative non lipophilic beta blocker medications. Lipophilic medications more easily pass the blood brain barrier, while hydrophilic ones do not. Tamoxifen and other chemotherapy medications cause fatigue/ depression. Oxybutynin for overactive bladder is highly lipophilic causing confusion and memory problems. Trospium is better hydrophilic alternative.

4. *Autoimmune diseases*. These cause all sorts of vague symptoms but usually have joint aches and fatigue. A simple screen with ESR and ANA can this rule out. Patients with a psychiatric history are often under assessed by primary care providers but a positive ANA awakens their curiosity to perform more diagnostic tests on your patient.

5. *Cardiovascular disease*, especially CVA, can produce both depressive and manic symptoms. Check for neurologic soft signs e.g. babinski, Hoffman's sign and palmomental reflexes.

6. *Diabetes* can cause a variety of symptoms particularly when blood sugars fall rapidly. Adrenaline release occurs as blood sugars fall producing anxiety, tremors and nightmares. Thyroid disorders can also present with psychiatric symptoms.

3. **Psychological problems that are not responsive to medications** are common. There are several classic scenarios that I have seen. These patients can seem very depressed and often have a brief benefit from medications but quickly relapse when they try to confront their issues. Here are three classic conflict situations that can cause refractoriness to medications.

1. *Unsolvable conflicts*: Here the patient has to make one of two bad choices and getting ill prevents them from having to make any choice. One example is the woman in a bad marriage who doesn't feel she can survive on their own and develops panic attacks and agoraphobia such that they remain frozen in the situation. Another is an individual with a high paying job that they hate or feel compromises their moral integrity. Getting severely depressed gets them on disability without the need to quit the job. Therapy can help reduce "either or thinking" and hopefully find a third path.

2. *Ego ideal depressions*. This is common at various life transition phases. The individual had a fantasy or expectation of goals that they would achieve by a certain age. When they reach that age they feel like a failure even if they came close. An example is the

premedical student who doesn't get into medical school or the school of their choice, or the upper management executive who didn't get their last promotion.

3. *Unrealistic work or home expectations.* This may be a reflection of what was called the "Peter principle" where individuals get promoted to their level of incompetence. A highly motivated person might be seen as more competent than they really are and start to get overwhelmed in the new task. Some limitations might be accounted for by undiagnosed ADHD but more than likely they had taken on more than they can do and need to figure out their capabilities and how to set limits with others.

For all of these scenarios medications are likely to have limited benefit. Medication might help some of the neuro-vegetative and cognitive symptoms but psychotherapy is essential to deal the conflicts and help with problem solving.

4. **Psychological resistance to treatment.** Psychiatric illness is the only illness where resistance to treatment is a symptom of the illness whether due to denial of illness, depressive nihilism, or paranoia. This can present in many ways in addition to overt paranoia or denial that can be missed if not looked for. Fear of side effects can lead to medication non compliance and somatic complaints including intolerable diarrhea, constipation, sedation, tremors, insomnia to name a few. I had a patient in an anxiety study where the first week was a single blind placebo trial. She called daily due to intolerable side effects accusing me of poisoning her until I had to admit that she was on a placebo and would have to drop out of the study. Some patients have clear secondary gain from their symptoms such as getting attention from family or providers or avoidance of work or other commitments. Secondary gain might include not having to make a decision as noted above (3.1). (See section on Treatment Non-compliance)

The psychodynamic concept of transference helps to explain some of the difficulty encountered in trying to accurately evaluate and treat patients. The patient brings with them a host of prior experiences, positive and negative, that occurred with them with other authority figures. This might have been controlling parents or physicians that were deceitful to them (e.g. "this is not going to hurt you.") Or sometimes the opposite occurs when the patient might be overly respectful of the doctor and not want to reveal embarrassing details about symptoms or side effects that might imply that the treatment decision was not well advised. I've had several patients keep regular appointments and continue to take my prescriptions for over a year before they informed me that they have not taken them due to side effects or lack of efficacy. Some even filled the prescriptions and stock piled the medication. I always ask each patient, in a very non judgmental way, "What are the medications they are taking now and on what schedule" even though I know what I have prescribed. I don't accept the line, "well doc you have it written down." If they simply can't remember, I ask them to bring in a significant other with all of their medications and make a list for them. I warn them, if they had an accident and went to the ER they should have a list of all their medications.

I would guess that 20% of the time the patient has changed what I recommended, often to their benefit. I always assume non compliance with complex medication regimens and give praise for strategies that patients take to remember them. I will ask, "how many pills do you think you miss in a week?" rather than "are you taking all of your medications?" Honesty and trust in the doctor patient relationship is essential for gathering accurate symptom information and determining the efficacy of an intervention. Psychological resistance can occur in many forms and intensities.

My approach is to address the resistance as you would in any psychodynamic therapy and encourage more regular therapy to identify the fears and consequences of getting well. I might predict that the patient is likely to have severe side effects before they might see improvement. In patients who clearly have borderline personality disorder, who seem bent on proving me to be as ineffective as all previous prescribers, I might detail several treatment options while refusing to initiate any medication until I feel they are ready to accept the consequences of side effects. This usually results in the patient demanding that I give them something. (Although this seems a paradoxical intervention, it is one that puts the patient in charge of making the decision.) I generally don't schedule visits too frequently so as to not create unrealistic expectations from a medication trial. I educate the patient that their next appointment is scheduled when I think a medication adjustment might be appropriate. But I strongly suggest that the patient see a therapist in between visits to help them work on coping strategies while waiting for a medication effect. Also avoid medication adjustments over the phone as these are likely to be done with limited data and create a false impression that side effects, need to be eliminated by medication changes even though they might clear with time. Making a special brief earlier appointment is preferable to a phone intervention as it can provide supportive psychotherapy for coping with side effects which foreshadow response. You can also reiterate the need for psychotherapy and identify therapy goals.

5. **True refractory illness**. This is fairly uncommon but does occur. The prescriber should rule out all of the above noted reasons before declaring severe refractory illness. ECT should be high on the list of treatment options for severe symptoms known to respond to ECT. Rational polypharmacy is indicated where care is given to medications that have different complementary mechanisms of actions and don't cause dangerous drug interactions. New interventions like TMS (transcranial magnetic stimulation) and ketamine are available for select patients.

The MTHFR (methyline tetrahydrofolate reductase) mutation is one cause of frequent relapse but not true refractoriness. I have tested individuals who seem to have frequent depressions lasting several days, often after periods of stress. They also have more complaints of memory problems. I have now tested over 130 of these patients and found 70% to have a single mutation and 20% have a double mutation with the C677t allele. Treatment with L methyl folate has been beneficial to most of the double mutation and many of the single mutation patients regardless of polarity. Folic acid is necessary to synthesize neurotransmitters which may be depleted under stress (similar to the alcohol effect). Individuals with the MTHFR mutations can't convert folic acid (which can't pass the blood brain barrier) to L methyl folate which does pass. As a water soluble vitamin, l methyl folate is not stored and depressed patients diets might be erratic. Unfortunately insurance has generally not covered the testing or the supplement.

    I am hopeful that in the future more pathways responsible for non responsiveness will be identified. I highly doubt that a more effective treatment will be discovered for treatment of all types of depression and anxiety disorders. It is more likely that treatments will be more specific and guided by newly identified abnormalities. Until then careful attention to individual patient details combined with thoughtful clinical trials and psychotherapeutic interventions can result in very successful outcomes for the vast majority of patients. I have proposed a strategy of assessing and treating patients with anxiety and depression discussed in another section

⌘⌘⌘⌘⌘

TREATMENT NON-COMPLIANCE OR FAILURE TO GAIN ACCEPTANCE OF ILLNESS?

Providers have a tendency to complain about their patients being non-compliant with treatment. This can be manifest in many ways. I have had patients take my prescriptions after each visit but never fill them. Some fill them but stockpile them in a draw. Some admit to me a year later that they never took the medication. Patients have missed appointments rather than confess that they didn't follow my treatment advice. The main circumstance when I find out about non-compliance is when they take more than is prescribed since I get a call requesting early refills. Some claim to have the pills spill in the sink, on the dirty floor and have the dog eat the pills. I have developed a different way of looking at non-compliance now. Patients don't follow through with requests for lab tests, psychotherapy recommendations, quitting smoking, drinking and drug use, or exercise. I don't place blame for this non-compliance on the patient and provide sympathy for the patient who has to struggle with my treatment plans. I assume the position that they will not follow through on most of my advice and congratulate the patient for anything that they did in the right direction. Anything that was done that was not according to my plan I ask why they did it and how it went. Often the patient had a better strategy even if it wasn't planned.

I once led an education class for family members of individuals who suffered from serious mental illness such as schizophrenia and bipolar disorder. I spent almost a half hour reviewing a long list of serious side effects from the commonly prescribed medications. At the end of my presentation several parents asked why their child would not take their medications as prescribed. I had to point to the blackboard with all the side effects and said "look at these side effects; you have to be crazy to take them." I thought I got their attention with this blunt and not appropriate remark, but instead they repeated the question ignoring my insensitive remark. I realized that the problem was that we all failed to convince the patient that one, they had a problem and two, that the treatment would help that problem. It was our failure, not that of the patient.

I referred to this as patient acceptance. Compliance comes when the patient accepts their illness and a treatment necessary to reduce symptoms or relapse. This is a very complex issue that has many facets. It is more complicated with mental illness because two of the main symptoms of mental illnesses are to be either in denial of the illness or feel hopeless about ever getting better. No other physical illness has this symptom as part of the illness. For some people a symptom is to not want to get better, but to die. Treatment in this case only would prolong their suffering. So it is imperative for the clinician to not only comes up with a treatment plan, but to provide an explanation for the symptoms which do not blame the individual. This explanation should lead to logical course of treatment which might take weeks or months to work. The provider must not only exude hope for recovery but be realistic about potential side effects. If an unrealistically rosy prediction of treatment course is described and even a relatively minor side effect emerges, trust in the prescriber may be lost and the treatment trial jeopardized. If the prescriber tells the patient, "no one usually has a side effect from this medication," and they have one, the patient will wrongly assume that this medication is not for them. On the other hand, if they are told that some people have a hard time starting on the medication but the side effects are likely to improve over time, many patients will put up with fairly severe side effects. Tolerating the side effects is nothing compared to the suffering from the underlying illness being treated, but uncertainty can be very disturbing. Some patients say that they already feel so bad that they couldn't tolerate feeling worse. Reassurance that things can be done to ameliorate the side effects and that they can be interpreted as the medication working not failing. It is the clinician's responsibility to be accurate in the prediction of possible outcomes so the patient has confidence that the trial is appropriate. This is a monumental task which puts the clinician in the role of educator, physician and minister.

Often, the family must be brought in so as to not only provide support for the patient but not sabotage the plan. I have had patients whose spouses or significant others discard the patients pills before they had a chance to work citing fear of addiction or adverse reactions attributed to the medication. Many patients experience the stigma of going for mental health treatment while suffering from criticism for their underperforming at work, home and socially. Medications alone will not solve all of these problems. As symptoms improve, concomitant psychotherapy can help the individual find solutions to problems that either preceded their illness or resulted as a consequence of it.

Jane had a very difficult depression to treat. She had failed multiple trials of medications. After several years of failed trials she confessed that she had to hide her pills from her husband since he would throw them out, so that many of the trials were incomplete. He would research the medications online and be concerned about the side effects and decide for her that she didn't need them. One day after she had been successful hiding her medications from her husband for several months and seemed to improve, her husband found the pills and threw them out. Shortly after that I got an urgent call from him telling me that I had to put her back on the medication as she was much worse off them. I then insisted that he accompany her to all of her appointments so that I could educate him as to why each medication was chosen, what side effects to expect and their lack of addiction. He became a much needed advocate for her taking her medications as well as an informant about how she was doing on each trial. I have many "Janes" and some are men. For some I do split sessions, spending part of the time alone with the patient and the rest together with the significant other.

One major fear of patients and their family is that of becoming addicted to the medications. Lewis Carroll, in *Alice in Wonderland*, understood the strange effects of drugs of abuse. They talk to you, "take me, and swallow me." Drugs of abuse all have the same quality. Their effects are very rapid so that they give immediate positive reinforcement. They also tend to wear off quickly reminding you that you need to take more. Unfortunately, the subsequent doses are not as positive, often requiring escalating quantities until the individual may be taking the drug more to avoid the horrors of withdrawal than for the positive effects. Patients don't need instruction on how to take drugs of abuse, after the initial ingestion, the drug tells them what to do. They intuitively take more each time as the effects fade until it no longer has its positive effects but the withdrawals are so unpleasant that they continue to use.

Medications on the other hand usually take days to weeks to have their benefits. Side effects often precede any positive effect. Patients need encouragement to continue with the trial based on hope and faith that it will help in the long run. That is a tough sell to convince a person to endure possible increased suffering in hopes of feeling better down the road. Additional medication might be prescribed to give some immediate relief without causing later problems but the primary tool for acceptance of this treatment is psychotherapy. Psychotherapy takes many forms. It must include a psycho educational component. Some techniques many help with symptom reduction such as relaxation techniques. Supportive counseling might provide guidance for coping with day to day needs until symptom reduction can improve function. The most important element is that of hope. Oncologists have to do this all the time. They offer the prospect of a longer life. We offer the prospect of a better life.

The next point of decision making often leading to conflict is how long to stay on the medication. Relapse studies have been done for depression but are not so definitive with other conditions. In depression the chance of a relapse after a first episode in someone younger than age 40 is about 50 percent. After two episodes this rises to 70 percent. By the time a patient has a third episode the chances are 90 percent that there will be a recurrence. In individuals over age 40 relapse rates are higher. But what if there was never a really well period? What if on the medications this may be the best someone has felt in years or as long as they can remember? This is often the case of many patients with anxiety prominent symptoms. The chances of recurrence here is very high but the individual can do several things that might reduce this without medication. Psychotherapy can teach better coping skills and relaxation techniques. Yoga and exercise can help with benefits that rival some medications. This takes dedication to a regular regimen which many patients find difficult to continue and even a break from the routine for several weeks might result in relapse. Also patients with more moderate to severe presenting symptoms, non pharmacologic interventions are more adjunctive and are not likely to be adequate to prevent recurrence.

In the case of bipolar disorder and psychosis, relapse is almost inevitable. Old reports of periodicity for bipolar disorder, in the days before effective treatments, noted on average a four year interval between the first episode and second episode. The interval between the second and third was on average 2 years. After that episodes were almost annually. Since medications we see much more variability and with patients given antidepressants the frequency is often much greater with several episodes in a single year. So for bipolar and psychotic disorders long term prophylaxis is almost always recommended.

But wait there's more. More recent evidence is that bipolar disorder and depression may be associated with shrinkage in parts of the brain. This has been observed in some patients at the onset of illness before medications have even been started. Depression, bipolar and Alzheimer's disease are associated with low brain derived neurotrophic factor (BDNF). Medications such as lithium and SSRIs have been shown to increase BDNF. Interestingly, exercise increases BDNF as well. There have only been small studies looking at the long term effects of medication on preventing dementia, but there is a hint that they might. I can say from my experience of over 30 years that the incidence of dementia in my long time medication compliant patients has been almost nonexistent. I realize that this is not study grade data as patient may have left me when they got demented. I have seen some develop vascular type dementias and many complain of work finding difficulty but these are often present early in treatment and don't lead to serious impairment. (See my chapter on RAM hypothesis) I will ask a patient wondering if they should stay on antidepressant long term, do they have family members with dementia. The answer is often affirmative. Then I ask if they were treated for depression. Here the answer is mixed. They had depression but didn't get treatment or got it late in life. The dots are not fully connected, but it seems to me that long standing depression and anxiety are related to later development of dementia and long term treatment with medications might reduce that risk. It is this kind of information that might help patients to accept long term treatments to prevent relapse.

There have been some recent population studies that are looking for risks of antidepressants in elderly patients. One study looked at records of patients given an antidepressant within a year of having a fall with subsequent fracture. The curious finding was that the risk of having a fall peaked at one month before they started the medication but increased risk lasted for a year. No matter how you want to interpret the data, you can't blame a medication for a problem that preceded taking it. However, it can be interpreted that the condition that a prescriber thought justified giving an antidepressant, for example depression, might be a risk factor for fracture. Individuals who are depressed don't eat well, don't exercise and might have physical deterioration from this lifestyle impairment. Subsequent treatment with antidepressants might get them more active again making the fall more likely. You can't surmise causation from correlation studies. Having depression is not healthy.

⌘⌘⌘⌘⌘

THE FIRST SHALL BE LAST: AN ALTERNATIVE APPROACH TO THE PSYCHIATRIC INTAKE EVALUATION

Most clinicians are taught in school to take a history by letting the patient tell their story mostly uninterrupted. This allows the patient to feel that they are being heard and imparts an empathic stance. It also results in a very disjointed intake that may turn out to be overly inclusive and rambling in areas irrelevant to an accurate assessment while missing some important data. When I was a psychiatry resident we were expected to take two to three visits before completing an evaluation, allowing plenty of time to collect data. This is not a luxury in these fast paced, results oriented times. Even in the old days gaps were evident. In my residency I had to present an elaborate history of every patient admitted. This included obtaining records from all hospitalizations and treatment from prior clinicians. I thought I had done an excellent job reporting on a 40 year old woman with multiple hospitalizations for psychosis and post traumatic stress disorder. The attending paid careful attention to my presentation and noted that the dates of treatment didn't correlate with her reported ages at the time and this left a two year gap in her long history. Rather than receiving accolades for my hard work I felt humiliated in missing this data. Subsequent interview of the patient revealed that during this gap she had worked as a prostitute and suffered from multiple traumas. All this was missed because I let the patient control each interview rather than try to organize the patient into giving a sequential history.

As an attending at University of Connecticut I learned how to do structured clinical interviews. The two were the SCID (Structured Clinical Interview for DSM Diagnoses) for DSM diagnoses and the SCAN (Schedules for Clinical Assessment in Neuropsychiatry) for ICD 10 diagnoses. In these interviews the initial questions were demographic and historical. This historical data is collected prior to questions about symptoms. A typical unstructured clinical interview begins with the chief complaint and history of present illness. Clinical symptoms are gathered during this initial phase while family, medical and social histories are left to the end. The taking of the history of present illness often bogs down such that much of the historical data is missed due to time constraints. Additionally, the patient may begin to breakdown emotionally while recanting the most acute symptoms which then distract the interviewer from asking questions that might seem less relevant to the current crisis.

My strategy is to take a pause after a brief description of the chief complaint and obtain a summary of past psychiatric and medical histories as well as completing a genogram for family history and then social history. This lets the patient recompose while telling more neutral and less acute issues while giving me a context for my more in depth exploration of current history and symptoms. I usually allow less than 5 minutes for the open ended initial chief complaint before politely telling the patient I will get back to that after I ask some questions for background history. The background questions take about 15 minutes which leaves plenty of time to go in depth into history of present illness. This also includes a SCID-like series of screening questions for major categories of DSM diagnoses, e.g. depression, mania, OCD, panic, substance abuse, and trauma.

Having obtained past history first it is easier to see patterns of symptom recurrence, familial inheritance, and trauma. Knowing the social history which includes highest level of education, work history and living situation you can surmise how severely the present symptoms are impacting upon the patients social and occupational functioning. The patient might appreciate the connections as well, such as appreciating relapses occurring after medication discontinuations or triggers associated with certain life milestones. Saving the current history for last also reduces resistance to telling important but highly emotionally charged details. The patient feels that you now know something about them, so their telling you about acute problems doesn't seems as embarrassing or irrelevant. Most psychodynamic clinicians know that often the most relevant information occurs in the end of the session.

Drafting a treatment plan with the patient is also easier when it follows the history of present illness. The plan flows from the exposition of current symptoms and problems. The one exception to my strategy is if the past psychiatric history is extensive. If there is an extensive past psychiatric treatment history, I might defer some of the detail of this to after the history of present illness. This is because the outcomes of past treatment trials are critical to my recommendations for current treatments.

Let me give some other examples from my experiences to help illustrate the good, the bad and the ugly. I was doing intake evaluations during a fourth year medical school Psychiatry outpatient elective. I already had experience with psychiatric patients in my six week clinical inpatient rotation at Hillside Hospital-Long Island Jewish Hospital and a six week psychopharmacology elective at Columbia. The clinic was attached to the brand new Stony Brook hospital tower. It was an all glass structure 334 feet tall that stands as a beacon visible from miles around. It was the tallest building in Suffolk County. The patient, JR, was in his mid thirties and wanted to be admitted to the newly opened psychiatric ward. He was depressed but gave little reason for his hospitalization. He didn't seem to have the severity of patients I had seen in the hospital but I gathered little information about his prior treatment, family or social history. He was unhappy with his current and past treatments and wanted into the new Mecca. As I expressed my reluctance, he began to escalate until he finally exploded. He shot up from his chair. Picked it up and exclaimed, "If I throw this chair against the glass you would have me immediately admitted with Haldol in my butt." I calmly told him I would get my supervising resident. He put down the chair and sat silently.

When the resident physician entered the room, JR proceeded to re-enact his performance of lifting the chair and displaying what he thought would be his admission ticket to the hospital. The resident more experienced than me, knowing that patients in glass hospitals shouldn't be allowed to throw chairs, calmly told him that his ticket was no good. "If you did that, I would call security and have you sent to the State Psychiatric Hospital." JR put down the chair and stormed out of the hospital clinic. I was relieved and initially impressed by the resident's fast processing but now realize it was a missed opportunity. Had I redirected him from his initial complaint and said, "I see that you are in great distress now, but let me get some background information first." I might have learned more about him and his past treatment failures. He was calm when not facing rejection for the treatment he thought he needed. We might have been able to have a more rational conversation about treatment options including an intensive outpatient or day treatment program. We could have discussed why he thought prior treatments had failed and maybe learned about what social supports he had. Instead, I let him tell his story the way he wanted which left large gaps and allowed him to escalate his anger until he was out of control.

      Jill was a 20 year old college student who presented depressed and anxious stating that she thought that she had been raped the prior year. She presented now because she had discovered that she had contracted herpes as a result of the rape. As she told her story she cried profusely but I told her to pause in her story so I could get some background information. Her tears quickly dried as I proceeded to get a systematic history. She didn't have prior treatment except for emergency room visits for alcohol intoxication. She was in a Sorority and drank heavily every weekend and sometimes during the week. Her grades were declining. The boy who she thought raped her was a close friend and she never reported the crime. Several of her family members had severe alcoholism and some had arrests for DUI and lost employment as a result. When I suggested that she had an alcohol problem she didn't concur as she wasn't as bad as her father and didn't drink daily. But having obtained past history of DUI and other unwanted sexual encounters while intoxicated as well as deteriorating grades, I was able to build a case for the harm that alcohol was doing to her. She even suggested that the rape might not have occurred if she were sober as he had been nice to her before and after the party and she couldn't remember the details of that night. While not minimizing that a rape had occurred, the information gained enabled me to empower her so she could regain control of her life if she included treatment for her alcoholism as well as her trauma. I was also able to point out the consequences of untreated alcoholism that she recounted in her family history. Had I let the interview go as it was unfolding, she might have come to the conclusion many alcoholics make that they needed the alcohol to deal with their problems rather than alcohol being a contributor to their problems.

A free flowing clinical interview directed by the patient seems like an ideal to strive for in an ideal world. This is the role of a friend of the patient. The patient may feel that they have been listened to but they came to see you not as a friend, but as a clinician who has the power to provide relief of symptoms. For some individuals you may still have time to complete a history after a free flowing present illness but you can't guarantee that you won't be taken down a tangential path. The results might be more successful if information is gathered in the more methodical way that I propose. The more complete the picture, the more likely the treatment plan will meet the needs of the patient. The patient might also appreciate you not letting them lose emotional control while telling their story.

A criticism of my approach is that I am not "listening" to the patient as I interrupt their train of thought to obtain background information. I remind the reader that this is an initial intake interview and not a therapy session. Obtaining as thorough a picture of the patient including past and present provides context and invaluable information necessary for a rapid yet thorough differential diagnosis assessment. While not preventing the patient from withholding invaluable information, it reduces the risk of missing important background information.

When I was on call as a resident in a walk-in clinic a young man with schizophrenia presented asking for additional antipsychotic medication. He was on a long acting injectable antipsychotic and told me he was anxious between injections and needed more. Ordinarily I would not question a patient requesting more antipsychotic medication but I had received a strange call from his father requesting that I keep him in the clinic. No reason was given. I tried to get him to talk but he would only say he just needed more medication since he had come back from a vacation with his family. Obtaining information from his record I questioned him about his girlfriend, "I haven't seen her, we broke up." I questioned him about a smell of gasoline that I detected, "I have been working on my car," he told me. I got him his medication and asked him to wait to see its effect. He took the pills and ran out the door. I had no information that would have allowed me to place a hold on his leaving. The police were waiting outside to arrest him as he had just doused his girlfriend with gasoline but didn't light it. Sometimes you miss things no matter how hard you try. The irony is that had he stayed the police couldn't have arrested him and he would have been admitted to the hospital for more treatment.

 While my intake approach is appropriate for general outpatient interviews, modifications are appropriate for different settings such as an emergency department where there maybe even less time for assessment and the goals are mostly triage decisions. In an inpatient setting, there are multiple clinicians collecting data. This situation may allow for some interviewers to be more open ended. The end goal is to obtain the most complete picture of the person, and not just a collection of acute symptoms, that may help guide in formulating the most appropriate treatment plan.

⌘⌘⌘⌘⌘

THE ROLE OF THE NOT SO SIMPLE 15 MINUTE "MEDICATION CHECK"

After an initial psychiatric evaluation of about 45 minutes most follow up visits are 15 to 25 minutes long. The goals initially may be straight forward such as assessing the success of prior treatment recommendations. This includes whether the patient understood and followed with the plan. Did they take whatever medications prescribed, at what times and consistently? I always take the stance that non compliance and mistakes are to be expected. This way the patient feels freer to acknowledge doubt about taking the medications and any missed doses. It also is good to compliment the patient if they actually stuck with the plan. Monitoring and assessing the outcome of specified target symptoms is the primary objective but untoward events and mistakes made in prescriptions are almost more valuable. I've learned tricks from these mishaps including best times to take a given medication and side effects that were not listed in the package inserts.

What is the purpose of the 15 minute visit? The brief office visit is not just a "medication check" but an opportunity to reassess the patient's progress and overall well-being. Reassessment is not just about renewal of medications but is about making new or validating prior formulations of what problems exist and their treatment needs. While not all of the following elements may occur in every visit, every visit will include more than one of these elements.

1. Maintain the doctor-patient relationship

2. Assess the periodicity of symptoms by season (quarterly check-ups)

3. Provide support and hope for the future

4. Reinforce availability of the psychiatrist in times of crisis.

5. Assess the general wellbeing of the patient.

6. Evaluate medical symptoms as part of psychiatric syndrome or in need of appropriate medical evaluation, i.e. review of systems. The psychiatrist is a physician first and is best suited to help differential psychiatric symptoms from potential medical ones. We may be the primary care giver for the patient and need to make referral for additional work up.

7. Validate medical concerns to empower and arm patient with needed jargon to inform the primary care physician with symptoms requiring further medical work up.

8. Monitor medications for side effects and access need for laboratory testing including review of recent lab results. General lab screening may be ordered as part of wellness check in patients who've neglected wellness visits to primary care physicians.

9. Provide ongoing informed consent to continued use of medications with risks and benefits.

10. Provide up to date information about treatments and consequences of lack of treatment.

11. Ensure acceptance of treatment, address concerns to facilitate continued compliance with treatment.

12. Assess mental status and symptom profile for maximum adequacy of response.

13. Assess the congruity between affect and stated emotional status and challenge the meaning of any incongruity.

14. Encourage further symptom reduction to achieve remission and make medication adjustments to induce remission.

15. Identify psychosocial stressors and conflicts that might be foci of psychotherapeutic interventions, i.e. propose goals for psychotherapy.

16. Make referral for psychotherapy and/ or medical interventions.

17. Reinforce prior interventions for general healthy lifestyle including, smoking cessations, drug and alcohol abstinence or safe usage, diet and exercise.

19. Determine the frequency of follow-up visits thereby renewing the treatment contract.

20. Refill prescriptions,

⌘⌘⌘⌘⌘

A Multiple Models Assessment and Treatment Strategy for Depression and Anxiety

In psychiatry, as in the rest of medicine, treatment is guided by an initial assessment which suggests possible differential diagnoses. The clinician must decide on which diagnosis is the most likely and initiate the appropriate treatment plan suited for that diagnosis. The problem lies in the inaccuracy of many of our diagnoses and the varied presentations for the same condition. Unlike in other medical conditions, psychiatry lacks objective laboratory measures. Psychiatry has relied upon clinician observations and reported symptoms. In the early years of psychiatry (Diagnostic and Statistical Manual or DSM I and II) diagnoses were based upon unproven theories of illness causation which led to considerable disagreement among diagnosticians. DSM III sought to improve the reliability of our psychiatric diagnoses so that different clinicians would be highly likely to agree upon the diagnosis. This reliability was achieved by creating check lists of symptoms that could be easily recognized by most clinicians. Less attention was paid to the validity of the diagnoses as there are few objective measures to prove the validity other than statistical clustering of symptoms. Subsequent DSM revisions have made little progress in validating diagnoses by either biological or treatment outcome markers. A particular cluster of symptoms (phenotype) might emerge from different underlying causes (i.e. genotypes).

Just like in weather prediction where forecasters use a variety of models to predict the future weather, I propose using several models for making a diagnosis prior to intervening for treatment of psychiatric symptoms. I propose three models for assessment to help achieve better validity for our assessments which might improve our treatment decisions and outcomes. The first is the traditional symptom based check lists that lead to a DSM diagnosis. The second is a family history/genetic based assessment. Finally there is a longitudinal-dimensional course of illness based assessment which includes branching decision trees informed by medication trials.

It is important to keep in mind that each model leads to a primary "working" diagnosis which could be one of several possible differential diagnoses. Ongoing treatment provides additional data both historical and longitudinal which might alter our working diagnosis. For example, certain medication effects might trigger state dependent recall of prior symptomatic periods or new symptoms. Medications might trigger new symptoms such as agitation or mania which would alter the diagnosis. Family members might report new data about their treatment or provide information about a patient's symptoms both current and historical. Regularly scheduled visits will provide data as to seasonality and stability of symptoms.

1. DSM Model

The DSM model should be familiar to all providers. Use of structured clinical interview tools such as the SCID or SCAN can provide a comprehensive interview that screens for major symptom clusters. This can be done quickly with a series of probe questions associated with each symptoms cluster. For example, does the patient have: depression, anxiety, panic attacks, OCD, history of trauma, attention/concentration difficulty, or psychotic symptoms? Also, medical problems and treatments are recorded that might be relevant to the diagnosis or treatment. The problem with the DSM is that it pays little attention to family history, genetics, longitudinal course or even symptom severity. The introduction of dimensional criteria in DSM V does little to remedy this deficit.

2. Family/Genetic Model

The DSM seeks to find clusters of symptoms that congregate together implying a common pathology. It is not the case that all patients with the same DSM diagnosis suffer from the same pathology. If this were true there would be better correlation between diagnosis and treatment outcome than we see. As an example, patients diagnosed with major depression respond to medications with totally different mechanisms of action and some only respond to medications that are indicated for bipolar disorder and not depression.

There are many factors including both genetic vulnerability and situational factors that lead to illness. Current genetic testing that is clinically available provides little guidance to what type of treatment someone needs with some exceptions. The MTHFR (methlytetrahydrofolate reductase) enzyme mutations do identify a treatable problem that is associated with folic acid deficiency or more appropriately, the inability to convert dietary folic acid into its activated form, l-methyl folate. L-methyl folate is essential in the synthesis of multiple neurotransmitters among other processes. The genetic tests of variations in P450 liver enzyme metabolism may guide dosages of medications but doesn't tell the prescriber which class of medication is necessary. Newer genetic tests of serotonin transporter genes and COMT variants might, in the future, help guide treatment but studies are lacking at this time.

The best predictor of which medication(s) has (have) the most potential benefit for a specific patient is what medication(s) the patient responded to in the past. Next best predictor is what medication(s) first degree relatives responded to. In my experience this is a better predictor than even DSM diagnosis. So an individual who presents with major depression symptoms but has a strong family history of bipolar disorder is likely to be more responsive to medications useful in bipolar disorder than unipolar depression. It would be helpful to look for bipolar "soft signs" such as early onset, severe depression, atypical features, highly recurrent episodes particularly with a seasonal pattern, episodic substance abuse, post partum onset, extreme diurnal variation of mood, frequent deliberate non-compliance with medications (often with awareness that the medications have stopped working or are making the symptoms worse), and erratic responses to antidepressant medications with temporary improvements fading or responses dependent on season of treatment initiation.

3. Longitudinal dimensional model

The third model I propose is an empirically based categorical system which I will describe in segments. Each segment represents a series of category or decision trees.

Acute vs. chronic: The first question to ask about the patient's symptoms is if they can recall their onset. If they can, do they recall any precipitants and decide if the symptoms are acute or chronic. I would define acute as existing less than 6 months and chronic as present over several years. There is a large gap in between which could represent a persistent unresolved acute problem or early stage chronic illness.

Acute symptoms require more focus on new onset medical problems such as starting a new medication (e.g. initiation of steroids, metoprolol, autoimmune disease or substance abuse). It can also be the result of recent traumatic events such as death of loved one or job stress or loss. Acute symptoms are addressed by dealing with the underlying causes or providing psychotherapy.

Chronic symptoms might also be related to trauma or even medications or physical illness but this is harder to identify unless the patient is able to recall precipitating factors. The chronic symptoms also result in adaptive changes (i.e. personality traits) in the patient that may require extra psychotherapeutic techniques to treat.

Chronic disorders are more likely to be biologic and require medications and maybe multiple medications plus therapy to deal with the negative cognitions and other consequences. However, early trauma can also precipitate chronic symptoms. This might be evident in rapid mood shifts in response to interpersonal encounters. These patients over-react to situations that are similar to past traumas. However, extreme rejection sensitivity may look similar but be reflective of major depression with atypical features which is responsive to SSRI or MAOI medications.

Sub chronic states are queried as an acute condition with the awareness that precipitants are less likely to be identified. Getting an accurate timeline for the onset of symptoms can be difficult but may point to causative or aggravating factors. Finding out about deaths, moves, job/position changes, marital/relationship issues, even vacations can facilitate construction of timelines. For example antidepressants may fail after a patient takes a cruise or tropical vacation. Careful questioning identifies an all inclusive package which led to increased alcohol intake which continued after return from vacation. A sub chronic depression lasting a couple of years may have its onset in post partum or after the death of a relative but the patient didn't make the connection. A good question to ask is "when did you last feel well or not depressed?" If they can pinpoint the time of onset you can make a timeline. If they can't this sub chronic syndrome is probably heading towards chronic condition.

Cyclical vs. stable: The next subdivision is cyclical or stable symptoms. Bipolar disorder is by definition cyclical but shift the curve down on bipolar disorder you get recurrent depression with either periods of normal mood or mild dysphoria. Cyclothymia, by definition, has only mild depressive symptoms so this pattern can only be labeled in DSM as recurrent major depression with possible seasonal pattern. I have proposed calling this rapid cycling unipolar depression "cyclical mood disorder." There have been many other names proposed for this condition including, rapid cycling unipolar, bipolar 3 or bipolar NOS. DSM V now has included a major depression modifier of mixed depression which might help characterize some of these individuals. In practice many of these cyclical disorders are better treated with mood stabilizers than antidepressants. While mood stabilizers are often the best treatments for cyclical mood disorder, confusion and stigma can be associated with the bipolar label and should be avoided.

A special note must be made for the acute worsening of a stable chronic disorder. This might give the appearance of a cyclical disorder but is due to treatment non adherence or drug and alcohol overuse. Missing or stopping medications deliberately or by accident is very common especially after a vacation, hospitalization or initiation of medications by another prescriber. This is best asked in a non judgmental way such as, "How do you remember when to take your medication" and "how many pills to you think you miss in a week?"

Similarly, episodic overuse of alcohol or drugs can give the appearance of a cyclical disorder. However, some patients use drugs or alcohol episodically to self medicate a cyclical disorder. Sorting this out can be difficult. If depression and anxiety medications worked for sustained periods this is likely a non cyclical or stable disorder.

A stable pattern of hyperactivity may be the major separating distinction for diagnosing a patient with ADHD complicated by major depression/ anxiety disorder or mislabeling them as bipolar. Or conversely a child with bipolar disorder may be misdiagnosed with ADHD being asymptomatic over the summer and depressed in the fall with inattention and acting out the predominant symptoms. The depression may lift somewhat with stimulant medication. When January comes with improving mood, they become non compliant with the stimulant preventing full blown mania but return to hyperactivity. Likewise a patient may have a cyclical pattern to their obsessive compulsive disorder demonstrating an erratic response to long term SSRI medications. Should this patient be labeled "bipolar" or be given a my new diagnosis of "cyclical mood disorder"?

When using this multiple model strategy the clinician can begin with a comprehensive history which would obtain family, medical and past psychiatric histories. This would suggest several differential diagnoses which are kept in mind while using an algorithm like one proposed below to generate either alternate diagnoses or support prior impressions.

Potential algorithm outline

Using the above diagnostic paradigm a possible treatment algorithm can be proposed using currently available medications and psychotherapies.

1. ***Known date of onset***: yes/ no

    a. **No**: go to acute/chronic

    b. **Yes**: Identify trauma vs. medical vs. interpersonal problems and decide if symptoms are acute or chronic.

2. ***Acute vs. chronic vs. sub acute:*** The final medication treatment for symptoms might be the same for either acute or chronic symptoms but the need to explore stressors and other causes is greater for acute. The focus of psychotherapy is likely to be very different. Also the target goals may be different.

    a. **Acute and sub acute**: re-review stressors, medical conditions, relationships, job. Goals are aggressive towards remission of symptoms. Treatment is focused on underlying causes with medical treatment for medical causes and psychotherapy for stressors. Use of benzodiazepines or trazodone for anxiety and insomnia may be indicated. Brief courses of antidepressants (SSRIs are first choice) are indicated for more serious and sustained symptoms lasting over one month that do not respond to psychotherapy.

    b. **chronic**: reassess PTSD, family history. Goals are still to remission but this is less likely to occur. A return to mild dysphoric baseline might be acceptable outcomes. Use of antidepressants (first choice is SSRIs or based upon algorithm B below) and alpha blockers with adjunctive benzodiazepines or trazodone are usually indicated.

3. ***Cyclical vs. stable symptoms:***

    A. ***cyclical pattern***: seasonal vs. annual vs. periodic, highs and lows or only lows, a1: **Past response to antidepressant**: a. No response/b. good response/c. Temporary or erratic response depends on season.

    a1a: **no response**: go to mood stabilizer, identify family history of response.

    a1b: **good response**: Restart same antidepressant or change within same antidepressant class based on avoidance of prior side effects (e.g. sertraline for patients with constipation, venlafaxine for those with diarrhea). Assess reasons for discontinuing and address concerns.

    a1c: **temporary response**: Reassess response, are all the original symptoms re-emerging or are they somewhat different. If initial anxiety resolved on SSRI but depression emerges add NE medication. If reemergence of anxiety reassess for agitation- add antipsychotic or mood stabilizer, then consider discontinuation of antidepressant. If good initial response then clear relapse of initial symptoms take careful drug and alcohol history (relapse will occur with >2 standard drinks for a woman per occasion per week or >4 drinks for a man. Encourage "Pepsi challenge" = no alcohol for one month to identify if this is cause of relapse and if can't do suggest alcohol treatment.

a2: **If no prior treatment and no family history**: Trial Lamictal for more depressive symptoms and irritability. Trial lithium or Depakote are indicated if more agitation is present. Screen for atypical depression with extreme rejection sensitivity (hysteroid dysphoria-see b2a)

a3: **Classic bipolar disorder**: With overt psychotic symptoms or severe vs. mild hypomania.

    a3a: **Psychotic**: start with atypical antipsychotic and add lithium or Depakote. Alternative medications are tegretol or Trileptal.

a3b: Non psychotic: start with lithium/ Depakote/ Trileptal. Depakote might be better for rapid cycling (>3-4 episodes/year), lithium might be better for more depressive and suicidal symptoms and OCD, Trileptal might be better if cognitive problems/ ADHD symptoms with impulsivity.

a3c: Bipolar depression: Very difficult to treat. The best treatment is prevention of manic and hypomanic states with mood stabilizers. Patients need to learn of the connection between these two states and that "surfing" (sustained hypomania) is not possible. All waves eventually crash into the shore.

Latuda and Seroquel XR are the only FDA indicated medications but I would start with lithium and Lamictal first and consider adding the antipsychotic if necessary. Trials of combinations of mood stabilizers (usually 2) and different atypical antipsychotic medications are usually preferable to adding an antidepressant. Atypicals have different receptor profiles. For example low dose aripiprazole is activating while quetiapine is sedating/calming. Sometimes an antidepressant trial is indicated and might produce a rapid although brief response. There are 3 short acting antidepressants that can be used for patients who have morning depression with diurnal afternoon/ evening improvement with their bipolar disorder. It is useful to question about diurnal variation of mood. Most patients are more depressed in the am but if antidepressants are on board, this might reverse with better mood in am but agitation in the pm. Use of antidepressant augmentation of a mood stabilizer when mood stabilizers alone have not been effective can be considered on a temporary or prn basis. For NE effect short acting bupropion between 37.5mg (half tablet) and 150mg given only in am or am and noon. For 5HT effect venlafaxine up to 75mg immediate release tablets only, or fluvoxamine up to 50mg can be tried often on an as needed basis i.e. prn. Studies fail to demonstrate long term efficacy of antidepressants so trial discontinuation periods are advised so as not to induce rapid cycling.

B: ***Stable depressive/anxiety symptoms***: Symptoms are fairly stable with minor variations through the year or over reactivity to situational stressors. This category can be subdivided into two major depressive types and

b1: Classic major depression: sequence med trials based upon symptom profile with color-coded medication trials (see Psychiatry in Techno colors). Some consideration for either genomic testing for prediction of side effects may be considered but I haven't found this too helpful. Some ultra rapid metabolizers may need higher doses of some medications. However, for bupropion slow 2d6 metabolizers may have a greater DA effect while ultra rapid metabolizers may have more of a NE effect.

b2: Is it double depression with dysthymia and episodes of more severe depression? This can be of two types with atypical features or melancholic subtype.

b2a: Atypical features: Patients with atypical depression may need SSRI + NE + DA, e.g. Lexapro + bupropion + Abilify (or other atypical) or MAOI. These patients have high anxiety with panic attacks (cause for 5HT medication), and fatigue with over sleeping (NE and DA symptoms). Extreme rejection sensitivity is a key feature with prolonged depression after actual rejection and panic attacks at the threat of rejection. Donald Klein labeled these patients with hysteroid dysphoria as counter to their borderline personality label from psychoanalysts. This new label called for medication treatment when others declared that only psychotherapy was indicated. There may be a downward drift in mating choice with the unconscious goal of finding a partner who wouldn't leave them. Consider PTSD with personality disorder. Consider aggressive medication trials giving hope to avert despair and suicidal ideation. Psychotherapy may have multiphase goals with initial focus on reducing despair and providing support, while later goals may be changing avoidant behaviors and reassessing negative interpersonal beliefs. Also, an exploration of maladaptive clinging behavior and unrealistic expectations in relationships is indicated.

b2b: Melancholic subtype. This is a more severe depression with near total loss of function, inability to think and concentrate, poor sleep, poor appetite and extended time doing nothing. Diurnal variation of mood can be more extreme than in atypical depression with worsening of mood in am and some improvement in the pm. Patients may deliberately avoid sleep to prolong this temporary reprieve of symptoms. Mood is non reactive to external events unlike in atypical depression where there is over-reaction to the interpersonal environment. Guilty rumination is common when they are able to think clearly enough to articulate their feelings. These patients usually require SNRI medications with an antipsychotic medication whether or not true psychotic symptoms are present. Be cautious in that many of these patients may turn out to have bipolar disorder where the cyclical nature of their illness is forgotten. State dependent memory phenomenon can cause patients not to recall times when they felt better or had manic symptoms.

b3: Panic anxiety: This is special case in that the symptoms are acute but the pattern is chronic. There is less value in focusing on the cause since it is usually not meaningful and delays remission of symptoms. Although, it is helpful to question what was occurring at the onset of symptoms to see if there are situations that occurred with the panic attacks which might have been paired with them as a form of classical conditioning. Sometimes the onset was in the context of a traumatic event indicating a co-morbid diagnosis of PTSD and a need for additional therapy. Pharmacotherapy is classically low dose Klonopin less than or equal to 1mg/ day (I usually start 0.5mg HS the first night followed by 0.25mg bid the next morning with initiation of the SSRI e.g. escitalopram 5-10mg) The SSRI is begun on second day after this loading dose of Klonopin. Klonopin and other benzodiazepines might be withheld if there is a history of alcohol abuse. No value in waiting to start treatment. CBT is essential for all to prevent or reduce agoraphobia. When the panic attacks are in control, therapy for co-morbid PTSD is in order.

b4: Obsessive compulsive disorder (OCD): Similar to panic it may be waxing and waning but has features of a chronic and stable pattern. About 10-20% of patients have a cyclical pattern with intervals of spontaneous remission of symptoms-these patients are likely to have cyclical mood disorder (i.e. bipolar spectrum) and need a mood stabilizer.

b4a: Classical OCD: Here the OCD symptoms are more prominent than depression or panic symptoms, although, anxiety and depression is almost always present in OCD. If these are not co-occurring the diagnosis is likely OCPD or Obsessive compulsive personality disorder for which more in-depth questioning of possible underlying ADHD symptoms (see b4c) or history of trauma should be done. Treatment is with SSRI at doses near the top end of dosage range is usually required for a good response. Medication response is longer, often needing two months to get significant symptom reduction and the goal is symptom reduction not elimination. CBT is essential. Augmentation of SSRIs can be done with Depakote or lithium, lamotrigine, or some atypical antipsychotic medications. Memantine as an alternative glutamate antagonist can have a mild augmenting effect. Some atypicals may worsen OCD like Zyprexa, clozapine and Saphris. Seroquel, Risperidal and possibly Geodon might be better to reduce agitation. More data are necessary to support which antipsychotic meds might be best to augment since some may block serotonin receptors that interfere with SSRI but other might augment. I might try a typical antipsychotic like loxapine if atypicals make the OCD worse. Buspirone may be another augmenting agent but some patients can get agitated on it.

b4b: Cyclical OCD: This is co-morbid OCD and bipolar spectrum disorder. This is very difficult to treat as SSRI might make the patient agitated while mood stabilizers may not be adequate for controlling OCD symptoms. Here, two antidepressants which have short half life (see a3c above) might help if given in low doses in the am so they wear off by evening (venlafaxine up to 75mg immediate release tablets only, and fluvoxamine up to 50mg). Note that this is counter to treatment for non-cyclical OCD where high dose of the SSRI is appropriate. As in bipolar disorder there may be a seasonal pattern to symptoms such that serotonin antidepressants could be used when needed while the mood stabilizer is taken year round.

b4c: OCD with underlying ADHD. This is a special case often in high functioning patients who used compulsive behavior as an adaptation to manage attention problems. Childhood ADD is often acknowledged but these patients are often intelligent and found school so easy as to not require much attention. As they got more advanced in their careers, OCD symptoms worsened when tasks overwhelmed them. SSRI medications alone may initially reduce anxiety but performance worsens which in turn makes anxiety worse. Adding Strattera or a stimulant carefully may help while reducing the dose of SSRI. Some eventually won't need the SSRI. CBT techniques are very helpful in reducing the need for SSRI medication. I have also found vilazodone to be helpful in these patients as it provides just enough SSRI effect with less cognitive impairment. Vilazodone is generally not helpful in classic uncomplicated OCD. Trintellex may also be a preferred antidepressant. It is helpful to point out the useful function of organizational skills with limited checking of work. Telling the patient not to check at all might result in careless errors that increase anxiety which in turn could reinforce excessive checking.

b5: Generalized anxiety: This type of anxiety can exist by itself or co-occur with other specific anxiety. Of note is that both benzodiazepines and SSRI medications can help but tolerance to the benzodiazepines can develop rapidly. If a patient requires more than 1.5mg of clonazepam equivalents, the addition of an antidepressant is advised rather than increasing the dosage of the benzodiazepine. It seems that the benzodiazepines almost lose their benefit when the dosage increases beyond this amount. Be observant to rule out agitation masquerading as extreme anxiety which might be part of a cyclical mood disorder or agitated depression. Agitation has more of a physical, almost vibrating feel that persists longer than panic anxiety. Agitation is treated with "major tranquilizers", i.e. atypical and typical antipsychotic medications. Psychotherapy is almost always indicated for generalized anxiety to identify the stressors and cognitively reframe catastrophic thinking. Patients with agitation have difficulty in psychotherapy and often can't tolerate some relaxation techniques until the agitation is reduced.

Affective cues

Affective cues might provide additional data helpful in confirming diagnoses. I include this discussion to point out that we might miss information or misinterpret symptoms if we are not careful in observing the context or manner in which they are obtained. Unfortunately, it is difficult to standardize these criteria in a reliably reproducible way so they have generally been removed or reduced in significance in our current diagnostic criteria. Prior to DSM III, diagnoses were more dependent upon the clinician's observations in contrast to patient reported symptoms. The original criteria of Bleuler for schizophrenia (or dementia praecox) included the four "A" of autism, affect, association and ambivalence which required clinical skill to observe. DSM III chose the more easily reported criteria of Schneider for its schizophrenia criteria (presence of delusions, hallucinations and ideas of reference). But these criteria might not be as valid or specific to the diagnosis of schizophrenia. (Schizophr Bull (2011) 37 (3): 471-479.doi: 10.1093/schbul/sbr016).

A skilled clinician can make many observations in a diagnostic interview that are hard to capture on a strict structured clinical interview with check lists pertinent to DSM criteria (e.g. SCID). For example, a patient's hesitancy to answer questions might reflect paranoia, distracting racing thoughts, hearing loss, comprehension difficulty due to language differences or negative transference towards the interviewer. This transference might relate to prior traumas or prejudice towards the gender, ethnicity or race of the clinician. A skillful clinician can identify these psychodynamic issues and interpret the resistance with hopes of finding out the true underlying symptoms necessary to make an accurate diagnosis.

As a medical student on a consult service, I observed a psychiatric resident of Middle Eastern origin interview an acutely distressed Hispanic woman. She was only 16, had delivered a baby and was suffering from acute pancreatitis. She was explaining her condition as the work of the devil and referred to God's wrath for getting pregnant. The resident in presenting the case to the attending described her as psychotic and probably schizophrenic. The attending perceptively realized the cultural differences and carefully questioned the woman. She had no clear hallucinations or delusions but made these remarks in the context of her evangelical religious beliefs. Of note, her affect was appropriate to statements in that there was no flattening of affect consistent with a schizophrenia diagnosis or incoherent loosening of associations that would point to a manic or other psychotic state. This resident would have inappropriately prescribed antipsychotic medication instead of treating her panic disorder.

An inappropriate affect might be exaggerated by being more intense or more flat compared to what might be expected by the content of speech. Rather than take the content on face value, it is appropriate to question the incongruity of affect. For example, "you describe these distressing events rather calmly, can you tell me why?" Or conversely, "Can you explain to me why these things that you say make you so upset?" This line of questioning often leads to new data such as secretly held delusions or past trauma. One of my long term patients, knowing my line of questioning pre-empted my response to her incongruent affect. When I asked how she was doing she responded: "I've been doing well, I don't need a medication change. I know you are going to ask why I don't look like I'm doing well now. It is because I just had a minor car accident coming here."

Sometimes the clinician might misread or misinterpret these affective incongruities and need to appreciate their own counter transference issues. I supervised a trainee who was a refugee herself. She failed to appreciate the significance of traumatic events in one of her patients since they seemed insignificant compared to her life story. When I pointed out the counter transference issues, she demonstrated resistance to acknowledging that her history influenced her dealing with her patient. Years ago psychiatric trainees were almost expected to have their own personal psychotherapy partly so they could learn about themselves to be able to identify transference and counter transference phenomenon.

In summary, it is necessary to make accurate observations in order to collect the data necessary to formulate appropriate diagnoses. These formulations usually entail a differential of several possible diagnoses. As treatment progresses new observations are made with each visit and medication trial. Medication trials become our diagnostic tests of different neurotransmitter systems. Positive outcomes provisionally confirm our diagnoses, while incongruities in response to treatment, both pharmacologic and psychodynamic, become the bases for reassessment of diagnoses and their treatments.

⌘⌘⌘⌘⌘

How to do a Medication Trial

Medication trials are psychiatry's lab tests. Since we have a general idea about the mechanism of action of most of our psychiatric medications they can be used as probes into the function or dysfunction of different neurotransmitter systems in the brain. These probes are less about discovering new diagnostic realities than about trying to find the best treatments for an individual patient. With the goal of helping patients recover, each trial becomes both a chemical probe and a therapeutic treatment trial. Medication selection can be informed by data derived from clinical trial studies, known mechanisms of action and hypotheses derived from clinical practice as described above.

Therapeutic medication trials are different from clinical trials done by pharmaceutical companies whose goal is to gain approval of a new medication for a given indication. They are also different from researchers' comparative studies aimed at identifying the best treatments for a given population. In these studies one treatment is compared to another or a placebo and statistics are used to determine if differences are significant or due to chance. It is unusual for subjects in these studies to receive multiple treatments at the same time other than placebo wash out periods. A wash out period is usually done to prevent misinterpretation of withdrawal symptoms of previous medications with side effects of the new medication. Placebo run-ins also help to reduce the number of placebo responders who might dilute differences between treatment arms. The assumption is made that all subjects suffer from the same illness (or underlying pathology) and any differences, reflecting unknown variables, will be statistically accounted for by randomization of large enough study populations. In most clinical trials, patients are not matched to treatments fitting their individual symptoms and not all groups are expected to improve the same. In my opinion, if a medication proves superior to placebo in these heterogeneous populations, that is good evidence for its efficacy, which might be even better if we had more specific criteria to match candidates to the given treatment.

These clinical trials are extremely valuable for identifying useful medications for populations with similar conditions. This provides evidence for how best to treat a population of individuals with an identified condition but it does not provide definitive information about how to treat a specific individual. Evidence based medicine is a starting point for individualized medicine. Most studies of this kind rarely give remission rates above 40-50 % which means more than half of the patients are still clinically ill. Psychiatric syndromes in particular are a heterogeneous mix of mechanisms with complexities in genetics, metabolism, co-occurring medical and substance abuse as well as life stressors and life style differences. The only way to find the best treatments for the individual patient is to use the patient as his or her own control.

Therapeutic trials are done with one subject or patient using an A: B or A: B: A study design. Each patient serves as their own control. Each medication is compared to a previous medication or no treatment. The first treatment or "A" is compared to second treatment "B". If the trial result is doubtful the patient may return to treatment "A" or switch to another medication "C". Since each patient is their own control inter-subject variables are eliminated. However, this does not means all variables are the same for each intervention. The patient does each trial in sequence so other variables are introduced such as co-occurring illness when medications are added, or seasonality variables or incident stressors or life events. The good news is since the goals are symptom reduction, not publication; placebo responses are helpful and not discouraged.

Since we want to find the efficacy and need for each medication only one medication is begun for each trial. If there is a need to begin a second medication in close proximity e.g. a sleep aid or side effect medication or minor tranquilizer, at least 12 to 24 hours should be placed between initiations so that side effects are not associated with the wrong medication. If an adverse effect occurs when multiple medications are started simultaneously the risk is that all medications will be rejected as options by the patient even if one might have been very beneficial alone.

Therapeutic trials should be done with appropriate expectations. Medications are selected to alleviate specific target symptoms. These target symptoms should be documented as well as general global impression of function. I assess global function in three spheres: psychological distress, interpersonal function and occupational function. Since medications generally have a delayed response I inform the patient of an expected time course of response. I inform that side effects of most medications may precede clinical benefit. I generally wait 4 weeks between observations for an antidepressant trial. This sets a realistic duration for an effect and reduces the impulse to push a medication to higher dosage with more risk of side effect without proven necessity. More important than placebo effect are side effects.

Psychotherapy is indicated for the time interval between medication adjustments. At the four week evaluation the effect of the medication is assessed as change in target symptoms and global function. Side effects and any other effects positive or negative are made note of. Rate and form of progress is noted by asking when was improvement observed and if the past week is better or worse than the previous week. If the current week is better than the previous one, more time can be given to the current treatment without dosage adjustment. If improvement stalled, a dosage increase or augmentation strategy might be employed. If there is no benefit for a medication trial, it is important to review all symptoms as there might have been reduction of symptoms not initially identified as target or some intervening event or illness occurred. For example, a patient might state that they don't feel any better, meaning that they are still depressed, but on questioning, their anxiety and irritability have improved greatly.

A re-evaluation of target symptoms and decision to either increase dosage or change treatment is then made. For more impaired patients, the observations of significant others can be very helpful. A patient might deny any improvement while the significant other might report improvement in activity, interpersonal connection, and/ or level of distress.

The timing of medication trials should be adjusted to the urgency and severity of symptoms. An acutely manic or suicidal patient who doesn't quite meet hospitalization criteria might need a more rapid escalation of medication dose. They are more likely to begin on antipsychotic medications (with or without a mood stabilizer) which usually have more rapid response times. This also would merit a follow up appointment sooner than the four weeks suggested above. As an outpatient, compliance with treatment is paramount so flexibility in dosing might be given to the patient in the titration. Also the rule of starting only one medication per day except to treat emergent side effects is followed.

When changing medications or augmenting a given medication, care must be given to potential drug interactions or withdrawal symptoms. This doesn't mean there should be a wash out period between medication trials. This is only necessary for certain changes such as between trials with an MAO inhibitor. In fact, switching from one antidepressant to another is best done without a gap or with a cross taper, overlapping the medications while titrating off the previous medication and increasing the second. This avoids SSRI withdrawal symptoms and initial activation of panic anxiety with SSRIs. The same can be said for mood stabilizers and antipsychotic medications.

Rational polypharmacy should be the tenant of any combination. Selection of two medications with the same or similar mechanisms of action doesn't make rational sense, e.g. two SSRI medications. Addition of a noradrenergic medication e.g. bupropion, to an SSRI creates the effect of an SNRI. Other rational additions to an SSRI might include 5HT 1A partial agonists like buspirone, aripipizole or vilazodone. There are many rational combinations but that is the topic of another section.

"But doc, this means I am just a guinea pig!" many patients will complain. To this I say, "You're right, but you are the primary beneficiary of the study." This leads to the discussion of the stressors and rigors of switching medications. I warn my patients that I will work to find the best medication combination that makes them feel back to their "old self" or better than they can remember or until they cry "uncle, please don't change my meds anymore." Any initial trial that leads to a partial response is at risk of losing this benefit in a subsequent trial. Augmentation with additional medication may reduce the risk of this loss but adds the complication of multiple medications and maybe more cost. Every step of the way calls for an informed consent discussion of the risks and benefits of moving forward. This includes the risk of relapse when response is not to remission or the risk of doing nothing.

Some patients are initially enthusiastic about finding the best medications but are unrealistic about having no side effects. This might lead to a patient who has an excellent response to their symptoms wanting to try a new medication with purported fewer side effects. This can lead to falling into a rabbit hole of endless failed trials. I have had patients go on like this for years ending in hospitalization before I get to review their chart and remind them that they did well on a previous combination of medication. Suddenly, minor sexual dysfunction seems quite manageable compared to the nightmare of unhelpful new medications. For this reason, I make a prominent mark in the margin of my chart "restore point" so that I can easily find the last best combination of medications. This is what computers do to mark a point in time before a software upgrade is installed allowing the frustrated user to go back in time when their computer was working properly.

⌘⌘⌘⌘⌘

Choosing medication cocktails: Top shelf brands "neat" vs. mixed generic "well" drinks

Much of what I have been writing has been about selection of medications for different symptoms and efforts to identify subtypes of disorders. The goal of this effort has been to look beyond just DSM diagnoses and medication indications and use known mechanisms of action as they relate to symptom clusters in order to make better, rational choices of medications. I have not given much discussion to the costs of medications. I have noted that most of the data we have come from studies sponsored by the manufacturers of these medications. FDA approval for specific indications requires very expensive efficacy trials. Therefore, almost all these studies occur when medications are still branded and patent protected resulting in high costs to consumers and insurers. When medications are about to lose patent protection manufacturers often raise prices to squeeze out the most profit. The largest price increases in brand medications usually occur when multiple generic versions become available and the manufacturer tries to make the most from doctors and patients fear of generic medications since they can't compete with the inexpensive generics.

Pharmaceutical companies hold many patents on a given medication. There are patents on the compound, the fillers, the shape, color and form of the pills as well as the name. In order for a generic manufacturer to make a competing generic, it must challenge all of these patents. This can be very expensive. In the past, the brand manufacturers paid the generic company not to challenge their patents delaying release of competition. Years ago, Congress passed legislation to stop this delay tactic and gave incentive to companies to challenge the patents. The first company to challenge a patent can be granted a six months period of being the only competing generic. This usually results in the price of the new generic going down only about 10% from the brand price for the first six months until new generic manufacturers have the opportunity to compete.

Generic medications must contain the same active compound at a quantity plus or minus 10% of the brand name. Most of the time there is very little variance. Most patients will respond to psychiatric medications with considerable variance in dosage. Also dosages can be easily adjusted up or down to compensate for different generic versions. My seventh grade shop teacher used to refer to this as "boob factor." By this he meant that in constructing wood projects, we could be off slightly in our measurements without negatively affecting the final product (referring to us sloppy craftsmen as "boobs"). With the side effects of most of our psychiatric medications being relatively mild, patients can tolerate higher than needed dosages. The manufacturers of these medications knew this and often study higher than necessary doses of the medications in their clinical trials so to assure that there would be an effect that separates from placebo. In many of these trials the study was designed to optimize a separation from placebo which meant dosages were raised as high as tolerated without having the subjects drop out of the trial due to side effects. This meant that many patients in non research settings can get away with lower doses than were suggested by the original studies.

I began using Klonopin for panic disorder when it was still only available as a brand name medication. It worked very well in a low dose (as I noted in other chapters.) When it became generic, many of my patients complained that it didn't work as well and wanted to go back to the brand. When the price of the brand exceeded 5 to 10 times the cost of the generic version, these patients worked with me to tweak the dosage to compensate for any slight differences. Subsequent patients who began on the generic rarely had any problems as this tweaking process occurred with the initial generic medication. The same thing happened with other medications. One woman whose insurance covered brand names at minimal extra cost told me she wouldn't give her dog the generic version of Celexa. When her insurance changed and the cost became ten times that of the generic, she did quite well on the generic "dog unworthy" version.

Studies done by most pharmaceutical companies may provide only limited information about the effects of very low or very high dosages of medications. In order to minimize side effects that might come from other medications, these studies also greatly limit adjunctive medications and most polypharmacy. This means there are very few studies on the risks and benefits of multiple medications given simultaneously, i.e. polypharmacy. Limited literature has claimed that polypharmacy creates the risk for more side effects than mono therapy, but these studies often use high doses of at least one of the medications. Prescribing more than one medication for a patient is not usually done without careful consideration of the consequences and benefits. A patient may not get a complete remission of symptoms despite being on the highest dosage of medication that they can tolerate. This dosage may not be the top approved dosage, but does the clinician torture the patient into getting used to the higher dose, switch completely to another medication with the risk of losing any benefits gained, or augment the low dose of the first medication which is giving partial benefit with a second medication? My experience suggests that rational polypharmacy with low dosages of multiple medications can result in fewer side effects, a more complete remission of symptoms, and lower costs.

How can it result in all of these benefits? Most side effects of medications are dose related. So keeping each medication below the point of side effect minimizes these side effects. There have been studies that advocate pushing dosages of medications so high to change their effect. For example, when Prozac (fluoxetine) is raised to high levels it affects norepinephrine in addition to serotonin. However, by doing so you have raised the serotonin effect so high that you have much worse serotonin side effects (e.g. sedation, sexual dysfunction, affect flattening, and weight gain.) If you give a low dose of bupropion with a low dose of fluoxetine you can get the same norepinephrine benefits without the excess serotonin side effects. Also since many generic medications are priced on a per pill basis, you have fewer pills taken and thus a lower cost.

Brand name medications are also priced on a per pill basis. A patient might need an antipsychotic medication as a mood stabilizer. A low dose of aripiprazole might boost an antidepressant but this may not help with sleep. Raising the dose higher might help with sleep by causing some sedation but may also cause greater risk of weight gain and tardive dyskinesia. The price of aripiprazole is tiered by dosage but pills can be broken when low dosages are used cutting the price in half. Branded Latuda for bipolar depression can cost over $1000 per month. It also can cause insomnia at a low dose which can often be overcome by raising the dose. Breaking the pill can reduce this cost by at least half. Alternatively a low dose of inexpensive quetiapine can be added to a half of the other medication for a lower cost than raising the dose of either medication. In addition, you may have reduced the side effects of a high dose antipsychotic medication since the long term risks of side effects of antipsychotic medications are related to dose and duration.

Lithium has been the standard for treatment of bipolar disorders. It has a very powerful neurotrophic benefit which means it may protect and heal the brain. The dosages recommended for treatment of bipolar disorder are close to levels that might cause toxicity with risk of kidney damage. The simple act of using ibuprofen or other ANSAID medications can double the blood levels of lithium resulting in toxicity. Periods of accidental toxicity may account for subsequent accounts of kidney damage on lithium that was supposedly kept in the therapeutic range. Now that there are several alternative medications to lithium, we can avoid the high doses of lithium or not use lithium at all. However, I have encountered many patients for whom lithium was the only medication that gave complete remission of symptoms. I have found that by combining low blood levels of lithium with an adjunctive mood stabilizer such as lamotrigine or divalproex (Depakote) I can achieve the same results as a high dose of lithium without the side effect risk. All of these medications are available in inexpensive generic versions which achieve the same benefit of the much more expensive brand name medications.

The argument against polypharmacy leads to other problems as well. Anxiety treatment is a case in point. The most common medications approved for treatment of anxiety are benzodiazepines such as Xanax and Klonopin (clonazepam). If only a benzodiazepine is used to treat anxiety, i.e. mono-therapy, the initial treatment often fails as tolerance develops. This leads to higher and higher doses of the medication being used until a pattern resembling abuse ensues. Benzodiazepines act in similar parts of the brain as alcohol. As many imbibers of alcohol know, if they binge drink even one day per week they develop a tolerance to the alcohol. However, the casual cocktail drinker knows, having one drink per day doesn't cause this tolerance. The same is true for benzodiazepines. From my experience, using up to 1mg of clonazepam per day doesn't induce a tolerance to its anti-panic effect (see chapter on panic). However, tolerance to the generalized anxiety benefit is common. The answer is not to increase the dose of benzodiazepine but to add an antidepressant for this generalized anxiety. This avoids the addiction cycle of escalating benzodiazepine dependence. You might appropriately ask, why not start with the antidepressant? The problem here is that many patients with anxiety experience an initial worsening of their anxiety when begun on the antidepressant and stop the medication before it has a chance to work. So this is another case of the benefits of polypharmacy leading to a safer and better outcome.

One final point in this discussion of the treatment of anxiety is the need for psychotherapy. It is nearly impossible to have a good outcome in anxiety treatment without some psychotherapy. Psychotherapy helps in so many ways. Most importantly is helps channel the anxiety into a productive force for change. While excessive use of pharmacology runs the risk of taking away motivation and drive.

Patients and prescribers are bombarded with advertising for new brand name medications. This leads people to believe that the latest medications are also the greatest. This is often untrue. Rarely are the new medications compared to the old medications in a manner that proves superiority. All that the FDA requires is for the medication to be safe and effective for the stated indication, not whether or not it is superior. The goal of the marketers of these new medications is to convince prescribers that there is some superiority. For some patients the new medications offer a new hope and prove better than prior trials. But this is not always the case. I have to concur here with insurance companies which usually require "step therapy" meaning to try at least one or two less expensive generic medications before jumping to an expensive brand name. Pharmaceutical companies used to hire sales representatives that had a science background so they might relate better to the physicians. Now the most common educational background for a pharmaceutical representative is in marketing or a related major. This way the representatives can be trained to parrot the marketing materials from the manufacturer and be less likely to go off script. This is partially to protect the company from claims of "off label" marketing of the drug which may result in large fines but it also means there is less depth to the sales pitches.

One talented pharmaceutical representative did a very successful pitch to my new nurse practitioner. Claiming that their medication had fewer sexual side effects, she convinced her that their $300 per month medication should be tried on all of our new patients needing an antidepressant. The nurse was pleased with her new found knowledge and potential treatment algorithm. Unfortunately she had to suffer from my wrath. First I had to explain that there were no valid head to head comparisons of the new medication to old ones showing equal efficacy and fewer side effects. Second, whatever studies done that suggested fewer side effects didn't necessarily merit the cost which was over ten times that of the generic medication. Third, the fact that the manufacturer gave a coupon to reduce the cost of the medication for the patient, we were still raising the overall cost of medical care to the system that could result in cuts elsewhere. All of this would be done without evidence that the patient wouldn't benefit from the old medication without troubling side effects. Recall my experience, noted above, with patients switching for brand name Klonopin to generics compared to those started on the generic in the first place. The pharmaceutical companies know that patients don't like to change medications if they are working, and that transitions aren't always smooth, so better to start them on their medication first. Finally, my experience with the new medication only showed superiority in some areas but weakness in other areas that cancelled out any overall advantage for most patients.

I still see pharmaceutical representatives to obtain the knowledge of FDA approved studies and guidance about use of these medications. It also informs me of new and novel treatment strategies but I always keep in mind the sources and scrutinize the studies. I can often ask the representative to forward questions I have about the new medications such as mechanisms of action that will be directed to the company's medical liaisons. I have enough scientific knowledge and clinical experience to try to appreciate the relative merits of a new medication. At times this new knowledge from a scientific liaison has led me to identify an older medication that I had ignored that might have a new use. This is partly why the companies don't want their frontline representatives from knowing too much. (See chapter on marketing of a slightly better medication.)

In conclusion, the latest is not always the greatest. But don't ignore the latest since there may be subgroups that will greatly benefit from novel treatments. Generic "well drinks" may be just as effective as their brand names that they emulated. A talented psychiatric bartender can mix up a medication cocktail that can beat out a "neat" medication while reducing the hangover of side effects.

⌘⌘⌘⌘⌘

(Is this the end? Nope, it's hopefully, the beginning of a better life.)

Notes:

Made in the USA
Monee, IL
17 January 2022